THE SINS OF T

M000028167

For nearly two millennia, Western law visited the sins of fathers and mothers upon their illegitimate children, subjecting them to systematic discrimination and deprivation. The graver the sins of their parents, the further these children fell in social standing and legal protection. While some reformers sought to better the plight of illegitimate children, only in recent decades has illegitimacy lost its full legal sting. Yet the social, economic, and psychological costs of illegitimacy still remain high even in the liberal, affluent West.

John Witte, Jr. analyzes and critiques the shifting historical law and theology of illegitimacy. This doctrine, he argues, misinterprets basic biblical teachings on individual accountability and Christian community. It also betrays basic democratic principles of equality, dignity, and natural rights for all. There are no illegitimate children, only illegitimate parents, Witte concludes, and he presses for the protection and rights of all children, regardless of their birth status.

JOHN WITTE, JR. is Jonas Robitscher Professor of Law, Alonozo L. McDonald Distinguished Professor, and Director of the Center for the Study of Law and Religion at Emory University. He has published two dozen volumes, including *Law and Protestantism: The Legal Teachings of the Lutheran Reformation* (2002), *The Reformation of Rights: Law, Religion and Human Rights in Early Modern Calvinism* (2007), and *Christianity and Law: An Introduction* (2008), with Frank S. Alexander.

THE SINS OF THE FATHERS

The Law and Theology of Illegitimacy Reconsidered

JOHN WITTE, JR.

Emory University

CAMBRIDGE UNIVERSITY PRESS

Cambridge, New York, Melbourne, Madrid, Cape Town, Singapore, São Paulo, Delhi

Cambridge University Press

The Edinburgh Building, Cambridge CB2 8RU, UK

Published in the United States of America by Cambridge University Press, New York

www.cambridge.org
Information on this title: www.cambridge.org/9780521548243

First published 2009

Printed in the United Kingdom at the University Press, Cambridge

A catalogue record for this publication is available from the British Library

ISBN 978-0-521-83941-9 hardback
ISBN 978-0-521-54824-3 paperback

In memory of Ponkie
(1964–1980)

[T]he gods visit the sins of the fathers upon the children.

Euripides, *Phrixus*, fragment 970

For the sins of your fathers you, though guiltless, must suffer.

Horace, *Odes*, III, 6:1

I the Lord your God am a jealous God, visiting the iniquity of the fathers upon the children to the third and the fourth generation of those who hate me, but showing steadfast love to those who love me and keep my commandments.

Exodus 20:5–6

Thou, Nature, art my goddess; to thy law
My services are bound. Wherefore should I
Stand in the plague of custom, and permit
The curiosity of nations to deprive me,
For that I am some twelve or fourteen moonshines
Lag of a brother? Why bastard? Wherefore base,
When my dimensions are as well compact,
My mind as generous, my shape as true,
As honest madam's issue? Why brand they us
With base? with baseness? Bastardy base? Base?
Who, in the lusty stealth of nature, take
More composition and fierce quality
Than doth within a dull, stale, tired bed,
Go to th'creating a whole tribe of fops
Got 'tween sleep and wake? Well then
Legitimate Edgar, I must have your land.
Our father's love is to the bastard Edmund
As to the legitimate. Fine word "legitimate."
Well, my legitimate, if this letter speed,
And my invention thrive, Edmund the base
Shall top the legitimate. I grow. I prosper.
Now, gods, stand up for bastards!

Shakespeare, *King Lear,* I.ii (Edmund the Bastard)

Contents

Illustrations

Figure 1 Cristofo Savolini?, *The Expulsion of Hagar and Ishmael.*

Preface and acknowledgements

"Bastards have no place in this assembly of the Lord; even to the tenth generation none of his descendents may enter here." That was the startling admonition that I heard from the pulpit of the conservative Protestant church of my youth. These harsh words, taken from Deuteronomy 23:2, I now realize, were intoned gravely as the final public step of banishing a single woman and her illegitimate child from our church. Even as a youth, I remember being shocked. How could our church, so filled with sinners, banish a fellow sinner who just wanted to have her new child baptized? Furthermore, how could the church banish this little baby and withhold from him the sacrament of baptism? Was fornication so much worse a sin against the Decalogue than the sins of lying, stealing, or dishonoring parents – all of which were already on my ample roll of youthful follies? Perhaps I was next out the door. Even worse, what would come of my little foster-brother, Robert, given his illegitimate birth? Surely, he would be banished soon, too. I remember being terrified.

I also remember that the issue of banishing this mother and her illegitimate child was controversial in our tight-knit little Christian community. When challenged, the minister had stuck to his guns and fought off dissenters with the ammunition of the Law – not least the Decalogue's call to "visit" the "sins of the fathers" and mothers upon their children. Other leaders of the community struck back with the Gospel. Who were we, after all, to "cast the first stone" against a fornicator, or to disobey Christ's commandment to "suffer the little children to come unto me"? Here, in miniature, was my first real encounter with the great dialectics of Law and Gospel, justice and mercy, discipline and love. Happily, the glum minister soon left our church, and with him went the stark discipline and dark sermons that marked his troubled tenure. But the memory of that sad day has never left me. It explains a bit of the motivation for this book.

This book is a brief historical essay, not a thick, note-strewn monograph. It is intended to provoke new thinking about the historical doctrine of illegitimacy, not to challenge settled accounts of its history. My main aim is to retrace what warrants there are for and against illegitimacy doctrine in Scripture and tradition. My main findings are that the weight of Scripture is against the doctrine of illegitimacy, and that both early Jewish and Christian interpreters taught this. It was only in the second millennium that Christian theologians and jurists together took up the doctrine of illegitimacy in earnest, as part of their effort to shore up the doctrine of marriage. Using both Roman law precedents and selected biblical passages, sundry medieval Catholics and early modern Protestants visited the extramarital sins of parents upon their children. They set up something of a caste system of illegitimacy, making the rights of illegitimate children a function of the sins of their parents. The greater their parents' sin, the lower these children fell in social rank and legal protection. While early modern reformers in church and state alike sought to better the plight of illegitimate children, only in the course of the twentieth century did illegitimacy lose its full legal sting. Yet the doctrine of illegitimacy persists in some conservative theological and political quarters to this day, and the economic and psychological consequences of illegitimate birth remain grim even in the affluent West.

This book may surprise some readers who have grown accustomed to my more favorable treatments of law and religion in the Western tradition, particularly in the history of marriage and family life. I am not turning a new leaf in this book. I have always tried to avoid nostalgia in my historical writing, and have always tried to compare the evolving teachings of the tradition with the enduring teachings of Scripture. On the topic of illegitimacy, in my view, the tradition comes up shorter than on many other family topics; hence my call to reconsider the doctrine and its alternatives. There are no easy solutions to the problem of illegitimacy. But forcing illegitimate children to bear the sins of their fathers and mothers – as parts of the tradition and a few of our neo-traditionalists teach – is neither just nor necessary.

I have incurred a number of debts in the preparation of this volume. I express my profound appreciation to Dr. Craig Dykstra and his colleagues at the Lilly Endowment, Inc. for a generous grant that provided me with release time and research support to work on this volume and others on the interaction of law and Christianity in the Western tradition. I wish to thank Gina Weiser, a graduate of the Candler School of Theology, for her outstanding and prodigious research on the theological sources of Western illegitimacy doctrine, and Colleen Flood, a graduate of Emory Law School, for unearthing several valuable classical and medieval legal sources on point. I also wish to thank Chris Hudson, Will Haines, and Kelly Parker for their excellent library support and Trevor Pinkerton for his research and review. Special thanks as well go to my friends and colleagues – Frank S. Alexander, Michael Ausubel, Patrick M. Brennan, Don S. Browning, Michael J. Broyde, M. Christian Green, Judith Evans Grubbs, E. Brooks Holifield, Timothy P. Jackson, Martin E. Marty, Charles J. Reid, Jr., and Robert Wilken – for their valuable constructive criticisms and guidance on draft chapters. Finally, I wish to thank Kevin Taylor and Kate Brett at Cambridge University Press for soliciting this volume and collecting such helpful reviews of the preliminary manuscript.

This volume is part and product of a major project on the "The Child in Law, Religion, and Society," undertaken by the Center for the Study of Law and Religion at Emory University. This project is focused on children *qua* children – in their being and becoming, in their birth and growth. As a team of twenty scholars, directed by Professor Martin E. Marty, we are studying the rites and rights attached to birthing and naming, baptism and circumcision, education and discipline. We are examining the steps and stages in a child's physical, emotional, sexual, moral, and spiritual formation, as well as the rituals and ordeals, and the rights and responsibilities, attached to each. We are examining the pathos of child abuse and rape, child poverty and homelessness, juvenile delinquency and violence, and illegitimacy and infanticide. And we are probing the mystery of the child – that combination of innocence and imagination, acuity and candor, empathy and healing, sharing and caring that uniquely become a child. I wish to express my deep gratitude to Rebecca Rimel and her colleagues at The Pew Charitable Trusts for their very generous support of our Center and this project on children. I also offer my profound thanks to Amy Wheeler for her excellent work on the manuscript and illustrations, and my other Emory Center colleagues in addition to Ms. Wheeler, namely, April Bogle, Eliza Ellison, Anita Mann, and Linda King, for their extraordinary work on this project on children, which is scheduled to yield a score of other volumes.

This volume is dedicated to the memory of my brother Robert, whom our family nicknamed "Ponkie." Though dumped by his natural parents on account of his illegitimacy and severely plagued by physical and mental handicaps to which he succumbed by the age of sixteen, he was the best model I have ever seen of the pure faith and simple joy that become the true Christian life. He brought out the angels in my parents and siblings, and he taught me more than a thousand books and sermons could ever do what it means to be a humble and happy child of God. May his name and memory be blessed forever.

JOHN WITTE, JR.

Introduction: The paradoxes of illegitimacy

Sex has long excited an intimate union between theology and law in the Christian West. Western clerics and magistrates have long collaborated in setting private laws to define and facilitate licit sex. These include rules and procedures for sexual etiquette, courtship, and betrothal; for marital formation, maintenance, and dissolution; for conjugal duties, debts, and desires; for parental roles, rights, and responsibilities. Western churches and states have also long collaborated in setting moral and criminal laws to police and punish illicit sex. For many centuries, these two powers kept overlapping rolls of sexual sin and crime: adultery and fornication, sodomy and buggery, incest and bestiality, bigamy and polygamy, prostitution and pornography, abortion and contraception. They also operated interlocking tribunals to enforce these rules on sex. The church guarded the inner life through its canons, confessionals, and consistory courts. The state guarded the outer life through its policing, prosecution, and punishment of sexual crimes. To be sure, church and state officials clashed frequently over whose laws governed sex, marriage, and family life. And their respective laws on these subjects did change a great deal – dramatically in the fourth, twelfth, sixteenth, and nineteenth centuries. But for all this rivalry and change, Christianity – and the Jewish, Greek, and Roman sources on which it drew – had a formative influence on Western laws of sex, marriage, and family life.

Most of these classic legal doctrines have now been eclipsed by the dramatic rise of new public laws and popular customs of sexual liberty and personal privacy in much of the West. Courtship, cohabitation, betrothal, and marriage are now mostly private sexual contracts with few roles for church and state to play and few

Figure 2 Matthias Stomer (*c.* 1600–*c.* 1650), *Sarah Presenting Hagar to Abraham.*

restrictions on freedoms of entrance, exercise, and exit. Classic crimes of contraception and abortion have been found to violate constitutional liberties. Classic prohibitions on adultery and fornication have become dead or discarded letters on most statute books. Free-speech laws protect all manner of sexual expression, short of obscenity. Constitutional privacy laws protect all manner of voluntary sexual conduct, short of child abuse and statutory rape. The classic prohibitions on incest, polygamy, and homosexuality still remain on some law books, but they are now the subjects of bitter constitutional and cultural battles.

One other such classic doctrine has persisted in the West but without too much critical reflection. That is the doctrine of illegitimacy – or, more historically accurate but less politically correct, the doctrine of bastardy.[1] In the Western tradition, the

---

[1] The term "bastard" first appeared in English in the later eleventh century to describe William the Conqueror, known as "the bastard king." Though the etymology of the word is unclear, it is thought to derive from the word "bent," conceived "on a pack saddle," or "in a

bastard was defined as a child born out of lawful wedlock – a product of fornication, adultery, concubinage, incest, prostitution, or other sexual crime and sin. A bastard was at once a child of no one (*filius nullius*) and a child of everyone (*filius populi*) – born without name and without home, the perennial object of both pity and scorn, charity and abuse, romance and ribaldry. Absent successful legitimation or adoption, bastards bore the permanent stigma of their sinful and criminal birth, noted on certificates of baptism, confirmation, marriage, and death as well as on tax rolls, court records, and property registrations. For many centuries, bastards lived in a sort of legal limbo, with some claims to charity and support but with severely truncated rights to inherit or devise property, to hold high clerical, political, or military office, to sue or testify in court, and more. These formal legal disabilities on bastards were often compounded by their chronic poverty, neglect, and abuse, assuming that they escaped the not so uncommon historical practice of being secretly smothered or exposed upon birth, or put out to nurse or lease with modest odds of survival.[2]

grange." "Bastard" was in regular legal usage by the thirteenth century. See Nicholas Orme, *Medieval Children* (New Haven, CT: Yale University Press, 2002), 57. "The adjective 'illegitimate,' meaning 'not born in lawful wedlock' (the earliest sense of the term in English), joined its predecessor '*bastard*' in written English . . . in Shakespeare's *Henry VIII* (1536), in which Elizabeth is described as 'the kynges doughter illegyttimate borne under same mariage [sic]'. By the early seventeenth century 'illegitimate' was a synonym for 'bastard'" and has remained so in Anglo-American law and literature. Gail Reekie, *Measuring Immorality: Social Inquiry and the Problem of Illegitimacy* (Cambridge: Cambridge University Press, 1998), 23. See further Jenny Teichmann, *Illegitimacy: An Examination of Bastardy* (Ithaca, NY: Cornell University Press, 1982). Historically, a whole series of separate and shifting terms attached to the child, depending on the non-marital sexual act of the parents – *mamzerim, spurii, nothi, filii naturalis, incestui, adulterini, favonius, illegitimus, vulgo quaesitus, vulgo conceptus,* and more; by the fifteenth century, the term "*bastardi*" became the common generic term to describe any child born out of wedlock. See below pp. 52–9, 67–8, 89–99, 107–11, and John Brydall, *Lex Spuriorum, or the Law Relating to Bastardy Collected from the Common, Civil, and Ecclesiastical Laws* (London: Assigns of Richard and Edwards Atkins, 1703), 1–14. I shall be using "bastard" and "illegitimate" interchangeably herein in discussing the historical material, with a preference for the milder term "illegitimate." Current terminology favors "non-marital child."

2   Mark Jackson, *New-Born Child Murder: Women, Illegitimacy, and the Courts in Eighteenth-Century England* (Manchester: Manchester University Press, 1996); T.E. James, "The Illegitimate and Deprived Child: Legitimation and Adoption," in Ronald H. Graveson and F.R. Crane, eds., *A Century of Family Law: 1857–1957* (London: Sweet & Maxwell, 1957), 39–55; Lionel Rose, *The Massacre of the Innocents: Infanticide in Britain 1800–1939* (London: Routledge and Kegan Paul, 1986); Mason P. Thomas, "Child Abuse and Neglect. Part I:

Illegitimacy doctrine has been a common feature of most legal and religious traditions of the world. It has long served to regulate the scope of the *paterfamilias'* power and responsibility within the household, and to regularize the transmission and inheritance of property, title, lineage, and (in some cultures) to ensure control over the household religion.[3]

In the Western tradition, the legal doctrine of illegitimacy was given special support by Christian theology. Illegitimacy doctrine was a natural concomitant of the church's repeated attempts to shore up marriage as the only licit forum for sex and procreation. Illegitimacy doctrine was also viewed as an apt illustration and application of the biblical adage that "the sins of the fathers [and mothers] shall be visited upon their children" (Ex. 20:5, 34:7; Num. 14:18; Deut. 5:9).[4] The Bible itself seemed to condone this reading in its story of Ishmael, the illegitimate son of Abraham, who was condemned already in the womb as a "wild ass of a man" (Gen. 16:12) and was ultimately cast out of his home with minimal prospects of survival. Mosaic laws banned bastards and their descendents "from the assembly of the Lord . . . for ten generations" (Deut. 23:2). Later Hebrew prophets threatened that "the offspring of an unlawful union will perish," for they are "witnesses of evil against their parents when God examines them" (Wisd. 3:16–17; 4:6). Both Christ and St. Paul analogized bastards with those stubborn souls who refused to accept the life and liberty of the Gospel and were thus condemned to slavery and repression (John 8:31–59; Gal. 4:21–31). From the Middle Ages forward, Christian theologians and jurists alike found in these biblical passages ample sanction for the legal doctrine of illegitimacy. The doctrine became a perennial teaching of Western civil law, canon law, and common law alike. And today, in some Christian and other fundamentalist circles, the

---

Historical Overview, Legal Matrix, and Social Perspectives," *North Carolina Law Review* 50 (1972): 293–349.

[3] See generally John C. Ayer, Jr., "Legitimacy and Marriage," *Harvard Law Review* 16 (1902): 22–42; Shirley Hartley, *Illegitimacy* (Berkeley: University of California Press, 1975); Peter Laslett, Karla Oosterveen, and Richard M. Smith, eds., *Bastardy and Its Comparative History: Studies in the History of Illegitimacy and Marital Non-Conformism in Britain, France, Germany, Sweden, North America, Jamaica, and Japan* (Cambridge, MA: Harvard University Press, 1980).

[4] Unless otherwise noted, I am using the Revised Standard Version of the Bible throughout.

doctrine is gaining renewed support as out-of-wedlock births have skyrocketed.

The doctrine of illegitimacy, however, does not sit so easily with other biblical teachings. The doctrine finds no firm anchor in the familiar biblical adage that "the sins of the fathers shall be visited upon their children." Four times that passage occurs in the Bible. Twice, it appears in the Decalogue. "You shall not make for yourself a graven image . . . for I the Lord your God am a jealous God, visiting the iniquity of the fathers upon the children of the third and the fourth generation of those who hate me, but showing steadfast love to thousands of those who love me and keep my commandments" (Ex. 20:4–6; Deut. 5:8–10). The sin at issue in this commandment is idolatry, not adultery or fornication. And nothing is said here to distinguish between the legitimate or illegitimate children of the next generations. Those children who love God and keep his commandments are promised God's "steadfast love," regardless of their status. Those children who continue to "hate God" or perpetuate idol worship will suffer God's eternal punishment, even if they are legitimate. But even then, a merciful God, who is "slow to anger," will give his people time to redeem themselves. Rather than punish them right away as they deserve, God will "visit" the question three or four generations later and punish the people only if they have persisted in the idolatry of their forebearers. Exactly the same promise is repeated in the other two "sins of the fathers" passages that threaten "visiting iniquity upon children" (Ex. 34:7; Num. 14:18) for violations of the whole Decalogue. These passages do not teach a doctrine of double original sin for illegitimates. They underscore the need for all to repent and to be righteous before a merciful God.

Other biblical passages reflect this more benign teaching. The Bible repeatedly enjoins believers not to "pervert the justice" due to "the fatherless" (Deut. 24:17; 27:19; Ps. 94:6; Is. 9:17; Lam. 5:3). Mosaic criminal laws make clear that "the fathers shall not be put to death for the children, nor shall the children be put to death for the fathers; every man shall be put to death for his own sin" (Deut. 24:16). Later Hebrew prophets insisted that "the son shall not suffer for the iniquity of the father, nor the father suffer for the iniquity of the son; the righteousness of the righteous shall be upon himself, and the wickedness of the wicked shall be upon himself" (Ezek. 18:19–20). The New Testament underscores this teaching of individual accountability. If Christ's atonement for sin means anything, it means that no one, not least unborn or newborn children, need be a scapegoat for the sins of their parents or of any others. Each individual soul will stand directly before the judgment seat of God to answer for what he or she has done in this life, and to receive God's final judgment and mercy. Here, there will be no vicarious liability charges to answer.

Moreover, the Bible teaches the doctrine of adoption as a sublime remedy for the illegitimate and ill-born. The Hebrew Bible hints several times that adoption may have been used to remedy the plight of illegitimate, conquered, emancipated, and orphaned children (Gen. 30:1–13; 48:5–6; Ex. 2:7–19; Judg. 11:1–2; I Chr. 2:34–5; Ezra 10:44, Ruth 4:16–17; Esther 2:7). The prophet Jeremiah further hints at the image of adoption to describe how God makes Israel his chosen people and promises them a "beauteous heritage" (Jer. 3:14). The New Testament endorses adoption more directly. First, there is the adoption of five illegitimate children – Perez, Zerah, Boaz, Obed, and Solomon – into the genealogy of Christ (Matt. 1:1–17), and other bastards like Jephthah into the drama of salvation (Heb. 11:32). Next, there is Joseph's adoption of Christ, the purportedly illegitimate child of Mary (Matt. 1:20–5). Finally, there is the promise to all who have faith that they shall be "adopted as heirs of salvation," despite the sins that they inherited through birth or committed in life (Rom. 8:14–15, 23; 9:4; Gal. 4:4–5; Eph. 1:5).

The doctrine of illegitimacy runs counter not only to standard theological teachings, but also to standard legal doctrines. First, illegitimacy is an unusual kind of status offense that, by definition, forgoes required proof of the three main elements of any prima-facie case of crime: (1) a defendant's voluntary act or omission (*actus reus*), (2) that is done intentionally, knowingly, recklessly, or negligently (*mens rea*), and (3) that causes or threatens harm to a victim or society (*causa*). All three of these basic elements of crime – grounded as they are in classic Western teachings on will, reason, and causation – are missing in this case. Yet classically, illegitimates are treated as if criminals.

Second, illegitimacy doctrine is an unusual form of deterrence that threatens harm to an innocent third party in order to dissuade a non-marital couple from sexual intercourse. This instrumentalizes innocent children, making them a means to the end of achieving the common good of licit sex and procreation. Punishing a duly convicted criminal severely and giving him a criminal record in order to deter others is one thing: upon proper conviction, a criminal "belongs to society for that purpose."[5] But punishing an innocent child without trial, and giving that child a record of its illegitimacy in order to deter others from illicit sex, is simply cruel and unjust.

Finally, illegitimacy is an unusual species of vicarious liability, a sort of *respondeat inferior* doctrine that imposes upon innocent children some of the costs of their parents' extramarital experimentation. The law is replete with examples of *respondent superior* cases, where liability is imposed on parents, principals, or employers because of the actions of their children, agents, or employees. The point of this vicarious liability scheme is to encourage those in authority to teach, supervise, and control those for whom they are responsible. Illegitimacy doctrine stands this simple legal logic on its head: it imposes liability on the newborn child, the party least able to supervise or control the actions of others.

To be sure, a good deal of the classic law and lore of illegitimacy is now falling aside in the United States and other Western countries. Most Western nations have removed the majority of the chronic legal disabilities on the illegitimate child's rights to property, support, and standing in courts. State welfare and education programs have relieved some of the traditional social and economic pressures on illegitimates. And the legal doctrine of adoption, which came to be accepted at Anglo-American common law for the first time at the turn of the twentieth century, has provided still further relief for some illegitimate children. Many of the remaining statutory disabilities on illegitimates have recently been struck down as violations of the non-discrimination provisions in the European Convention on Human Rights and as violations of the equal

[5] Sydney Smith, *Elementary Sketches of Moral Philosophy* (New York: Harper and Bros., 1856), 252. Cf. Immanuel Kant, *The Metaphysics of Morals*, 6:336 re: the punishment and killing of illegitimates.

protection clause of the Fourteenth Amendment to the United States Constitution.

But, in the United States, what the Fourteenth Amendment gives with one clause it takes back with another. The Fourteenth Amendment equal protection clause does spare illegitimates from most vicarious liability for their parents' extramarital experimentation. But the Fourteenth Amendment due process clause spares sexually active adults from criminal liability for engaging in extramarital sex. With the legal stigma of both illegitimacy and promiscuity removed, it is perhaps no accident that illegitimacy rates in the United States have soared. More than 38 percent of all American children, and more than 69 percent of all African-American children, are now born out of wedlock. While illegitimate children no longer suffer many formal legal disabilities, they continue to suffer chronic social disabilities in the form of markedly higher rates of poverty and poor education, deprivation and child abuse, juvenile delinquency and criminal conduct. Moreover, a new species of *in utero* illegitimates has emerged in the past four decades, sometimes condemned to death by the very same Fourteenth Amendment that protects the rights of their mothers to abort them. If the historical doctrine of illegitimacy was a Christian theology of sin run amuck, this new form of illegitimacy is a constitutional theory of liberty run wild.

This little volume parses some of these paradoxes of the historical doctrine of illegitimacy. "The sins of the fathers," I submit, consists not only in the sinful acts of having children "out of wedlock." It also consists in the sinful acts of "visiting the iniquity of the fathers" and mothers upon the innocent children born of these illicit unions. Historically, the sins of the fathers of illegitimate children were compounded by the sins of the fathers of church and state. Their theology and law of illegitimacy, which crystallized in the second millennium, was, in my view, wrongly conceived and improperly nurtured. While illegitimacy doctrine lent itself to clear moral instruction and to clean family legacies, it condemned innocent children to an inferior status which the church's pastoral services and state's equitable remedies could only partly offset. The common law tradition exacerbated these problems by rejecting the civil law tradition of adoption and legitimation until the turn of the twentieth century, leaving illegitimate children even more dependent than in civil law communities upon the "kindness of strangers."[6]

Today, the sins of the fathers (both real and metaphorical) consist more of omission than commission, of indifference to the plight of illegitimate children more than condemnation of them in their cradles. This indifference comes in many forms: in the rise of unsafe sex in a day of easy contraception; in the scourge of drive-by conceptions and one-night stands; in the rise of non-marital cohabitants who flee in the face of unexpected pregnancy and children; in the reality that anti-abortion campaigns claim far more attention and resources than pro-adoption ministries in the United States; in the shame that America, the richest nation on earth, has left untold millions of its illegitimate children underinsured, undereducated, and undersupported.

Chapter 1 of this volume analyzes the classical Western sources and limits of illegitimacy and legitimation – in the Bible and its elaboration by early Jewish rabbis and early Church Fathers. Chapter 2 analyzes the classical Roman law of legitimacy and legitimation, which was well developed before the time of Christ and then transformed by Christian morality in the fourth through sixth centuries. Chapter 3 takes up the medieval canon law, whose intricate theology of marriage provided a more refined gradation of illegitimacy, and whose sacramental theology provided a more refined system of legitimation. Chapter 4 takes up the English common law, which in deliberate departure from Roman law and canon law shifted the focus of illegitimacy doctrine from sin and morality to land and inheritance. Chapter 5 analyzes the gradual eclipse of illegitimacy law in American by an emerging law of natural rights and equal protection for all children, regardless of their birth status. The "Concluding reflections" probe a few remedies for the modern problem of illegitimacy that can be responsibly drawn from Scripture and tradition.

---

[6] John Boswell, *The Kindness of Strangers: The Abandonment of Children in Western Europe from Late Antiquity to the Renaissance* (New York: Pantheon Books, 1988).

ABRAHAM RENVOIE AGAR.

Figure 3 Gustav Doré (1832–1883), *Sarah Watching the Expulsion of Hagar.*

CHAPTER I

Suffer the innocent children: Illegitimacy in early Judaism and Christianity

The Western doctrine of illegitimacy was born in the biblical story of Ishmael, the bastard son of Abraham and Hagar. The facts, as recorded in Genesis, are these: At seventy-five years old, Abraham, a rich and powerful man, grew concerned about his lineage and legacy. He complained to God that he and his wife Sarah were without child, and he contemplated selecting a slave born in his household to be his heir, as was customary for childless couples in the day (Gen. 15:2–3). God told Abraham that a slave would not be his heir, and instead promised that he would have his own son as his heir, who would yield countless descendents – as many "as the stars of the heavens and the sand on the seashore" (Gen. 15:2–6; 22:17). But for ten years thereafter Abraham and Sarah had no children (Gen. 16:3, 16). Concerned that time was running out, Sarah urged Abraham to take her slave maid Hagar and have children by her, following the custom of the day for childless couples. Abraham obliged. Hagar conceived. Newly pregnant, Hagar "looked with contempt" upon Sarah, her barren mistress (Gen. 16:4). Sarah was livid. She dealt harshly with Hagar, who fled into the wilderness (Gen. 16:6).

An angel enjoined Hagar to return. The angel promised that her child would survive and indeed have many descendents (Gen. 16:7–10). But the angel also spoke ominously of the bane that would befall her bastard child: "Behold, you are with child, and shall bear a son; you shall call his name Ishmael [meaning "God hears"]; because the Lord has given heed to your affliction. [But] [h]e shall be a wild ass of a man, his hand [will be] against every man and every man's hand against him; and he shall dwell over against all his kinsmen" (Gen. 16:11–12).

Ishmael was born and raised in Abraham's household (Gen. 16:16). Abraham embraced him as his first-born son and circumcised him to signify him as one of God's own (Gen. 17:18, 23–6). Fifteen years later, however, Abraham and Sarah were miraculously blessed with the birth of their own son Isaac, as God had promised (Gen. 17:15–21; 21:1–7). Sarah grew jealous of the adolescent Ishmael "playing with" – perhaps (sexually) abusing[1] – her newly weaned son Isaac. She grew concerned about Isaac's claims to Abraham's vast wealth. "Cast out this slave woman with her son," she enjoined Abraham; "for the son of this slave woman will not be heir with my son Isaac" (Gen. 21:8–10), echoing God's own earlier commandment (Gen. 15:4). After anguished reflection and prayer, Abraham obliged Sarah, contrary to his own affection for Ishmael and to the custom of the day that a master care for his slaves and their children, however conceived (Gen. 21:11–14).

Abraham sent Hagar and Ishmael away into the desert, meagerly supplied with food and water. Their provisions ran out. Ishmael grew weak. Hagar cast him under a bush, walked away, and sat with her back to him, not wishing to see or hear him die. Ishmael cried (Gen. 21:15–16). The angel returned to his mother and proclaimed: "Fear not; for God has heard the voice of the lad where he is. Arise, lift up the lad, and hold him fast with your hand; for I will make him a great nation" (Gen. 21:17–18).[2] Miraculously, Hagar found a water well and saved Ishmael. Ishmael grew up to be a skilled huntsman and warrior (Gen. 21:19–21). Hagar later found Ishmael a wife from among her kin. Ishmael fathered twelve (legitimate) sons, who became princes of the tribes of the ancient Middle East (Gen. 25:12–18).[3] Abraham gave Ishmael and his other children born of concubines various gifts and then "sent them away from his son Isaac" (Gen. 25:5). While Ishmael received no inheritance, he joined his half-brother Isaac in burying their father Abraham (Gen. 25:9).

---

[1] *Tzad chet hoof,* the Hebrew words for "playing," often have a sexual overtone in the Hebrew Bible. See, e.g., Gen. 17:17; 18:12–15; 19:14; 21:6–9; 26:8; 39:14–17.

[2] In Gen. 21:12–13, God tells Abraham: "I will make a nation of the son of the slave woman also, because he is your offspring."

[3] See the biblical references to the "Ishmaelites" who sold Joseph into exile in Egypt (Gen. 37:25, 27; 39:1); and who are later listed among the enemies of ancient Israel (Judg. 8:24; Ps. 83:6). Biblical scholars dispute whether these are the descendents of Abraham's son, Ishmael.

Ishmael lived a full life and died at 137 years (Gen. 25:17). Thus far the facts as reported in the Book of Genesis.

The harsh treatment of Ishmael the bastard is echoed later in the Bible.[4] Several passages denounced bastards and bastardy, sometimes in rhetorically violent terms. The Mosaic law precluded bastards and their progeny from corporate worship, if not from the community altogether: "No bastard (*mamzer*) shall enter the assembly of the Lord," Deuteronomy provided; "even to the tenth generation none of his descendents shall enter the assembly of the Lord" (Deut. 23:2). At minimum, this verse seemed to preclude illegitimate sons from serving in the temple as priests – since Mosaic law prohibited priests from unions with widows, divorcees, prostitutes, concubines, or other defiled women (Lev. 21:7–14). The prophet Zechariah suggested further that bastards had no place as political leaders either. "A bastard shall dwell at Ashdod, and I will cut off the pride of the Philistines," he proclaimed, suggesting the illegitimacy of this bastard's rule (Zech. 9:6).

During the time of the Judges, Gilead's sons drove out their half-brother Jephthah, because he "was the son of a harlot." "You shall not inherit in our father's house," they said to him; "for you are the son of another woman" (Judg. 11:1–2). The Book of Judges underscored the fact that Jephthah, like Ishmael, was unruly: "worthless fellows collected around Jephthah and went raiding with him" (Judg. 11:3). After a remnant of the Jews returned from exile in Babylon, their leader Ezra rounded up all those children who were born of forbidden mixed marriages with foreign women and "banned them from the congregation of the exiles" (Ezra 9:10–10:44).

Through the prophet Hosea, God condemned the children of the adulteress: "Upon her children also I will have no pity because they are the children of harlotry. For their mother has played the harlot; she that conceived them has acted shamefully" (Hosea 2:4–5). The prophets Jeremiah and Ezekiel both complained that because "[t]he fathers have eaten sour grapes," their "children's teeth are set on edge" (Jer. 31:29, Ezek. 18:2–3). "Our fathers have sinned, and we

---

[4] In this section, I am simply presenting the literal biblical texts, using the Revised Standard Version. Later in this chapter, and again in Chapter 2 and the "Concluding reflections," I shall be treating the history of exegesis of these texts.

bear their iniquities," another prophet lamented (Lam. 5:7). The Book of Sirach made clear that while "the glory of a man is from the honor of his father," "a mother in dishonor is a reproach to the children" (Sir. 3:11).[5] Indeed, the children of the adulteress must bear vicarious liability for the sins of their mother: "She herself will be brought before the assembly, and punishment will fall on her children. Her children will not take root, and her branches will not bear fruit. She will leave her memory for a curse, and her disgrace will not be blotted out" (Sir. 23:24–6). The Wisdom of Solomon struck an even more threatening tone for illegitimates: "[C]hildren of adulterers will not come to maturity, and the offspring of an unlawful union will perish. Even if they live long they will be held of no account, and finally their old age will be without honor . . . For children born of unlawful unions are witnesses of evil against their parents when God examines them" (Wisd. 3:16–17; 4:6). All these threats of vicarious liability for illegitimate children seemed to vindicate God's repeated promise to "visit the sins of the fathers" upon their children "until the third and fourth generation of those who hate me" (Ex. 20:5; 34:7; Num. 14:18; Deut. 5:9).

The New Testament echoed some of these teachings. St. Paul suggested that the sins of an unbelieving couple would be visited upon their children, just as the faith of believers would render their children holy: "If any woman has a husband who is an unbeliever, and he consents to live with her, she should not divorce him. For the unbelieving husband is consecrated through his wife, and the unbelieving wife through her husband. Otherwise, your children would be unclean, but as it is they are holy" (1 Cor. 7:13–15). The Letter to the Hebrews echoed the familiar assumption that an illegitimate child would be unruly and undisciplined – "a wild ass of a man," as Ishmael had been described. "It is for discipline that you have to endure. God is treating you as sons; for what son is there whom his father does not discipline? If you are left without discipline, in which all have participated, then you are illegitimate children and not sons" (Heb. 12:7–8).

---

[5] I am treating the Apocryphal books (as Protestants call them) as part of the biblical canon, since they were included in the Septuagint and Vulgate, on which a good part of the tradition based its views on illegitimacy.

The New Testament went further and labelled as bastards (*nothos*) all those who reject the Gospel's promise of Christian freedom from the Mosaic law. Christ said as much to the Jewish scribes and pharisees of his day in a testy exchange about Christian truth and freedom. The true "sons of God," Christ announced, are all those who accept the truth of the Gospel and its "promise of freedom" from the bondage of the law (John 8:31–3). The scribes replied: "We are descendents of Abraham, and have never been in bondage to anyone. How is that you say, 'You will be made free'?" (John 8:33). Christ retorted: Unlike Abraham, you are bound by sin, to the point that "you seek to kill me" (John 8:34–8). But "Abraham is our father," the scribes replied to Christ, unlike you who must be "a Samaritan" (John 8:39, 48). No legitimate child of Abraham would threaten to kill me, God's son in whom "father Abraham rejoiced," Christ shot back (John 8:40, 42, 56). "We were not born of fornication," rendering us illegitimate, the scribes rejoined. In fact we all are children of "one Father, even God," and that is what makes us all legitimate (John 8:41). "If God were your father, you would love me," for I am God's son, Christ replied, now escalating his rhetoric. And because you don't love me and listen to the truth of my word, but instead threaten to kill me, you are not only the illegitimate sons of Abraham, but you are also the true sons of the devil, "liars," "thieves," and "murderers" who deprive the people of the truth and life of God. "You are of your father the devil, and your will is to do your father's desires. He was a murderer from the very beginning, and has nothing to do with truth." "He who is of God hears the words of God; the reason why you do not hear them is that you are not of God" (John 8:42–4, 46). The scribes charged back: It is you who is possessed by "a demon," and thereafter "they took up stones to throw at him" (John 8:48, 57, 59).

St. Paul tied this contrast between free Christians and enslaved (if not possessed) Jews directly to the story of Abraham and Ishmael. The legitimate children of Abraham are those who accept the Gospel. The illegitimate children of Abraham are those who stubbornly cling to the Law, notably the Jews. Legitimate children are free Christians whose lives are filled with promise. Bastards are enslaved non-Christians whose lives are without hope – and who accordingly live as the "wild man" Ishmael and need to be curtailed if not cast out. St. Paul captured this new variation on the Ishmael story in a jarring message to the new Christians in Galatia who insisted on continued adherence to the Mosaic law:

Tell me, you who desire to be under law, do you not hear the law? For it is written that Abraham had two sons, one by a slave [Hagar], one by a free woman [Sarah]. But the son of the slave was born according to the flesh, the son of the free woman through promise. Now this is an allegory: these women are two covenants. One is from Mt. Sinai, bearing children for slavery; she is Hagar. Now Hagar is Mt. Sinai in Arabia; she corresponds with the present Jerusalem, for she is in slavery with her children. But the Jerusalem above is free . . . Now we, brethren, like Isaac, are children of promise. But as at that time he who was born according to the flesh persecuted him who was born according to the Spirit, so it is now. But what does the Scripture say. "Cast out the slave and her son; for the son of the slave will not inherit with the son of the free woman." So, brethren, we are not children of the slave, but of the free woman (Gal. 4:21–31; see similarly Rom. 9:6–13).

This passage would become a *locus classicus* for all manner of later Christian theories and practices not only of illegitimacy but also of anti-Judaism.[6]

EARLY JEWISH TEACHINGS

Illegitimacy doctrine found only a modest place in early Jewish legal sources, and the category and consequences of illegitimacy were very narrowly defined.[7] The rabbis of the Talmud (the books of rabbinic law gathered from the first five centuries of the common era) started

---

[6] See below pp. 68, 96, 110 and 154. On anti-Judaic teachings, anchored in this and other texts, see Heiko A. Oberman, *The Roots of Antisemitism in the Age of Renaissance and Reformation* (Philadelphia: Fortress Press, 1984); James W. Parkes, *The Jew in the Medieval Community: A Study of his Political and Economic Situation*, 2nd edn. (New York: Hermon Press, 1976); Amnon Linder, ed., *The Jews in the Legal Sources of the Early Middle Ages* (Detroit: Wayne State University Press, 1997); Amnon Linder, ed., *The Jews in Roman Imperial Legislation* (Detroit: Wayne State University Press, 1987). On Judaic and Islamic interpretations, see Phyllis Trible and Letty M. Russell, eds., *Hagar, Sarah, and Their Children: Jewish, Christian, and Muslim Perspectives* (Louisville, KY: Westminster John Knox Press, 2006).

[7] For an overview of the various Jewish law texts, and how they came to be read by Christians in the common era, see David Novak, "Law and Religion in Judaism," in *Christianity and Law: An Introduction,* ed. John Witte, Jr. and Frank S. Alexander (Cambridge: Cambridge University Press, 2008), 33–52; David Weiss Halivni, *Midrash, Mishnah, and Gemara: The Jewish Predilection for Justified Law* (Cambridge, MA: Harvard University Press, 1986).

with Deuteronomy 23:2: "No bastard shall enter the assembly of the Lord, even to the tenth generation none of his descendents shall enter the assembly of the Lord." This same prohibition fell on all men who were castrated or sexually mutilated, on Ammonites and Moabites to the tenth generation, and on Edomites and Egyptians to the third generation (Deut. 23:1–8). This passage in Deuteronomy, the rabbis emphasized, is the only formal legal statement on bastardy in the entire Torah. All other biblical passages on point, including the story of Ishmael, might have homiletic or personal uses, but they had no direct legal significance.[8]

The rabbis defined bastardy more narrowly than the common Western view of "a child born out of lawful wedlock."[9] "The law laid down in Deuteronomy against the bastard (*mamzer*) and

[8] For the main Jewish legal sources on illegitimacy, see *The Mishnah*, trans. Herbert Danby (Oxford: Oxford University Press, 1987), *Yebamoth* 4.12–13; 5.2, 14; 7.1–8:3, 9:1–2; 10:1–9; *Hagigah* 1.7; 2.4; *Ketuboth* 1.8–9; 3.1; *Sotah* 8.3–5; *Gittin* 8.59.3–4; *Kiddushin* 2.3; 4.1, 8; *Horayoth* 1.4; *The Minor Tractates of the Talmud*, 2nd edn., trans. and ed. A. Cohen, 2 vols. (London: Soncino Press, 1971), 407, 424–7, 531–2; *The Schottenstein Edition Talmud: The Gemara* (Brooklyn: Mesorah Publications, 1990), *Tractate Yevamos* 44a–46a, 78a, 78b, 93b, 115a, 116b; id., *Tractate Kiddushin* 68b, 69a–70a; *The Hebrew–English Edition of the Babylonian Talmud*, trans. Israel W. Slotki, ed. I. Epstein (London: Soncino Press, 1984), *Yebamoth* 21b–22a, 44a–46a, 49a–50a. See also the later distillations of the law on point in *The Code of Maimonides (Mishneh Torah)*, Book 5, The Book of Holiness, ed. Leon Nemoy, trans. Louis M. Epstein (New Haven, CT: Yale University Press, 1965), 10–16, 97–105, and *The Shulchan Aruch*, trans. and ed. Eliyahu Touger (Brooklyn: Kehot, 2002), Family Law, Book 4.1, 4.14–16. See modern commentaries in Menachem Elon, ed., *The Principles of Jewish Law* (Jerusalem: Keter Publishing House, 1975); Menachem Elon, *Jewish Law: History, Sources, Principles*, trans. Bernard Auerbach and Melvin J. Sykes, 4 vols. (Philadelphia: The Jewish Publication Society, 1994); Joseph B. Soloveitchik, *Family Redeemed: Essays on Family Relationships*, ed. David Shatz and Joel Wolowelsky (New York: Meorot Harav Foundation, 2002); Louis M. Epstein, *Sex Laws and Customs in Judaism* (New York: Ktav Publishing House, 1967); id., *Marriage Laws in the Bible and the Talmud* (Cambridge, MA: Harvard University Press, 1942); Rabbi Elie Kaplan Spitz, "Mamzerut," *The Committee on Jewish Law and Standards of the Rabbinical Assembly* (March 8, 2000), 558–86; Stephen M. Passameneck, *Some Medieval Problems in Mamzeruth* (Cincinnati: Hebrew Union College Annual, 1966). I wish to express my deep thanks to my friend and colleague Professor Michael J. Broyde for guiding me to these Jewish law sources. See his own critical writings on Jewish marriage and family life: Michael J. Broyde, *Marriage, Divorce, and the Abandoned Wife in Jewish Law* (Hoboken, NJ: Ktav Publishing House, 2001); Michael J. Broyde and Michael Ausubel, eds., *Marriage, Sex, and Family in Judaism* (Lanham, MD: Rowman & Littlefield, 2005); Michael J. Broyde, "Adoption, Personal Status, and Jewish Law," in *The Morality of Adoption: Social-Psychological, Theological, and Legal Perspectives*, ed. Timothy P. Jackson (Grand Rapids, MI: Wm. B. Eerdmans, 2005), 128–47.

[9] See pp. 52–9 below on the origins of this view in Roman law.

against his distant offspring was so harsh that every opportunity was taken to confine it to the narrowest limits."[10] This demand became even more pronounced after the destruction of the Temple in Jerusalem (68 CE) and the ensuing diaspora rendered local Jewish populations fragile and vulnerable. No Jew was to be excluded from the community who did not have to be.

The rabbis thus restricted the category of bastards to children born of a "forbidden" (*ervot*) sexual union that was punishable by death, banishment, or extirpation (*karet*) (Lev. 18:29).[11] These were principally children born of adultery or of incest. Adultery was narrowly defined, however, as proven sexual intercourse between a Jewish man and a Jewish woman who was validly betrothed or married to another Jewish man at the time of the sexual union (Lev. 20:10; Deut. 22:22).[12] Excluded from this definition of adultery was sex between a married Jewish husband and another woman (whether Jewish or Gentile) or sex between a married Jewish woman and a Gentile man. While such unions were regarded as sinful and impure, any children born of such unions were considered to be legitimate and were accepted as full members of the Jewish community.

Some early rabbis narrowed this category of adulterine illegitimacy even further. While adulterous sex between a Jewish wife and a Jewish man not her husband was a punishable offense for the parents, they argued, the child born of this adultery was not necessarily a bastard. Only if the adulterous couple were permanently precluded from a valid marriage, because of an absolute impediment of incest, would their child be condemned as a bastard. But if the couple were theoretically capable of marriage, say after the woman was divorced or widowed, their child would be regarded as legitimate.

---

[10] "Bastard," in *The Universal Jewish Encyclopedia*, ed. Isaac Landman, 10 vols. (New York: The Universal Jewish Encyclopedia, Inc., 1942), X:587.

[11] Yev. 4.13.

[12] The burden of proof of illegitimacy was set very high, however. If a husband and wife lived together, but the wife was notoriously promiscuous, the husband was still presumed to be the father of her children, and those children were regarded as legitimate. Only if the husband was absent for a number of years and his wife married or cohabited with another Jewish man would adultery be stipulated, and the children deemed illegitimate. See below pp. 115–16 for comparable rules in English common law.

While adultery was narrowly defined in classical Jewish law, incest was broadly defined to include the Torah's long list of prohibited incestuous unions that were punishable by death, banishment, or other severe punishment. The Torah declared incestuous any sexual unions between a man and his mother, stepmother, mother-in-law, or mother-in-law's mother; between a man and his aunt or his father-in-law's mother; between a man and his sister, half-sister, or his brother's wife;[13] between a man and his daughter or daughter's daughter, his stepdaughter or stepdaughter's daughter, and his son's or stepson's daughter – and the equivalent illicit unions between a woman and her corresponding male relatives (Lev. 18:6–18; 20:12, 17; Ex. 20:11, 14, 19–21; Deut. 22:30; 27:20–3). Children born of any such prohibited incestuous unions were illegitimate.

The Talmudic rabbis disputed whether a child born of a couple who had reunited after being divorced from each other should be deemed a bastard as well, for such sexual unions were prohibited by the Torah (Deut. 24:4). Most Rabbis agreed that such children were to be viewed as legitimate but "profane," the latter taint only precluding them from serving as male priests or as wives to priests. Most rabbis assigned this same status of "legitimate but profane" to children born of a sexual union between a high priest and a widow, divorcee, prostitute, or defiled woman, or between a divorcee and a common priest. All these unions violated the Torah's rules on priestly purity (Lev. 21:7, 13–14), and the parents were punished for the sin. But their children were legitimate, although again foreclosed from serving as male priests or as wives to priests.

Bastards begat bastards, according to the Talmud. With narrow exceptions, if either party to a sexual union was a bastard at the time of the new child's conception, the child born of this union would be a bastard as well.[14] The rabbis debated at length about the status of

---

[13] Except in the case of a "levirate" marriage: the Torah stipulated that a brother (a *levir*) should marry his late brother's widow and have children by her in order to carry on his dead brother's lineage (Deut. 25:5–10). This was the obligation that Onan so famously flouted by having sex with his dead brother's wife but "spilling his semen upon the ground" for fear of impregnating her. For that failure of duty "God slew him" (Gen. 38:1–10).

[14] Yeb. 2.4, 5.2. The exception was to marry a Gentile slave, and have the child of that union later convert to Judaism. See Yev. 78a: "Mamzerim can be purified, i.e., there is a way that through which they do not transmit their illegitimacy to their offspring. How so? If a mamzer marries a slavewoman, the offspring is a slave and not a mamzer, for the offspring

foundlings, orphans, or newborns whose parentage was unknown or undisclosed: what if one or both of their parents were illegitimate? These "doubtful bastards," as these children came to be called, were regarded as presumptively legitimate if they were found within Jewish communities (especially if abandoned in the synagogue), if they bore evidence of Jewish parentage (such as being circumcised), or if their mother was a Jew and she declared the child to be legitimate. Absent such circumstances, it was safest for this child to convert formally to Judaism. The conversion eliminated all doubt about the child's lineage, and he or she was treated thereafter as a full-fledged legitimate member of the Jewish community.[15]

Classical Jewish law thus restricted the category of bastards to three main groups: children born of adultery, born of incest, or born to a bastard. Children born of many other forbidden or questionable unions were regarded as legitimate by most rabbis – though several of these cases remained disputed in the Talmud. Included on most rabbinic rolls of legitimacy were children conceived while a woman menstruated, even though this sexual union was explicitly forbidden by the Torah (Lev. 18:19; 20:18). Also included were children born of a Jewish–Gentile couple or between a Jew and his or her slave (even if this was an adulterous or incestuous relation). Also legitimate were children born of simple fornication, premarital fornication, prostitution, or concubinage, children born to a couple who had sex by mistake, fraud, fear, force, rape, or seduction, children born to a woman who was asleep during intercourse or who was brazen in seeking it out, or children born to a married couple who hated each other or were in the process of divorce. Even though their parents might well be punished for their sin in conceiving them, all such children were considered to be legitimate.

---

of a Jewish man and slavewoman is accorded his mother's legal status. If he then emancipates [the child] it turns out that the child becomes a freeman."

[15] On the Jewish conversion process, see Michael J. Broyde, "Proselytism and Jewish Law: Inreach, Outreach, and the Jewish Tradition," in *Sharing the Book: Religious Perspectives on the Rights and Wrongs of Proselytism,* ed. John Witte, Jr. and Richard C. Martin (Maryknoll, NY: Orbis Books, 1999), 45–60. For a detailed treatment of children born of ritual impurity in the Talmud, see Christine E. Hayes, *Gentile Impurities and Jewish Identities: Intermarriage and Conversion from the Bible to the Talmud* (Oxford: Oxford University Press, 2002), 164–92.

Only one main legal restriction was imposed upon the illegitimate at classical Jewish law. Bastards could not marry legitimately born Jews – though they were free to marry other bastards (whether Jew or Gentile, slave or free) or to marry converts to Judaism (regardless of that convert's lineage). This was how most early rabbis drew the sting from the hard passage in Deuteronomy 23:2 that banned bastards and their seed for "ten generations" from "the assembly of the Lord." This passage, the rabbis argued, meant only that a bastard could not enter the temple for the sake of getting married. And since bastards always begat bastards, this was a permanent prohibition on him and his seed – "to the tenth generation," that is, forever.[16] Bastards were free to enter the temple, however, for any other purpose besides getting married. Indeed, they were free to enter any part of the Jewish community for any legal purpose. Most early rabbis made clear that bastards were free to hold rabbinic or political offices, to litigate claims or to testify in court, to inherit, acquire, hold, sell, and devise property, and to engage in all other aspects of ritual, social, and commercial life just like any other member of the community.

The rabbis based this equal treatment of illegitimates and legitimates in all aspects of life, besides marriage, on the silence of the Torah. After all, Deuteronomy 17:15 said: "One from among your brethren shall you set as a king over you" – making no distinction between legitimate or illegitimate brethren who could serve as political rulers. The Torah set precise purity laws for the priesthood, but had no rule precluding bastards from serving as scholarly rabbis. Thus, a famous adage has it, "a bastard who is a scholar takes precedence over a high priest who is an ignoramus."[17] The Torah's rules on property and inheritance made clear that children born within and without marriage, as well as before and after divorce, were to inherit

---

[16] See esp. Yev. 78b. Some Rabbis softened this passage further by arguing that it applied only to illegitimate men who sought marriage, not illegitimate women.

[17] Hor. 3.8. But Sof. 1.13 says that Torahs copied and other texts written by bastards should not be used in the temple, and Hor. I.4 disqualifies bastards, among several others, from serving as judges in ordinary courts and from the Sanhedrin. These texts led to a minority view that illegitimacy was an impediment to political and priestly advancement in some communities. See Alexander Guttmann, *Rabbinic Judaism in the Making* (Detroit: Wayne State University Press, 1970), 26; Judah Goldin, *Studies in Midrash and Related Literature* (Philadelphia: The Jewish Publication Society, 1988), 208–9.

from their fathers, again without regard for their status (Ex. 25:46; Deut. 21:15–17). Only children born of slaves or of Gentiles could be limited in their inheritance rights. But that was because of their economic and religious status, not because they were illegitimate. All other Torah rules governing Jewish ritual, social, and economic life made no distinction between legitimate and illegitimate children, and the Talmudic rabbis largely maintained this equal treatment.

The rabbis found no reason to change these rules of equal treatment in light of the four Torah passages on the "sins of the fathers" being "visited" upon their children. Two of these "sins of the fathers" passages appear as a gloss on a specific Commandment:

You shall not make for yourself a graven image, or any likeness of anything that is in heaven above, or that is in the earth beneath, or that is in the water under the earth; you shall not bow down to them or serve them; for I the Lord am a jealous God, visiting the iniquity of the fathers upon the children to the third and the fourth generation of those who hate me, but showing steadfast love to thousands of those who love me and keep me commandments (Ex. 20:4–6; see also Deut. 5:8–10).

The sin at issue here is idolatry, not adultery or any other sexual offense, the rabbis made clear. And these passages draw no distinction between legitimate or illegitimate children. Those children, whatever their status, who love God and keep his commandments are promised God's steadfast love. Those children, of whatever status, who hate God and continue to practice idolatry like their ancestors are threatened with divine punishment. Moreover, the rabbis argued, because it was God himself who threatened divine punishment for breach of his Commandment, it was for God to mete out the punishment, not for a human tribunal. As one modern authority put it, quoting earlier rabbis: "In any case presented to a court where there is liability by divine law, the court must inform a party so liable: 'We will not apply sanctions against you, but you should fulfill your duty in the sight of Heaven, because Heaven will be your judge.' The court should so declare in order that the party will consider the matter carefully, placate his neighbor, and so fulfill his obligations to Heaven."[18]

The two other "sins of the fathers" passages appear as a gloss on the story of God in conversation with Moses on Mount Sinai

---

[18] Elon, *Jewish Law*, I:147.

during the preparation of the Decalogue. The conversation focused on the people obeying the Decalogue and being assured of God's covenant promise in return:

The Lord passed before him [Moses] and proclaimed: "The Lord, the Lord, a God merciful and gracious, slow to anger, and abounding in steadfast love and faithfulness, keeping steadfast love for thousands, forgiving iniquity and transgression and sin, but who will by no means clear the guilty, visiting the iniquity of the fathers upon the children, and the children's children, to the third and fourth generation." And Moses made haste to bow his head toward the earth and worshiped. And he said, "If now I have found favor in thy sight, O Lord, let the Lord, I pray thee, go in the midst of us, although it is a stiff necked people; and pardon our iniquity and our sin, and take us for thy inheritance" (Ex. 34:5–9; see also Num. 14:18–19).

This passage does not contain a formal law, the rabbis made clear, but a story about the law and about the mercy of God its author. Jewish laws about bastardy or any other matter are to be based on the commandments of the Torah, not on the stories about how the commandments came about. Moreover, the point of this passage is to underscore the mercy of God, even in meting out the divine punishment that he threatens for breach of one of his specific commandments. The rabbis point to this divine restraint several times in the Talmud.[19] But the clearest passage is in the Aggadah, a text drawn from the sermon literature of the early common era. Rather than imposing punishment immediately upon idolaters and their children as they deserve, God is quoted as saying:

I wait until the fourth generation to visit punishment upon the offenders, but if these generations are one after the other sinful, I will wait no longer with punishment. But those who love me, or fear me, I will reward even unto the thousandth generation. When Moses heard these words, according to which God would visit upon the descendents the sins of their fathers only if the consecutive generations were one after another sinful, he cast himself upon the ground and thanked God for it, for he knew that it never occurred among Israel that three consecutive generations were sinful.[20]

[19] See, e.g., San. 111a–b and analysis of various texts in Reinhard Neudecker, "Does God Visit the Iniquity of the Fathers upon their Children? Rabbinic Commentaries on Ex. 20,5b (Deut 5,9b)," *Gregorianum* 81(1) (2000): 5–24.

[20] Louis Ginzberg, *The Legends of the Jews*, trans. Henrietta Szold and Paul Radin (Philadelphia: The Jewish Publication Society, 2003), 605. See further ibid., 1021–2, citing

Even if one wanted to read these "sins of the fathers" passages as warrants for visiting the iniquity of parents upon children, the rabbis continued, this reading would violate a specific Torah prohibition against such vicarious liability. The Torah does have a doctrine of vicarious liability. For example, it punishes owners for the damage done by their animals, even executing owners whose repeated failure to control their oxen leads to the death of others (Ex. 21:28–36; 22:5). But the Torah makes clear that no vicarious liability charges are to be imposed on parents and children for the crimes of the other: "The fathers shall not be put to death for the children, nor shall the children be put to death for the fathers; every man shall be put to death for his own sin" (Deut. 24:16).[21] By the time of the Talmud, the rabbis saw this text as a bar not only to vicarious liability, but even to testimony by parents and children against each other: "Parents shall not be put to death because of the [crimes of] their children, nor shall children be put to death because of [the crimes of] their parents. But does not the verse already say that 'a person shall be put to death only for his own crime'? Rather, it means that a parent shall not be put to death on the basis of his children's testimony, nor children on the basis of their parents' testimony."[22]

Though classical Jewish law did not formally visit the sins of the fathers and mothers upon their children, the rabbis knew well that children born of forbidden or questionable unions could suffer miserably, even if they were legitimate. "Whoever marries a genealogically blemished [woman] will have children who are unworthy, i.e., genealogically blemished," reads the Talmud. "Woe to him who disqualifies his children and taints his family and who marries a woman who is not fit for him. Elijah ties him and the Holy One, blessed is he, whips him."[23] A later commentator wrote: "The very conception of the bastard (*mamzer*) is exceedingly evil,

---

Koh. 4.1; Hash 3b. See also the sympathetic discussion of the bastard's plight by Daniel the Tailor in the Midrash Vayikra Rabbah, quoted in Spitz, "Mamzerut," 562–4.

[21] San. 28a. The next verse underscored this lesson in individualized justice by commanding: "You shall not pervert the justice due . . . to the fatherless" (Deut. 24:17).

[22] Elon, *Jewish Law*, I:304, quoting *Sifrei Deuteronomy*, Ki Teze, sec. 280 (p. 297). See further San. 28a, and Babylonian Talmud San. 27b.

[23] Kid. 70a2.

having been brought about in impurity, abominable intention, and counsel of sin, and there is no doubt that the nature of the parent is concealed in the child. Consequently, God, in His love, has kept his holy people away from [this], just as He has separated us and kept us far away from all that is evil."[24]

Licit procreation through valid and proper marriages was by far the better course of action for parents and children. While a child ill-conceived might not suffer formal legal disabilities as a bastard, that child might well suffer other disabilities. The rabbis thus repeatedly warned couples against having children out of lawful wedlock. This counsel of prudence comes through in a striking passage in the Talmud:

Ten categories of persons are like bastards, but are not [legally] such, and they are: the children of a *niddah* [a menstruating woman], the children of one who is under a ban of excommunication, the children [born] of fear, the children of a woman who is forced [to cohabit or have sex], the child[ren] of a hated wife, the children of a seduced woman, the children of a wife divorced in the heart, the children of a woman thought to be another, the children of a drunken woman; and some say, the children of a brazen woman, of a woman asleep and of one who has intercourse with his betrothed in his father-in-law's house.

The children of *niddah* ultimately become leprous; the children of one under excommunication will ultimately be banned from the congregation of Israel, the child[ren] of fear will ultimately remove themselves from the source of holiness [the Torah], the children of a woman who is forced will themselves be violated, as for the children of a seduced woman ultimately others will seduce their heart, the children of a woman divorced in the heart will ultimately divorce themselves from all good and cleave to evil, the children of a woman thought to be another will ultimately change their faith, the children of a drunken woman will have children who will [be thought of] as though they were drunk, as it is written, *"How long wilt thou be drunken?"* [1 Sam. 1:14] which is rendered in the Targum "demented." "Some say the children of a brazen woman": these are persons who are bold-faced; "the children of a woman asleep": these are the sluggish. With regard to the children of "one who has intercourse with his betrothed in his father-in-law's house" there is a difference of opinion between Rab and Samuel: one says that the child is a bastard, and the other that he is a child of unknown paternity [a doubtful bastard].[25]

[24] *Sefer HaHinukh,* Mitzvah 560, quoted in Spitz, "Mamzerut," 567.
[25] *The Minor Tractates of the Talmud,* 424–5.

The Talmudic rabbis explicitly rejected the doctrine of adoption that prevailed in Roman law[26] and in other legal systems of their day. Adoption gave childless couples their own children and heirs, and it gave orphans and foundlings new parents who could nurture and support them. "Judaism did not recognize the Roman institution of adoption," one authority writes, "since the Roman concept is directed toward substituting a legal fiction for a biological fact and thus creating the illusion of a natural relationship between the foster parents and the adopted son. Judaism stated its case in no uncertain terms: what the Creator granted one and the other should not be interfered with; the natural relationship must not be altered. Any intervention on the part of some legal authority would amount to interference with the omniscience and original plan of the Maker."[27] None of the purported instances of adoption elsewhere in the Hebrew Bible (Gen. 30:1–13; 48:5–6; Ex. 2:7–19; Judg. 11:1–2; 1 Kings 11:20; 1 Chr. 2:34–5; Ezra 10:44; Ruth 4:16–17; Esther 2:7) were real adoptions in the legal sense, the rabbis contended – and most took place in locations outside of formal Jewish rule. And even if these could be regarded as legal adoptions per Roman law, no formal law of adoption was prescribed in the Torah to make this practice normative for the Jewish community.

This did not mean that an illegitimate child whose parents had abandoned him or her was without support. The local Jewish law court was considered to be "the father of all orphans," with responsibility to ensure that every child in the Jewish community was cared for. Moreover, Jewish law recognized the doctrine of guardianship (*apotropos*), which allowed a fit adult to be put in the position of the natural parents, with the right and the duty to provide for most of the child's upbringing, education, maintenance, and finance.[28]

---

[26] See further below pp. 62–4, and sources in Bruce W. Frier and Thomas A.J. McGinn, *A Casebook on Roman Family Law* (Oxford: Oxford University Press, 2004), 304–14.

[27] Soloveitchik, *Family Redeemed*, 60–1; see further Broyde, "Adoption, Personal Status, and Jewish Law," 140–5.

[28] See Broyde, "Adoption, Personal Status, and Jewish Law," 140–5 and Elon, ed., *Principles of Jewish Law*, 440–5.

EARLY CHRISTIAN TEACHINGS

Such were some of the main rabbinic teachings on childhood and illegitimacy that were available to the Church Fathers in the first six centuries of the common era. The Fathers did not develop a systematic theology or law of illegitimacy as part of their emerging teachings on sex, marriage, and family life.[29] But what little they did offer was often similar in tone to these rabbinic teachings on illegitimacy. Like the early rabbis, most Fathers rejected the notion of visiting the sins of the fathers upon children, and the later Fathers dismissed the story of Ishmael as grounds for imposing such vicarious liability. Also like the rabbis, the Fathers greatly narrowed the consequences of illegitimacy within the Christian communities – even while recognizing that out-of-wedlock births could cause great harm and pain. Unlike the early rabbis, however, the early Fathers drew on the full biblical canon, not just the Torah. This allowed them to counter some of the harsh texts against illegitimacy with other biblical passages that called for the protection and adoption of these children. Also unlike the rabbis, the Church Fathers greatly expanded the list of serious sexual sins as part of their emerging teachings on sex, marriage, and family life, but they did so without a corresponding expansion of the doctrine of illegitimacy. That last step would come only in the next millennium.

Sex, marriage, and family. Before sifting through their scattered texts on illegitimacy and adoption, it is worth tracking the emerging teachings of the Church Fathers on marriage and family life, since these teachings would shape Christian understandings of licit and illicit sex until modern times. The Church Fathers made clear from

---

[29] See generally Philip L. Reynolds, *Marriage in the Western Church: The Christianization of Marriage During the Patristic and Early Medieval Periods* (Leiden: E.J. Brill, 1994). See translations of most of these patristic writings in *The Ante-Nicene Fathers: The Writings of the Fathers Down to A.D. 325*, trans. and ed. Alexander Roberts *et al.* [1885], repr. edn., 10 vols. (Peabody, MA: Hendrickson Publishers, 1995) [hereafter "ANF"]; *Early Church Fathers: Nicene and Post-Nicene Fathers*, First Series, trans. and ed. Philip Schaff, [1886–9], repr. edn., 14 vols. (Peabody, MA: Hendrickson Publishers, 1994) [hereafter "CF 1"]; and *Early Church Fathers: Nicene and Post-Nicene Fathers*, Second Series, trans. and ed. Philip Schaff and Henry Wace, [1886–9], repr. ed., 14 vols. (Peabody, MA: Hendrickson Publishers, 1994) [hereafter "CF 2"].

the start that heterosexual monogamous marriage was the only place for licit sex and that all forms of extramarital sex were sinful. They also made clear that procreation was a main good and goal of marriage, and that non-procreative sex was suspicious even within marriage.

The Church Fathers anchored these views in a number of New Testament verses. Christ taught that marriage was created by God as a union of a man and a woman: "[H]e who made them from the beginning made them male and female, and said, 'For this reason a man shall leave his father and mother and be joined to his wife, and the two shall become one flesh'" (Matt. 19:4–6). Christ opened his ministry by blessing the wedding feast at Cana with his first miracle of changing water into wine (John 2:1–11). He reserved one of his last words on the cross for bringing his mother Mary and his apostle John into a new family: "Woman, behold your son." Son, "[b]ehold your mother" (John 19:26–7). Christ also used the image of marriage and the family to teach the basics about the Kingdom of God. "The kingdom of heaven may be compared to a king who gave a marriage feast for his son," he proclaimed. Only those who are invited may come to the feast. Only those who are ready for the feast when the bridegroom comes will gain entrance (Matt. 22:1–14; 25:1–13). The Kingdom of God may also be viewed as an extended spiritual family. "My mother and my brothers are those who hear the Word of God and do it" (Luke 8:21). "Let the children come to me and do not hinder them; for to such belongs the kingdom of God" (Luke 18:16–17). Even the most "prodigal son" and daughter, who come in childlike faith to seek forgiveness, can be part of this divine family (Luke 15:11–32). To be both a child of God and a brother or sister in Christ were the defining features of the new Christian community.

Christians were not, however, to elevate the temporal demands of their own families above the spiritual demands of the Kingdom of God. Christ commanded his twelve disciples to leave their families and vocations behind them and follow him. He commanded a man mourning the death of his father: "Follow me, and leave the dead to bury their own dead" (Matt. 8:21–2). "Truly, I say to you," he said to his disciples, "there is no man who has left house or wife or brothers or parents or children, for the sake of the kingdom of God, who will not receive manifold more in the age to come in eternal life" (Luke 18:29–30). Christians were also not to subordinate the moral laws of marriage and sexuality taught by Moses to sinful calculus. In the Beatitudes, Christ set forth the letter and spirit of the new Christian law. "You have heard that it was said, 'You shall not commit adultery'. But I say to you that every one who looks at a woman lustfully has already committed adultery with her in his heart." "It was also said, 'Whoever divorces his wife, let him give her a certificate of divorce'. But I say to you every one who divorces his wife, except on the ground of unchastity, makes her an adulteress; and whoever marries a divorced woman commits adultery" (Matt. 5:27–32). "What God has joined together, let not man put asunder" (Matt. 19:6).

St. Paul elaborated these Gospel teachings in his letters to the new Christian churches. He used the image of marriage not only to describe the Kingdom of God, as Christ had done, but also to define the nature of such unions in Christ. The church is the bride, Christ is the bridegroom, he argued. And in this metaphor lie the first principles of authority and submission, love and sacrifice that become both the Christian church and a Christian marriage. "[T]he husband is the head of the wife as Christ is the head of the church," Paul wrote to the Ephesians. "As the church is subject to Christ, so let wives be subject in everything to their husbands . . . [H]usbands should love their wives as their own bodies. He who loves his wife loves himself. For no man ever hates his own flesh, but nourishes and cherishes it, as Christ does the church, because we are members of his body" (Eph. 5:23–8). Paul translated Christ's teaching about the superiority of the Kingdom of God to earthly families into a more general counsel about the superiority of celibacy to marriage. "It is well for a man not to touch a woman," Paul wrote; "I wish that all of you were [celibate] as I myself am" (1 Cor. 7:1, 7). Paul advised virgins to remain celibate and widows and widowers to avoid remarriage if they could. For marriage divided persons between spiritual and temporal loyalties, and distracted them from divine service (1 Cor. 7:8–39; 1 Tim. 5:3–16). But Paul condoned marriage for those tempted by sexual sin, saying it was "better to marry than to be aflame with passion" (1 Cor. 7:9). And within marriage, he commended equal regard and rights for the sexual needs of both spouses.

> [B]ecause of the temptation to immorality, each man should have his own wife, and each woman her own husband. The husband should give to the wife her conjugal rights, and likewise the wife to her husband. For the wife does not rule over her own body, but the husband does; likewise the husband does not rule over his own body, but the wife does. Do not refuse one another except perhaps by agreement for a season, that you may devote yourselves to prayer; but then come together again, lest Satan tempt you with lack of self-control (1 Cor. 7:2–7).

Paul glossed Christ's prohibitions on adultery and lust with a number of specific prohibitions against sexual sins outside of marriage. These included incest, homosexuality, sodomy, prostitution, polygamy, seduction, immoderate dress and grooming, and other forms of sexual "immorality" and "perversion" (Rom. 1:24–7; 1 Cor. 5:1; 6:9, 15–20; Eph. 5:3–4; Col. 3:5–6; 1 Tim. 2:9–10; 3:2). "Flee fornication!" was his most famous admonition (1 Cor. 6:18).

Even before they were formally gathered into a canonical Scripture, these biblical passages of sex, marriage, and family life inspired the early church to develop a number of canon law rules to govern the sexual and marital morality of its members and clergy. The earliest surviving church laws – from the *Didache* (c. 90–120) onward – prohibited the sins of sodomy, adultery, pedophilia, and fornication, and commended chastity, modesty of dress, and separation of the sexes during bathing and education.[30] The ecumenical church councils from 325 to 451 repeated and refined this emerging Christian ethic somewhat. Several local synods and councils from the third to the sixth centuries added further rules. The earliest such councils ordered bishops, clergy, monks, and other leaders of the church to be chaste, heterosexual, and monogamous. By the fifth century, several councils ordered high clerics to be celibate, and to avoid prostitution, concubinage, and other sexual activities on pain of losing their clerical offices. Lay Christians, in

---

[30] *The Teaching of the Twelve Apostles, Didache, or The Oldest Church Manual*, trans. and ed. Philip Schaff, 3rd rev. edn. (New York: Funk & Wagnalls, 1889), 161, 168, 172; *Didascalia Apostolorum*, trans. R. Hugh Connolly (Oxford: Clarendon Press, 1929), chaps. 2, 3, 4, and 14.

turn, were enjoined to live in peaceful, monogamous, and hetero-sexual unions. They were prohibited from sexual sins of all sorts, with Paul's lists of sins repeated and sometimes supplemented with strong rules against incest, bestiality, and polygamy. Christians were further forbidden from marrying Jews, heretics, or heathens and from marrying parties with whom they had fornicated (save in the case of pregnancy).[31]

A good concrete example of this early conciliar legislation comes from the Council of Elvira in Spain, which issued a collection of disciplinary rules around 300–9 CE – just before the Edict of Milan granted new tolerance to the Christian church in the Roman empire. More than a third of Elvira's eighty-one canons dealt with issues of sex, marriage, and family life. Most of these canons threatened church members with the severe spiritual discipline of bans from the Eucharist or excommunication from the church altogether for their violation.

A number of the Elvira canons dealt with questions of proper marital formation and dissolution:

8. Women who without acceptable cause leave their husbands and join another man may not receive communion even when death approaches.

9. A baptized woman who leaves an adulterous husband who has been baptized, for another man, may not marry him. If she does, she may not receive communion until her former husband dies, unless she is seriously ill.

10. If an unbaptized woman marries another man after being deserted by her husband who was a catechumen, she may still be baptized. This is also true for female catechumens. If a Christian woman marries a man in the knowledge that he deserted his former wife without cause, she may receive communion only at the time of her death.

11. If a female catechumen marries a man in the knowledge that he deserted his former wife without cause, she may not be baptized for five years unless she becomes seriously ill.

61. A man who, after his wife's death, marries her baptized sister may not commune for five years unless illness requires that reconciliation be offered sooner.

---

[31] See illustrative provisions in *The Seven Ecumenical Councils*, CF 2, XIV:11, 46–51, 70, 73, 79, 81–2, 92, 95, 98, 129, 149, 156, 157, 279, 280, 452, 460–2, 569–70, 604–13. See discussion in David Balch and Carolyn Osiek, *The Family in Early Christianity* (Louisville: Westminster John Knox Press, 1997); David Balch and Carolyn Osiek, eds., *Early Christian Families in Context: An Interdisciplinary Dialogue* (Grand Rapids, MI: Wm. B. Eerdmans, 2005).

The Council of Elvira also prohibited marriage between Christians and non-Christians:

15. Christian girls are not to marry pagans, no matter how few eligible men there are, for such marriages lead to adultery of the soul.

16. Heretics shall not be joined in marriage with Catholic girls unless they accept the Catholic faith. Catholic girls may not marry Jews or heretics, because they cannot find a unity when the faithful and the unfaithful are joined. Parents who allow this to happen shall not commune for five years.

17. If parents allow their daughter to marry a pagan priest, they shall not receive communion even at the time of death.

A number of canons dealt with issues of sexual immorality, particularly the burning issues of fornication and adultery, on which the Council came down hard:

7. If a Christian completes penance for a sexual offense and then again commits fornication, he or she may not receive communion even when death approaches.

31. Young men who have been baptized and then are involved in sexual immorality may be admitted to communion when they marry if they have fulfilled the required penance.

44. A former prostitute who has married and who seeks admission to the Christian faith shall be received without delay.

47. If a baptized married man commits adultery repeatedly, he is to be asked as he nears death whether or not he will reform should he recover. If he so promises, he may receive communion. If he recovers and commits adultery again, he may not commune again, even as death approaches.

64. A woman who remains in adultery to the time of her death may not commune. If she breaks the relationship, she must complete ten years' penance before communing.

65. If a cleric knows of his wife's adultery and continues to live with her, he shall not receive communion even before death in order not to let it appear that one who is to exemplify a good life has condoned sin.

69. A married person who commits adultery once may be reconciled after five years' penance unless illness necessitates an earlier reconciliation.

70. A husband who knows of his wife's adultery and who remains with her may not commune even prior to death. If he lived with his wife for a period of time after her adultery and then left her, he may not commune for ten years.

72. If a widow has intercourse and then marries the man, she may only commune after five years' penance. If she marries another man instead, she

is excluded from communion even at the time of death. If the man she marries is a Christian, she may not receive communion until completing ten years' penance, unless illness makes earlier communion advisable.

78. If a Christian confesses adultery with a Jewish or pagan woman, he is denied communion for some time. If his sin is exposed by someone else, he must complete five years' penance before receiving the Sunday communion.

Several other canons also dealt directly with children, providing a modicum of spiritual and physical protection from delinquent or abusive parents, including adulteresses who might be tempted to abort or smother their illegitimate children:

12. Parents and other Christians who give up their children to sexual abuse are selling others' bodies, and if they do so or sell their own bodies, they shall not receive communion even at death.

22. If people fall from the Catholic church into heresy and then return, let them not be denied penance, since they have acknowledged their sin. Let them be given communion after ten years' penance. If children have been led into heresy, it is not their own fault, and they should be received back immediately.

54. Parents who fail to keep the betrothal agreement and who break their child's engagement are to be kept from communion for three years. If the bride or groom has committed a serious crime, the parents are justified in such an action. If both the bride and groom are involved in the sin, the first rule applies and the parents may not interfere.

63. If a woman conceives in adultery and then has an abortion, she may not commune again, even as death approaches, because she has sinned twice.

68. A catechumen who conceives in adultery and then suffocates the child may be baptized only when death approaches.

66. A man who marries his stepdaughter is guilty of incest and may not commune even before death.

71. Those who sexually abuse boys may not commune even when death approaches.[32]

Not only a body of new church laws, like those issued by the Council of Elvira, but also a body of new Christian theology

---

[32] See Hamilton Hess, *Sexuality and Power: The Emergence of Canon Law at the Synod of Elvira* (Philadelphia: University of Pennsylvania Press, 1972), with translation by Kenneth Pennington, posted at http://faculty.cua.edu/pennington/Canon%20Law/ElviraCanons. htm (visited April 16, 2008). Historians dispute whether these canons were all issued by a single council, or were the products of several councils and later compiled.

emerged from the second century forward.[33] The Church Fathers, who wrote prior to the fourth-century Christianization of Rome, sometimes set their teachings in sharp contrast to those of Roman law and society. They singled out for harshest criticism the Roman practice of temple harlotry, concubinage, transvestism, homosexuality, incest, polygamy, abortion, infanticide, and child abuse.[34] The later Church Fathers repeated and embellished these criticisms at great length, and their efforts eventually helped effectuate some modest changes in Roman law.[35]

The fullest patristic teachings on marriage and family life came from St. Augustine at the turn of the fifth century. Augustine called marriage a "true and loyal partnership" of faith, the "seedbed of the city," the "first step in the organization of men." God has ordained marriage to attain three goods (*bona*) in the life of man and society, he wrote. Marriage "is the ordained means of procreation (*proles*), the guarantee of chastity (*fides*), and the bond of permanent union (*sacramentum*)." As a created, natural means of procreation, Christian marriage rendered sexual intercourse licit. As a contract of fidelity, marriage gave husband and wife an equal power over the other's body, an equal right to demand that the other spouse avoid adultery, and an equal claim to the "service, in a certain measure, of sustaining each other's weakness, for the avoidance of illicit intercourse." As a "certain sacramental bond," marriage was a source and symbol of permanent union between Christians. "[M]arriage bears a kind of sacred bond," Augustine wrote; "it can be dissolved in no way except by the death of one of the parties. The bond of marriage remains, even if offspring for which the marriage was entered upon, should not follow because of a clear case of sterility, so that it is not

---

[33] Reynolds, *Marriage in the Western Church*, 121–240.

[34] See, e.g., Tertullian, *Apologeticus* and *De Spectaculis*, in *Tertullian*, trans. and ed. Gerald H. Rendall (New York: G.P. Putnam's Sons, 1931), 32, 35–48, 79, 105, 179, 274–81; Tertullian, *Against Marcion*, ANF, III:294, 385–7; Clement, *The Instructor*, ANF, II:212–22, 250–3, 259–63; Clement, *Stromata*, ANF, II:377–9.

[35] See further below pp. 70–2. See Jean Gaudemet, "Les transformations de la vie familiale au bas empire et l'influence du christianisme," *Romanitas* 4 (1962): 58–85; id., "Tendances nouvelles de la legislation familiale aux ivme siècle," *Antiquitas* 1 (1978): 187–207; John T. Noonan, "Novel 22," in *The Bond of Marriage: An Ecumenical and Interdisciplinary Study*, ed. W.J. Bassett (Notre Dame/London: University of Notre Dame Press, 1968), 41–90; Engbert J.J. Jonkers, *Invloed van het Christendom op de romeinsche wetgeving betreffende het concubinaat en de echtscheiding* (Wageningen: H. Veenman, 1938).

lawful for married people who know they will not have any children to separate and to unite with others even for the sake of having children."[36]

Procreation, fidelity, and sacrament: these were the three goods of marriage, in Augustine's view. They were the reason that the institution of marriage was good. They were why participation in marriage was good. They were the goods and goals that a person could hope and expect to realize upon marrying. Augustine usually listed the goods of marriage in this order, giving first place to the good of procreation. At least twice, he underscored this priority by writing that "the institution of marriage exists for the sake of procreation; for this reason did our forebearers enter into the union of marriage and lawfully take to themselves their wives, *only* because of the duty to beget children."[37]

Augustine, however, did not call procreation the primary good of marriage, and the others secondary. He sometimes changed the order of his list of marital goods to "fidelity, procreation, and sacrament," passages that inspired later canonists and theologians to develop theories of "marital affection" as the primary marital good.[38] Even when he listed procreation as the first marital good, Augustine made clear that spousal fidelity and sacramental stability were essential for a marriage to be good and sufficient when married couples were childless or their children had left the household. And in doing so, he followed the classic authors in highlighting some of the benefits of marriage to the couple themselves:

[Marriage] does not seem to me to be a good solely because of the procreation of children, but also because of the natural companionship

---

[36] Augustine, *The Good of Marriage*, in R.J. Deferrari, ed., *St. Augustine: Treatises on Marriage and Other Subjects* (New York: Fathers of the Church, Inc., 1955), 17, 31–2; Augustine, *On Marriage and Concupiscence*, in CF I, V:271; Augustine, *On Original Sin*, in CF I, V:251; Augustine, *City of God*, XIV:10, 21, 22; XV:16; XIX:7, 14, in CF I, II.

[37] Augustine, *Adulterous Marriages*, in *St. Augustine: Treatises on Marriage*, 116 (emphasis added).

[38] Augustine, *Commentary on the Literal Meaning of Genesis*, 9.7.12, trans. J.H. Taylor, in Johannes Quasten *et al.*, eds., *Ancient Christian Writers: The Works of the Fathers in Translation* (New York: Newman Press, 1982), 42:78. See later medieval theories in John T. Noonan, Jr., "Marital Affection among the Canonists," *Studia Gratiana* 14 (1967): 489–99; Jean Leclerq, *Monks on Marriage: A Twelfth Century View* (New York: Seabury Press, 1982), 11–38, 71–81.

(*societas*) between the two sexes. Otherwise, we could not speak of marriage in the case of old people, especially if they had lost their children or had begotten none at all. But, in a good marriage, although one of many years, even if the ardor of youth has cooled between man and woman, the order of chastity still flourishes between husband and wife . . . there is observed that promise of respect and of services due to each other by either sex, even though both members weaken in health and become moribund, the chastity of souls rightly joined together continues the purer, the more it has been proved, the more secure, the more it has been calmed.[39]

Augustine's account of the goods of marriage was more positive than most early Christian formulations. Many Church Fathers, before and after him, not only treated marriage as less virtuous than chastity and celibacy, but also spoke of marriage and of sexual intercourse even within marriage in increasingly deprecatory and discouraging terms. A few of them pressed this preference to the point of outright opposition to any sexual intercourse, sometimes even to marriage itself. By the later fourth century, it was commonplace to treat marriage as the least virtuous Christian estate, and to countenance sexual intercourse only for the limited purpose of procreation.[40] This emphasis became even more pronounced in the penitential literature of the later first millennium.[41]

Illegitimacy and adoption. This heavy emphasis upon licit and limited sex within marriage alone and this new emphasis on marriage as the only proper locus for procreation seemed tailor-made for an expansive doctrine of illegitimacy within the early Western church. But nothing of the kind occurred in the church writings of the first six centuries. The surviving canon laws from this period were virtually silent on the subject of illegitimacy. The church councils called only for parents and children to remain supportive

---

[39] Augustine, *The Good of Marriage*, 12–13.
[40] Ambrose, *Concerning Widows*, chap. 4.23, in CF 2, X:395. See also Gregory of Nyssa, *On Virginity*, in CF 2, V:342–71; Jerome, *Letters*, in CF 2, VI:22–42, 66–79, 102–11, 141–8, 260–72, and Jerome, *Against Jovinianus*, in CF 2, VI:346–86. See further analysis in David G. Hunter, *Marriage, Celibacy, and Heresy in Ancient Christianity: The Jovinianist Controversy* (Oxford: Oxford University Press, 2007).
[41] James A. Brundage, *Law, Sex, and Christian Society in Medieval Europe* (Chicago: University of Chicago Press, 1987), 77–175.

of each other and for the church and its leaders to care for orphans and abandoned children.[42]

The individual Fathers who spoke to the doctrine of illegitimacy condemned extramarital sex of every sort. But they did not condemn the children of these unions or condone easy application of the biblical texts on illegitimacy. In the early third century, for example, Cyprian of Carthage rebuked his fellow Christians who refused to associate with the children of adulterers, fornicators, and prostitutes – and those whose parents had been in association with schismatic bishops. Such persons were "unclean idolaters," the local church argued, citing St. Paul (Eph. 5:5; Col. 3:5–6), and they were thus to be shunned and banished to keep the local congregation pure and holy. This is not how the church should operate, Cyprian countered. "According to our faith," each person is guilty only "of his own sin; nor can one become guilty for another, since the Lord forewarns us, saying, 'The righteousness of the righteous shall be upon him, and the wickedness of the wicked shall be upon him' (Ezek. 18:20). And again: 'The fathers shall not die for the children, and the children shall not die for the fathers. Everyone shall die for his own sin' (Deut. 24:16). Reading and observing this, we certainly think that no one is to be restrained from the fruit of satisfaction, and the hope and peace, since we know ... both that sinners are brought to repentance, and that pardon and mercy are not denied to penitents" regardless of the legitimacy of their birth or the sins of their parents.[43]

Another third-century Church Father, Methodius, taught similarly that the perfection of Christ masks any taint of illegitimacy, even in the church's bishops and other clergy. "Very many who are begotten of unrighteous seed are not only numbered among the brethren, but are often called even to preside over them." "[T]hose who are born of adultery do come to perfection." "[T]hose who are begotten, even though it be in adultery, are committed to guardian angels."[44]

---

[42] See, e.g., the conciliar decrees in CF 2, XIV: 98–9; ANF, VII:433.
[43] Cyprian, *The Epistles*, Epistle 51, in ANF, V.
[44] Methodius, *The Banquet of the Ten Virgins*, Disc. 2, chaps. 3, 6, in ANF, VI.

The prolific third-century Father, Origen, denounced the notion of visiting the sins of the fathers upon their children. He let loose a barrage of biblical texts that in his view trumped the condemnations of illegitimate children offered by a pagan Greek critic named Celsus:

> How much better are those words of Scripture: "The fathers shall not be put to death for the children, nor the children for the fathers. Every man shall be put to death for his own sin" (Deut. 24:16). And again, "Every man who eateth the sour grace, his teeth shall be set on edge" [not his children's teeth] (Jer. 31:30). And, "The son shall not bear the iniquity of the father neither shall the father bear the iniquity of the son: the righteousness of the righteous shall be upon him, and the wickedness of the wicked shall be upon him" (Ezek. 18:20). If any shall say that the response, "To children's children and, to those who come after him," corresponds with that passage, "Who visits the iniquity of the fathers upon the children unto the third and fourth generation of them that hate Me" (Ex. 20:5), let him learn from Ezekiel that this language is not to be taken literally; for he proves those who say, "Our fathers have eaten sour grapes, and the children's teeth are set on edge," and then he adds: "As I live, saith the Lord, every one shall die for his own sin" (Ezek. 18:2–4).[45]

These texts from Deuteronomy 24, Ezekiel 18, and Jeremiah 31 that condemned vicarious liability for (illegitimate) children came in for endless repetition among the Church Fathers. In the mid-fourth century, Jerome, famous for his translation of the Bible into the Latin Vulgate, cited these texts in proclaiming that "an old man's countless sins cannot fairly be avenged upon a harmless infant." "Nor can a mother's harlotry be counted against her children." After all, Jerome argued, five bastards appear in the genealogy of Christ (Matt. 1:1–17) – including Perez and Zereh, who were born of the adultery, incest, and prostitution of Judah (Gen. 38:12–30), and Solomon, who was born of David's polygamous adultery with Bathsheba and his arranged murder of Bathsheba's husband Uriah (2 Sam. 11:1–12:25). Moreover, someone as unruly as Jephthah, the "son of a harlot," is included on the roll of great judges of ancient Israel and "reckoned by the apostle in the roll of righteousness" (Heb. 11:32).

---

[45] Origen, *Against Celsus*, bk. 8, ch. 40, in ANF, IV. For prevailing Greek views, see Daniel Ogden, *Greek Bastardy in the Classical and Hellenistic Periods* (Oxford: Oxford University Press, 1996).

"Birth from adultery imputes no blame to the child but to the father."
"[N]either the virtues nor the vices of parents are imputed to their
children." This is the real point of the "sins of the fathers" passages in
the Pentateuch, Jerome wrote, echoing rabbinic teaching:

> It is thus that he visits the sins of the fathers upon the children unto the
> third and fourth generation; not punishing those who sin immediately but
> pardoning their first offenses and only passing sentence on them for their
> last. For if it were otherwise and if God were to stand forth on the moment
> as the avenger of iniquity, the church would lose many of its saints, and
> certainly would be deprived of the apostle Paul.[46]

Augustine came to the same conclusion, and emphasized the
need for all persons, regardless of their status at birth, to be reborn
in Christ. "Not only the children of wedlock, but also those of
adultery, are a good work in so far as they are the work of God, by
whom they are created: but as concerns original sin, they are all
born under condemnation of the first Adam; not only those who are
born in adultery, but likewise such as are born in wedlock, unless
they be regenerated in the second Adam, which is Christ." All persons
are liable for the sin of Adam and Eve, and all are "conceived and born
in the sin of their parents," Augustine elaborated in his writings on
original sin. As such, "all persons are bastards." But all persons are also
promised salvation from sin if they seek God's grace in faith and are
reborn in Christ. The quality of a person's parents or the legitimacy
of a person's birth makes no difference in this economy of salvation.
"No man can return to his mother's bowels and be born again."
Everyone must be reborn in Christ and "received into the church –
being now . . . not bastards but sons of God."[47]

Christians must read the "sins of the fathers" passages in the Bible
in light of this promised "covenant of regeneration," Augustine went
on. Notice that "to these words, 'I will visit the sins of the fathers
upon the children' is added 'who hate Me'; that is, hate Me as their
fathers hated Me: so that as the effect of imitating the good is that

---

[46] Jerome, *Letters,* Letters 39, 60, 107, 147, in CF 2, VI; Jerome, *To Pammachius against John
of Jerusalem,* ch. 22, in CF 2, VI.

[47] Augustine, *Tractates on John,* Tractates 11–12, in CF 1, VII; Augustine, *On Marriage and
Concupiscence,* bk. 2, ch. 35, bk. 2, ch. 50 in CF 1, V; Augustine, *On the Psalms,* Ps. 51, ch. 10,
in CF 1, VIII; Augustine, *Against the Donatists,* bk. 6, ch. 29, in CF 1, IV.

even their own sins are blotted out, so the imitation of the wicked causeth men to suffer not their own deservings only, but also of those whom they have imitated." The prophets Jeremiah and Ezekiel confirm this reading by insisting that sons shall not bear the iniquity of their fathers nor daughters be punished for the sins of their mothers, a teaching already foreshadowed under the old covenant in Deuteronomy 24:16.[48]

Christians must also read the ancient story of Abraham and Ishmael in light of this same biblical teaching of individual accountability, Augustine insisted. This story is not an illustration of how the "sins of the fathers" are to be visited upon their children, as some earlier Church Fathers had assumed.[49] Ishmael was banished for his own sin, not for Abraham's sin, Augustine argued. In fact, Abraham committed no sin at all in this story. He was eager to have a son as his heir, as God had promised him. As a good husband, he devoted his body to his wife, Sarah. Sarah was the one who convinced Abraham to take Hagar, her handmaid, as a way of fulfilling God's promise. Sex with a maid was a common practice in the day for childless couples, the maid serving as a surrogate mother for her mistress. God had not yet ruled out this option as a way of fulfilling his promise of countless descendents, though he had

---

[48] Augustine, *On the Psalms*, Ps. 119, ch. 14, in CF 1, VIII. But cf. Augustine, *The Enchiridion*, chaps. 46–7, in CF 1, III: "For that divine judgment, 'I shall visit the iniquities of the fathers upon their children' (Ex. 20:5, Deut. 5:9) certainly applies to them [children] before they come under the new covenant of regeneration. And it was this new covenant that was prophesied of, when it was said by Ezekiel, that the sons shall not bear the iniquity of the fathers, and that it should no longer be a proverb in Israel, 'The fathers have eaten sour grapes, and the children's teeth are set on edge' (Ezek. 18:2). Here lies the necessity that each man should be born again, that he might be freed from the sin in which he was born. For the sins committed afterwards can be cured by penitence. Whether God threatens to visit the iniquity of the fathers upon the children unto the third and fourth generations, because in His mercy He does not extend his wrath against the sins of the progenitors further than that, lest those who do not obtain the grace of regeneration might be crushed down under too heavy a burden if they were compelled to bear as original guilt all the sins of their progenitors from the very beginning of the human race, and to pay the penalty for them; or whether any other solution of this great question may or may not be found in Scripture by a more diligent and more careful interpretation, I dare not rashly affirm."

[49] See, e.g., the more literal reading of this Abraham–Ishmael story as a warrant for banishing illegitimate children in Clement, *Stromata*, bk. 1, ch. 5 in ANF, II; Irenaeus, *Against Heresies*, bk. 1, ch. 18, in ANF, I; Justin Martyr, *Dialogue of Justin*, ch. 56, in ANF, I; Hilary of Poiters, *On the Trinity*, bk. 4, chaps. 26–7, in CF 2, IX.

specifically ruled out adoption of an existing slave, which was also a common practice in the day. And, Augustine insisted, there is not a whiff of lust or fraud in the whole story.

Abraham is in no way to be branded as guilty concerning the concubine, for he used her for the begetting of progeny, not for the gratification of lust; and not to insult, but rather to obey his wife . . . Here there is no wanton lust, no filthy lewdness. The handmaid is delivered to the husband by the wife for the sake of progeny, and is received by the husband for the sake of progeny, each seeking, not guilty excess, but natural fruit.[50]

Ishmael was banished from Abraham's household and deprived of his inheritance because of his own sin, Augustine argued. Ishmael was "obstinate" toward Sarah and was guilty of "deceiving and mocking" his little brother, Isaac, even "persecuting him." It was for that sinful act that Ishmael was punished – "not because he was the son of a bondwoman [Hagar], but because . . . he was proud to his brother, proud in playing, that is in mocking him." It was not because he was the illegitimate child of a bonded slave woman that he was banished; it was because of "his own stiff neck." "The children of bond women, when wicked are cast out; and the child of a free woman, when [evil] is cast out. Let none, therefore, presume on the birth of good parents" or despair because of their birth from bad parents.[51]

Even if the exact moral lessons of this ancient story might be disputed, Augustine continued, St. Paul makes clear that Christians should read the story of Hagar and Sarah allegorically, not literally. In Galatians 4:21–31, Augustine wrote in his *City of God*, Paul shows that "Sarah the free woman, prefigured the free city" of God, while Hagar, the bond woman, represented the enslaved city of men.

Citizens are begotten to the earthly city by nature vitiated by sin, but to the heavenly city by grace freeing nature from sin; whence the former are called "vessels of wrath," the latter "vessels of mercy." And this was typified

---

[50] Augustine, *City of God*, bk. 16, ch. 25, in CF 1, II. See further Augustine, *Tractates on John*, Tractate 11, ch. 8, 13 in CF 1, VII; Augustine, *Reply to Faustus the Manichaean*, bk. 22, ch. 32, in CF 1, IV.

[51] Augustine, *Against the Donatists*, bk. 1, ch. 10, in CF 1, IV; Augustine, *Tractates on John*, Tractate 11, chaps. 12–13 and Tractate 12, on John 3:16–21, ch. 4, in CF 1, VII. Another Church Father said that Ishmael "was wild and kicked at Isaac." See Ephraim Syrus, *Nineteen Hymns on the Nativity of Christ in the Flesh*, Hymn 8, in CF 2, XIII.

in the two sons of Abraham – Ishmael, the son of [H]agar the handmaid being born according to the flesh, while Isaac was born of the free woman Sarah, according to the promise. Both, indeed, were of Abraham's seed; but the one begotten by natural law, the other was given by divine promise. In the one's birth, human action is revealed; in the other, a divine kindness comes to light.[52]

While they rejected the doctrine of illegitimacy within the church, the later Church Fathers recognized that children born out of wedlock would bear undue shame and hardship given the prevailing law and culture of illegitimacy in the Roman empire.[53] The Fathers used this reality to urge their followers to avoid extramarital sex and to live by the letter and spirit of the Bible's teachings on proper sexuality. Augustine's Greek contemporary, John Chrysostom, put it well in pleading with his congregants to maintain their sexual morality:

Wherefore I beseech you flee fornication, and the mother of it, drunkenness. Why sow where reaping is impossible, or rather even if thou dost reap, the fruit brings thee great shame? For even if a child is born, it at once disgraces thyself, and has itself had injustice done it in being born through thee illegitimate and base. And if thou leave it never so much money, both the son of an harlot, and that of a servant-maid, is disreputable at home, disreputable in the city, disreputable in a court of law: disreputable too wilt thou be also, both in thy life time, and when dead. For it thou have departed even, the memorials of thy unseemliness abide. Why then bring disgrace upon all these? Why sow where the ground makes it its care to destroy the fruit? where there are many efforts at abortion? where there is murder before the birth? for even the harlot though does not let continue a mere harlot, but makest her a murderess also. You see how drunkeness leads to whoredom to adultery, adultery to murder; or rather to a something even worse than murder.[54]

Abortion, smothering, exposure, or abandonment of illegitimate and other unwanted children, practices tolerated by Roman law,

---

[52] Augustine, *City of God*, bk. 15, ch. 2–3, in CF I, II. See further Augustine, *Letters*, Letter 93, in CF I, I; Augustine, *On Christian Doctrine*, bk. 4, ch. 20, in CF I, II; Augustine, *On the Proceeding of Pelagius*, ch. 14, in CF I, V; Augustine, *A Treatise on the Grace of Christ and on Original Sin*, bk. I, ch. 31, in CF I, V; Augustine, *On the Psalms*, Ps. 120, ch. 6, in CF I, VIII.

[53] On this see further below, pp. 52–9.

[54] John Chrysostom, *Homilies on the Epistle of Paul to the Romans*, Hom. 24 on Rom. 13:14, in CF I, XI. See also John Chrysostom, *Homilies on Matthew*, Hom. 9, 74 in CF I, X.

were condemned by the Church Fathers.[55] Such acts, several Fathers pointed out, were in open violation of the Bible's repeated calls for God's people to care for the "fatherless," the bastards and orphans, in their midst with charity and benevolence (Deut. 24:17; Ps. 68:2; Job 29:12; Is. 1:17; Jer. 5:28; James 1:27).[56]

Some Fathers saw a far better solution in the doctrine of adoption, which was a common institution in Rome by the first century CE. Already an early church law urged that the faithful "who have no children should adopt orphans, and treat them as their own." Those who perform this "great work . . . shall receive the reward of this charity from the Lord God" who is "the father of orphans."[57] Bishops and other clergy, in particular, were called upon to provide for "the orphans the care of parents; . . . to the maiden, till she arrives at the age of marriage, and ye give her in marriage to a brother [in the church]: to the young man assistance, that he may learn a trade and be maintained by the advantage arising from it."[58]

Augustine was a particularly vocal champion of adoption, and he defended this institution against detractors who regarded it as a pagan Roman institution that Christians should avoid. For Augustine, adoption offered redemption to children in need and hope for parents without heirs. He believed that adoption was commonly practiced already in the Old Testament, contrary to prevailing rabbinic opinion.[59] He pointed to many passages that he considered examples of the simple adoption of the child(ren) of another: Abraham and Sarah adopted Ishmael born of Hagar. Jacob and Leah adopted her handmaid's son (Gen. 30:1–13). Jacob adopted his grandsons born of Joseph (Gen. 48:5–6, 15–16). Naomi adopted her grandchild Obed (Ruth 4:16–17). Other Church Fathers noted other such instances of adoption noted in the Hebrew Bible: Pharaoh's daughter adopting the infant Moses (Ex. 2:10), a later Pharaoh adopting Genubah (1 Kings 11:20), and Mordecai

---

[55] See below, p. 52. See further John Boswell, *The Kindness of Strangers: The Abandonment of Children in Western Europe from Late Antiquity to the Renaissance* (New York: Pantheon Books, 1988), 148ff.; John T. Noonan, Jr., *Contraception: A History of Its Treatment by Catholic Theologians and Canonists* (Cambridge, MA: Harvard University Press, 1986).

[56] See sources in Peter Brown, *Poverty and Leadership in the Later Roman Empire* (Hanover, NH/London: University Press of New England, 2000).

[57] *Constitutions of the Holy Apostles*, bk. 4, sec. 1, in ANF, VII:433.

[58] Ibid., 433–4.   [59] See above, p. 26.

adopting his cousin Esther (Esther 2:7). These examples, Augustine argued, show that "the word 'adoption' (*huiothesia*), or at least the reality, was of longstanding among the Jews."[60]

Christians should thus not suppose that "the custom of adoption is foreign to our Scriptures, as though it were something of the traditional laws of mankind that is worthy of censure, and so cannot be reconciled with the authority of the divine books. Adoption is something that has a long history and is familiar to the documents of the Church, that a son can be had by favor of a free choice as well as by natural begetting." And adoption is a good institution for parents and children alike, a valuable alternative to natural pro-creation. "Just look, brothers, just look at the rights conferred by adoption, how a man becomes a son of someone whose seed he was not born from, and as a result the one who adopts him has by this act of will more rights over him than the one who begot him has by nature. That being the case not only does [the man who adopts a child] have every right to be called a father, he ha[s] the greatest possible right."[61]

Moreover, said Augustine, adoption is the method that God uses to draw his people into an enduring covenant relationship with him. In the Old Testament, God embraced Israel as a "first-born son" and promised the people his divine inheritance (Ex. 4:22; 2 Sam. 7:14; Ps. 2:7; Jer. 3:19). In the New Testament, "the word adoption is of great importance in the system of our faith," for by it God redeems us from our sinful natures and brings us into the family of Christ. St. Paul used this image repeatedly, and Augustine quoted him at length. "God sent forth his Son, born of woman, born under the law, to redeem those who were under the law, so that we might receive adoption as sons" (Gal. 4:4–5; see also Rom. 9:4–5). "For all who are led by the Spirit of God are sons of God [and] heirs of God and fellow heirs with Christ" (Rom. 8:14, 17).

---

[60] Augustine, *Reply to Faustus the Manichaean*, bk. 22, ch. 32, in CF 1, IV; Augustine, *Sermons on Selected Lessons of the New Testament*, Sermon 1, ch. 28, in CF 1, VI; Augustine, *The Harmony between the Evangelists Matthew and Luke Concerning the Lord's Genealogy*, Sermon 51, in *The Works of Saint Augustine*, trans. and ed. John E. Rotelle (Charlottesville, VA: Intelex Corporation, 2001), 3.37.

[61] Augustine, *Reply to Faustus the Manichaean*, bk. 22, ch. 32, in CF 1, IV. Augustine, *Sermons on Selected Lessons of the New Testament*, Sermon 1, ch. 28, in CF 1, VI. The last quotation is from the translation in Augustine, *The Harmony between the Evangelists*, 3.37–8.

"[W]e ourselves who groan inwardly as we wait for adoption as sons, the redemption of our bodies" (Rom. 8:23). While "our Lord Jesus Christ is the only Son of God," Augustine concluded from these passages, "his brothers and fellow heirs, whom he is pleased to have, become so through a kind of adoption by divine grace."[62]

Augustine was more forthcoming on the doctrines of illegitimacy and adoption than most of the Church Fathers. But even he gave these doctrines only scant attention compared to his longer disquisitions on marriage and sexual ethics, let alone his voluminous writings on the major theological doctrines of God and man, sin and salvation, word and sacrament, church and state. Illegitimacy and its remedies were simply not major doctrinal or ethical issues for the Church Fathers of the first six centuries. But what they did say on the topic, counseled strongly against visiting the sexual sins of parents upon their children.

SUMMARY AND CONCLUSIONS

The Bible contains a number of "texts of terror" for illegitimate children.[63] Genesis and Judges record how Ishmael and Jephthah, born of concubinage and prostitution, were banished from their homes. Ezra records how children of interreligious marriage were banished from their land. Deuteronomy prohibits bastards and their seed from the assembly of the Lord. Zechariah discounts their capacity to rule in the state. Genesis, Judges, John, 1 Corinthians, Galatians, and Hebrews all describe bastards as wild, undisciplined, unruly, stubborn, unclean, unsavory, enslaved to misguided if not diabolical ideas. Hosea, Jeremiah, Lamentations, Sirach, and Wisdom treat bastards as both witnesses and victims of their parents' sexual sins. Their severe punishment, even to death, seems a painful but necessary expression of the Pentateuch's command that "the sins of the fathers" shall be "visited upon their children."

The Bible also, however, contains a number of texts of redemption for illegitimate children. Genesis reports that Ishmael

---

[62] Augustine, *The Harmony between the Evangelists*, 3.38–9.
[63] Phyllis Trible, *Texts of Terror: Literary-Feminist Readings of Biblical Narratives* (London: SCM Press, 2002).

survived and thrived, leaving a legacy of twelve sons and many
nations, despite being banished with his mother from his home and
disinherited. Judges and Hebrews record that Jephthah became one
of the great judges of ancient Israel and a key actor in the drama of
redemption. Deuteronomy, Jeremiah, and Ezekiel all explicitly
prohibit visiting the sins of the parents upon children, and command that each person be accountable only for his own acts, not
that of his parents. Matthew includes five bastards in the genealogy
of Christ, and Hebrews counts the child of a harlot on the roll of
the righteous. The Bible repeatedly calls God's people to do justice
and mercy to the fatherless and the orphan. In particular, the Bible
holds out adoption as a sublime human expression of love to a lost
child that reflects God's love in adopting his people as heirs to
salvation, despite their sinful birth.

The Talmudic rabbis reduced the sting of illegitimacy by redu-
cing the biblical texts that count and reading them very narrowly.
Only the laws of the Torah had enduring legal and moral significance for the community, they argued; all other texts could be
discounted. Only children of strict adultery and incest could be
regarded as illegitimate, and even these had loopholes to exploit.
The only stricture on illegitimates was that they could not marry
legitimate Jews; that is what Deuteronomy meant by barring them
from the assembly of the Lord. Little else was foreclosed to
illegitimates. "The sins of the fathers" passages had no bearing;
those are about how God, not humans, will punish idolaters, not
adulterers. The law says clearly that no child can bear liability for a
parents' sin.

The Church Fathers reduced the sting of illegitimacy by expanding
the texts that count, and reading them inventively. The story of
Abraham and Ishmael was not about the sins of the fathers being
visited upon children. It was Ishmael who sinned, not Abraham,
and he was punished, but not so severely that he did not thrive.
The sins of the fathers passages are not about vicarious liability for
children. They are about God's mercy in postponing punishment
for three or four generations, in hopes that later generations will
repent. Deuteronomy, Ezekiel, and Jeremiah make clear that children cannot be punished for the sins of the parents, and other texts
to the contrary are metaphors about how persistent idolaters should

fair. Rather than punish illegitimate children, Christians should embrace them as God's own, adopting them into their families, just as God adopts all sinners into the family of faith.

To mitigate the plight of the illegitimate child was not to deprecate the seriousness of their parents' sin. For the Church Fathers, Christian charity counseled tenderness for illegitimate children, but Christian morality declared anathema on the illicit sex that produced them. From the first to the sixth centuries, the church councils and Church Fathers condemned extramarital sex with increasing alacrity – eventually forbidding the clergy from all sex, and forbidding the laity from sexual unions with prostitutes, concubines, fiance(é)s, clergy, divorcees, relatives, Jews, heretics, heathens, and more. These increasingly stern views on sexual sin slowly soaked into the Roman law after the fourth century, and there they gradually combined with existing Roman laws on illegitimacy. It was this combination of the church's elaborate definition of extramarital sex and the Roman law's elaborate doctrine of illegitimacy that slowly gave shape to the emerging Western laws of illegitimacy – provisionally in the legal syntheses of the Christian Roman emperors, more fully in the canon law, civil law, and common laws of medieval and early modern times. That is the story of the next three chapters.

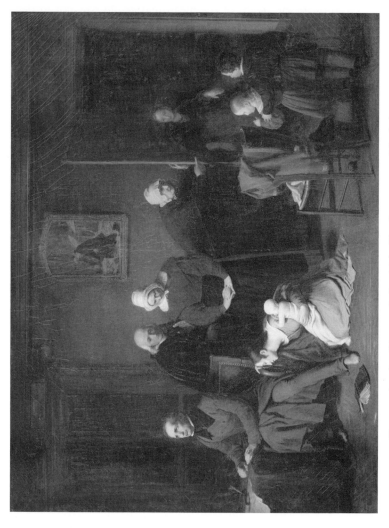

Figure 4 Antoine Béranger (1785–1867), *The Consequences of the Seduction.*

CHAPTER 2

Woe to bastards: The classical Roman law of illegitimacy and legitimation

The Western law of illegitimacy was born in ancient Rome. Rome had already developed a law of illegitimacy before the time of Christ, in the centuries of the republic. These early republican laws were greatly expanded in the pre-Christian Roman empire, particularly in the second century CE. In this pre-Christian period, however, "illegitimacy was neither a moral nor a social problem."[1] Illegitimacy was rather a convenient means to control citizenship and property in the empire, and to determine whether children came within the authority of their fathers or their mothers. The Roman state had no direct responsibility to support children. A legitimate child was the responsibility of its father and his extended household, called the *familia*.[2] "An illegitimate child was the responsibility of its mother or her *familia*, or it was disposed of in a way that resulted either in its death or its maintenance by another *familia*. The state thus incurred no expense. If the child was a slave, its mother's household was expanded; if a Roman citizen, the population of those eligible for civic or moral duties was expanded. The comparative lack of stigma is a striking feature of Roman society" before it was Christianized.[3]

The Christian emperors from the fourth to the sixth centuries confirmed and extended parts of this traditional Roman law of

---

[1] Beryl Rawson, "*Spurii* and the Roman View of Illegitimacy," *Antichthon* 23 (1989): 10–41, at 10.

[2] In classical Rome, the *familia* was the extended set of families under the authority of a single senior male, called the *paterfamilias*. It included not only all the children of the *paterfamilias*, but also the (great-)grandchildren born of his sons. It could also include slaves, wards, sojourners, students, and others who came within the *paterfamilias'* power. See Jane F. Gardner, *Family and* Familia *in Roman Law and Life* (Oxford: Clarendon Press, 1998).

[3] Rawson, "*Spurii*," 10–11.

illegitimacy, but they also added a heavy moral overlay. Drawing on the church's refined sexual morality, the emperors distinguished sharply between "spurious illegitimates," born of grave sexual sins, and "natural illegitimates," born of lighter sexual sins. Spurious children were treated as irredeemable and subject to increasingly onerous deprivations. Natural illegitimates were treated as innocent and eligible for legitimation, adoption, and other privileges.[4]

LAWFUL MARRIAGE AND ILLEGITIMATE BIRTH

Both before and after the Christianization of the empire, Roman law regarded as legitimate only those children who were born to, or adopted by, a couple who had entered into a "lawful marriage" (*matrimonium iustum, iustae nuptiae*). A lawful marriage was defined simply, per a mid-third century text, as "the union of a man and a

---

[4] The most important legal texts on point are in Gaius, *Institutiones*, ed. Paul Krüger and William Studemund (Berlin: Weidemann, 1877), 1.55–200 [hereafter "Gaius"]; *The Rules of Ulpian*, 5, 8, 13, 22, in S.P. Scott, *The Civil Law*, repr. edn., 17 vols. (New York: AMS Press, 1973), I:223–58; *The Opinions of Julius Paulus*, 19–26, in Scott, *The Civil Law*, I:259–332 [hereafter "Sent. Paul"]; Paul Krüger, ed., *Codex Theodosianus* (Berlin: Weidmann, 1923–6), translated by C. Pharr as *The Theodosian Code and Novels and the Sirmondian Constitutions* (Princeton: Princeton University Press, 1952), 3.5–3.16; 4.3.1; 4.6.1–8; 4.12.1–7; 9.9.1; 9.7–9.9; 9.24–9.26 [hereafter "C. Th."]; *The Code of Justinian*, in Paul Krüger, ed., *Corpus Iuris Civilis*, 3 vols. (Berlin: Weidmann, 1928–9), 5.4–27, 6.57 [hereafter "JC"]; *The Digest of Justinian*, ed. Theodor Mommsen and Paul Krueger, trans. Alan Watson, 4 vols. (Philadelphia: University of Pennsylvania Press, 1985), bks. 23–5; 37.7–15; 38.10–11, 16; 48.5 [hereafter "Dig."]; *Institutes of Justininan*, in *Corpus Iuris Civilis*, translated as *Justinian's Institutes*, ed. Paul Krüger, trans. Peter Birks and Grant McLeod (Ithaca, NY: Cornell University Press, 1987), 1.10–12 [hereafter "Inst."]; *The Novels of Justinian*, Nov. 12.1–4; 18.11; 22.1–48; 74.1–6; 89.1–15, in Scott, *The Civil Law*, XVI [hereafter "Nov."); *The Constitutions of Leo*, Nov. 18–35, 74, 85, 91, 93, 98, 100–1, 109–12, in Scott, *The Civil Law*, XVII [hereafter "Nov. Leo"]. For sample laws, see Bruce W. Frier and Thomas A.J. McGinn, *A Casebook on Roman Family Law* (Oxford: Oxford University Press, 2004); Judith Evans Grubbs, *Women and the Law in the Roman Empire: A Sourcebook on Marriage, Divorce, and Widowhood* (London/New York: Routledge, 2002). For analysis, see Gardner, *Family and Familia*, 114–208, 252–61; Judith Evans Grubbs, *Law and Family in Late Antiquity: The Emperor Constantine's Marriage Legislation* (Oxford: Clarendon Press, 1995), 96–100, 284–305; Anke Leineweber, *Die rechtliche Beziehung des nichtehelichen Kindes zu seinem Erzeuger in der Geschichte des Privatrechts* (Königstein: Peter Hanstein Verlag, 1978), 20–30. See more generally Suzanne Dixon, *The Roman Family* (Baltimore: The Johns Hopkins University Press, 1992); Susan Treggiari, *Roman Marriage: Iusti Coniuges from the Time of Cicero to Ulpian* (Oxford: Clarendon Press, 1991); P.E. Corbett, *The Roman Law of Marriage* (Oxford: Oxford University Press, 1930); Alan Watson, *The Law of Persons in the Later Roman Republic* (Oxford: Clarendon Press, 1967).

woman, a partnership for life involving divine as well as human law."[5] The man and woman had to be of the age of puberty and have the fitness and capacity (*conubium*) to enter into marriage with each other. This latter requirement of *conubium* precluded marriage between parties of different ranks or classes, notably between Roman citizens and non-citizens and between non-citizen freemen and slaves. Eligible couples had to give their consent to the union and to receive the consent of their *paterfamilias* or guardian. Their families or guardians would often exchange marital property (*dos*), sometimes executing elaborate dotal contracts in so doing. The later Christian emperors, particularly Emperor Justinian in the sixth century, legislated heavily about these and other marital formalities – seeking to make marital property transfers and public celebrations essential to the validity of marriages. But, despite these efforts, Justinian maintained the traditional Roman law belief that "reciprocal affection constitutes marriage, without it being necessary to enter into a dotal contract" or hold a public ceremony.[6]

The children born to or adopted by a married couple were legitimate. Legitimate children came automatically within the authority of their father (*patria potestas*), who had near absolute power over their person, property, and activities until his death or their emancipation. He also had responsibilities for them: caring for and supporting them, facilitating their later marriages and their entry into a proper profession, and making presumptive provision for them in his last will and testament – though he could disinherit any of his children by name. Legitimate children also automatically came to be members of the formal legal family or extended household, called the *familia*, which was headed by a *paterfamilias* – either the children's own father or their paternal (great-) grandfather if he was still living. The *paterfamilias* held virtually unchecked control over all the property of the children he had sired or adopted, as well as the property of children or grandchildren born to or adopted by his sons. And legitimate children were automatically

[5] Dig. 23.2.1.
[6] Nov. 22.1.3; JC 5.4–9. See further Judith Evans Grubbs, "Marrying and Its Documentation in Later Roman Law," in *To Have and to Hold: Marrying and Its Documentation in Western Christendom, 400–1600*, ed. Philip L. Reynolds and John Witte, Jr. (Cambridge: Cambridge University Press, 2007), 43–94.

related to the siblings, aunts, uncles, nieces, nephews, and other relatives by blood or adoption within this extended Roman *familia*. These relatives had basic responsibilities to support and protect the legitimate child throughout its lifetime, and this child could have claims to various parts of their estates, especially if they died intestate. These private domestic support systems were important considerations in a Roman society where the state provided virtually no public support for children, regardless of their status.

Children born outside of a lawful marriage were illegitimate at Roman law. These were principally children born of: (1) adultery; (2) incest; (3) other illicit sex; (4) unlawful unions; or (5) concubinage. Absent legitimation, all such illegitimates were not a formal part of any legal household. They were beyond the authority and responsibility of any *paterfamilias* and without the support of any paternal relatives. They could not be counted by the *paterfamilias* for purposes of taxation or of gaining rewards occasionally given to Roman citizens to have more children. Nor did they count in determining whether a *paterfamilias* with multiple children could be exempted from such public duties as guardianship or night watch.

Early Roman law allowed illegitimate children to be exposed upon birth or sold into servitude or slavery with virtual impunity – a tempting course of conduct for parents who lacked the means to support the child.[7] Illegitimates had little legal recourse if they were abused, banished, or cut off from longstanding support, even from their guardians or tutors.

Illegitimate children were not necessarily shut out or left destitute. Until the reforms of Justinian in the sixth century, Roman law required the mother to support her illegitimate children if she chose to keep them, and to make provision for them in her will. If she left them out of her will, her illegitimate children could make a claim against their late mother's estate. Maternal grandmothers for a time had to furnish them some support as well. This was no guarantee of survival, since principal wealth and property control usually rested with the *paterfamilias*, but it was some support. Roman law further allowed the fathers of illegitimate children to take custody of them

---

[7] See early sources in Gardner, *Family and* Familia, 252–60. This practice was outlawed by Justinian in Nov. 153. See also the more general prohibition on infanticide in C. Th. 9.14.1.

and support them during the father's lifetime, and evidently some fathers did so. Fathers could also assign guardians or tutors to protect these illegitimates and their property, or could place them with another *familia* through adoption. Early Roman law also made clear that illegitimates, including those born of adultery and incest, were not precluded from receiving private support from non-relatives, from appearing or testifying in cases, or from holding military or municipal political office. Just because a man was born illegitimate, one second-century jurist wrote in a striking passage, "he should not be excluded from office, for he has committed no crime."[8]

SPURIOUS VERSUS NATURAL ILLEGITIMATES

Beyond these common rules about illegitimacy, special rules gathered around each of these five classes of illegitimates. Children born of adultery were a perennial issue throughout the Roman empire. Roman law defined adultery as proven sexual intercourse between a married woman and another man, not her husband. (Extramarital sex by the husband was simple fornication until the Christian era.) Roman law maintained elaborate procedures and rules for proof of the wife's adultery. It stipulated severe punishment of the convicted adulteress – exile and confiscation of half her dowry and a third of her property. A child born of adultery remained illegitimate unless the husband of his adulterous wife took the child to be his own. If he did not, the husband could dismiss his adulterous wife and her child – and, after the fifth century, she could be sent to a convent, thereby losing her property and leaving the child to fend for itself. The convicted adulteress was forbidden to marry her paramour even after the divorce or death of her husband, though she did retain the right and the duty (if she had not been cloistered) to distribute her property to any illegitimate children born of adultery.[9]

Adultery was always viewed as a serious offense against the husband and his *familia*. It was given added moral stigma by Constantine and later Christian emperors as an "impious crime" against the law of God and the state, which was punishable by

---

[8] Dig. 50.2.6, preface.   [9] JC 9.9; Dig. 48.5.1–44.

death.[10] The criminal prohibition on adultery came to be applied, at least in theory, to both husbands and wives who strayed, though the procedural law remained focused on the adulterous wife. A later law by Emperor Leo III reflected the new opprobrium: "The crime of adultery is one for which I think a most severe and horrible punishment should be inflicted, no less severe than the punishment for homicide. For a murderer frequently only takes a life with his bloody hands, but the execrable adulterer assails many persons' lives at once – the husband, his children, their relatives, and others."[11]

The Roman law of incest varied a bit over the centuries, but it was close to Jewish[12] and other ancient laws of unlawful unions between relatives. Roman law generally prohibited unions between a man and his mother, mother-in-law, stepmother, and grandmother, his maternal or paternal aunt or grand-aunt, his sister, half-sister, stepsister, adopted sister, or sister-in-law,[13] his niece or grand-niece, his daughter, step-daughter, daughter-in-law, or granddaughter – and the equivalent male relatives of a woman, whether formed by blood or by adoption. It made no difference in determining incest whether such a relative was legitimate or illegitimate. All children of incestuous unions, even those born to parents who had lived in longstanding unions that later proved incestuous, "are in the same category as those whom a mother conceived in promiscuous intercourse," Justinian declared. "They are understood to have no father . . . conceived, as it were, at random."[14]

Random conception was also the mark of children born of "infamous" or "illicit unions." This was a shifting category in the first six centuries, but it generally included children born of rape (particularly of a virgin, widow, and, after the fourth century, a nun), seduction or fraudulent inducement to sex, sex with slaves, prostitutes, or minors, sex in groups, and various other forms of "debauchery." Children born of such unions were deemed illegitimate as well. The stigma of illegitimacy was customarily waived if

[10] Nov. 134.17.10   [11] Nov. Leo 32.   [12] See above p. 19.

[13] The Christian emperors explicitly banned levirate marriage, marrying one's dead brother's widow, and they declared all children of such unions illegitimate. C. Th. 3.12.2, 4.

[14] Inst. 1.10.12; JC 5.4.17. In Nov. Leo 24, Emperor Leo prohibited explicitly the marriage of siblings who were related only by adoption. The Roman law, however, did allow for marriage of first cousins (the children of two siblings whether natural or adopted). JC 5.4.19.

the man could and did marry the woman whom he had impregnated. But if the child was born before the actual marriage, or if the couple was precluded from marriage for whatever reason (such as lack of parental consent or disparity in class), their child was deemed illegitimate.[15]

The plight of these three groups of illegitimates – children born of adultery, incest, and illicit unions – worsened somewhat from the fourth to the sixth century. Reflecting the growing moral scruples about sexual immorality, the Christian emperors condemned these children as "vulgar," "defiled," "disgraceful," and "spurious," and condemned the sexual unions that produced them as "abominable," "wicked," "unnatural," and "execrable" offenses against the law of God and the state. Various Christian emperors imposed increasingly harsh penalties and deprivations on the fathers of such illegitimate children – forbidding them from holding public and military office and depriving them of control and disposition of their private property. The emperors visited these punishments on their illegitimate children as well, foreclosing them from public office as well as from private support and inheritance from their families. "All children born of the intercourse – for we do not want to call this marriage – which is either infamous, incestuous, or illicit," wrote Justinian, "are not designated natural and shall not be supported by their parents" – whether by gifts given during the parents' lifetime or by legacies left for them after their parents' death.[16] Justinian further specifically ordered mothers of high rank and their families to desist from supporting their illegitimate children as well, "for the preservation of chastity." This reversed a longstanding rule that obligated mothers and their *familia* to care for their illegitimate children.[17] Spurious children were now considered a permanent witness to the sexual sins of their parents.

---

[15] But see below p. 60 on the change introduced for premarital fornication. Nov. 12.4.

[16] Nov. 89.15. Earlier imperial laws, summarized by Justinian, had allowed some illegitimate children to make modest claims on their father's estates – up to one quarter of their estates under the most generous laws, one twelfth if there were competing legitimate children who stood to inherit. The argument was that such illegitimate children are "free from blame" and "innocent of the offense of their fathers" and yet "have been punished as if they were guilty." Nov. 12.7, pr.1, 3. This policy was reversed in Nov. 89.5.

[17] JC 6.57.5.1.

The fourth category of illegitimates – children born of unlawful unions – was probably the largest category of illegitimates in the first century but it largely disappeared by the end of the sixth century. Classically, Roman law maintained a complex system of social stratification that governed various interactions among groups, especially those involving sex and marriage.[18] Roman citizens could not marry non-citizens – notably freeborn foreigners or Juninan Latins (slaves who had not been properly emancipated). Children born of such unions were generally viewed as both illegitimate and non-citizens (though children born of unions between two freed slaves were legitimate). Active soldiers were prohibited from marriage until the early third century, and children born of their unions were illegitimate. Guardians or tutors were not permitted to marry their wards or pupils; sex, let alone marriage, between them was severely punished and any children born to them were illegitimate. Slaves were forbidden to marry altogether, and children born of any union involving a slave, even a consensual relation between two unrelated slaves which had been blessed by the *paterfamilias*, were illegitimate. While freed slaves could marry other freeborn or freed non-citizens, they could not marry their ex-patrons who had freed them. Such unions, too, produced illegitimate children.

Senators, provincial and municipal rulers (*decuriones*), and other high political officials (*perfectissimi*) and their male descendents faced further restrictions, especially during the fourth-century reign of Emperor Constantine. They were forbidden from marrying women and their daughters who were not freeborn, were of "low or degraded social condition," or were involved in such dishonorable professions as acting, tavern-keeping, pimping, merchandizing, or fighting as gladiators. Children of all such unions were also branded as irredeemable bastards and foreclosed from any support from their fathers and any succession to their father's professional position. "Whatever a father may have given to such children, regardless of whether he states that they are legitimate or natural," Constantine provided in a firm decree of 336, "it shall be taken from them in full,

---

[18] See generally Peter Garnsey, *Social Status and Legal Privilege in the Roman Empire* (Oxford: Clarendon Press, 1970); Grubbs, *Law and Family*, 261–316.

and delivered to his lawful offspring, or to his brother or sister, father or mother."[19]

Though a few later Christian emperors periodically revived these prohibitions on mixed-class marriages, particularly those involving high political officials, these rules were gradually relaxed in subsequent centuries, particularly as traditional distinctions between citizens and non-citizens blurred and became less important. By Emperor Leo III's reign in the eighth century, even slaves could enter into valid marriages – with other slaves or with freedmen who purchased the slave's freedom in consideration of their pending marriage. This new permissiveness, said Leo, is "what custom has now established regarding two persons of unequal status, who out of love, desire to get married."[20] If they are otherwise compatible and eligible for marriage, mere class or social differences should not stand in the way of their forming a valid marriage and producing legitimate children.

While social disparities with regard to marriage eventually melted away in the later Christian empire, religious differences become more important in defining illegitimate marriages and children. Orthodox Christians were precluded from marriage or sexual relations with Jews, heretics, apostates, and pagans; children born of any such unions were regarded as illegitimate. The Christian councils prohibited these interreligious marriages with increasing alacrity from the fourth through sixth centuries.[21] These prohibitions periodically entered into imperial law as well. Emperors Theodosius and Justinian specifically prohibited interreligious marriages with Jews: "No Jewish man shall marry a Christian woman, nor shall any Christian man marry a Jewish woman; for if anyone should be guilty of an act of this kind, he will be liable for having committed the crime of adultery" – leaving their children in the same position of irredeemable bastards.[22] Various Roman laws, from the time of Constantine forward, prohibited contacts and contracts of all sorts between orthodox Christians and various apostates, pagans, and heretics – and these general prohibitions presumably covered sexual contacts and marital contracts as well.

---

[19] C. Th. 4.6.3 repeated in JC 5.27. See analysis in Grubbs, *Law and Family*, 284–92.
[20] Nov. Leo 100. [21] See above pp. 31–3. [22] C. Th. 3.7.2; repeated in JC 1.9.5.

These later laws also prohibited any property transfers or testamentary support for any children who were pagans, heretics, or apostates.[23]

The fifth category of illegitimates – children born of concubinage – also underwent dramatic legal changes after the fourth century, most to the betterment of the children. Concubinage was a common institution in Rome, both before and after the Christianization of the empire.[24] It was a quasi-marital relation that was both legally permissible and legally regulated. Concubinage was generally reserved for men of ample means who sought a longstanding monogamous relationship with a woman for sex and companionship. This could be a young man not yet ready for the responsibilities of a wife and children, or a widower or divorced man who already had enough children. It could also be a man who had fallen in love with a woman whom he could not marry because of the social disparities between them. Such was the case with St. Augustine, who took a low-born woman as a concubine before he converted to Christianity. He could not marry her because of her inferior social status, and he painfully dismissed her after he turned to the faith and turned against concubinage as a violation of the Christian view of marriage.[25]

Most concubines in the Roman empire were freeborn or freed women but of lower status, and sometimes of doubtful origin, if not born illegitimate. But concubines kept by men of *dignitas,* such as senators, governors, and even occasional emperors, could be rich women who were citizens. While single men rather freely fornicated with single women of lower classes, including their slaves, Roman law, already before the Christian era, discouraged this promiscuity for male patrons who had a concubine. And this same pre-Christian law, confirmed famously by Constantine, prohibited a patron from keeping a concubine once he had become married to another woman. A man could marry his concubine if she was of proper

---

[23] See, e.g., C. Th. 16.5.7; 16.7.2–6; JC 1.5.4; 1.5.10; 1.7.2; 1.7–1.9.

[24] Paul Meyer, *Der römischen Konkubinat nach den Rechtsquellen und den Inschriften* (Leipzig: G.B. Teubner, 1895).

[25] See Augustine, *Confessions,* 4.2, 6.12–15 and discussion in Philip L. Reynolds, *Marriage in the Western Church: The Christianization of Marriage during the Patristic and Early Medieval Periods* (Leiden: E.J. Brill, 1994), 101–20.

status and not a relative, but he could not have a concubine and wife at once.[26] Men could give gifts to their concubines during their lifetimes, but most could not leave them property in their last wills and testaments. Concubines were expected to remain faithful to their patrons, and could be punished severely for fornicating with others. They could also be dismissed by their male patron or his *paterfamilias* without cause, and left without support from them or legal recourse against them thereafter.

Inevitably, concubinage sometimes yielded children, though that was not the goal of such relationships. Such children were declared illegitimate, and they usually inherited the social status of their mother. Until the later imperial reforms, these children fared much like other illegitimate children.[27] After the fourth century, however, the Christian emperors began to relax the rules against concubinage and the restrictions on children of concubines. Part of this was a function of relaxing the rules against marriage between parties of unequal social status. Even Roman citizens could now, for the first time, marry their low-born concubines, and were encouraged to do so or to dismiss them. By the fifth century, various Roman emperors also allowed fathers to leave up to one quarter of their estates to their illegitimate children born of concubinage – up to one twelfth if there were competing legitimate children who had claims to his estate as well. The Christian emperors also allowed these illegitimates greater access to political and military positions and other civil benefits, just at the time that they were clamping down on children born of adultery, incest, and illicit unions. These piecemeal legal changes, several of them reversed, qualified, and then reinstated by successive emperors, were cast into systematic and enduring form by Justinian in a famous law of 539, called Novel 89.

LEGITIMATION AND ADOPTION

Justinian's stated concern in Novel 89 was to show "greater humanity" toward all "natural children" (*filii naturalis*) who were

---

[26] JC 5.26.1 (quoting Constantine in 326). See also Sent. Paul. 2.20.1; JC 7.15.3.2 with discussion in Grubbs, *Law and Family*, 294–304.

[27] Dig. 38.8.

born illegitimate.[28] Natural illegitimates were the children born to a man who, "induced by pure affection," has formed a union with a woman whom he is eligible to marry and "has had children by her."[29] Most notably, these were children born of concubinage – but also those born of simple fornication between lovers who were free to marry, or children born of premarital fornication between fiancés whose child arrived before the wedding day.[30] Such children, born from "marriage-like affection," should not suffer as if they were slaves, Justinian reasoned. After all,

> before the enactment of any human laws, nature sanctioned the procreation of children and treated all children as if they were free and freely born. Indeed, the children of our first parents were all free and legitimate at birth. But then wars, legal disputes, licentiousness, and concupiscence introduced a new state of affairs. Slavery resulted from war, and inchastity produced natural [illegitimate] children. The law took cognizance of [the first of] these faults, however, and bestowed freedom upon slaves ... introducing ten thousand methods of liberating them.

It is time to do the same thing for "natural children" born out of wedlock, Justinian argued. They should at least be ensured support from their father and his *familia*, if not given a chance to be legitimated and treated equally with all other children in the family.[31]

Justinian offered four means by which fathers could legitimate their "natural illegitimates," several of these methods drawn from legal prototypes introduced by earlier Christian emperors beginning with Constantine. Both the father and his natural child generally had to consent to these arrangements, though evidently the consent of the mothers was not required.[32]

The first and least attractive method was called "curial oblation." This method required a father to offer his illegitimate child to the Roman state to serve as a municipal official called a *decurion*. After his father's death, an illegitimate son could also offer himself to

---

[28] For the complex evolution of the concept of "*filius naturalis*" from republican to imperial law, see Hans Julius Wolff, "The Background of the Post-Classical Legislation on Legitimation," *Seminar* 3 (1945): 21–45.

[29] Nov. 74, preface.   [30] Nov. 12.4.   [31] Nov. 89.1; see also Nov. 89.9.

[32] See detailed studies in Albert Weitnauer, *Die Legitimation des ausserehelichen Kindes im römischen Recht und in den Germanenrechten des Mittelalters* (Basel: Helbing & Lichtenhahn, 1940), 5–48.

serve in the court. Illegitimate daughters, in turn, could be offered or offer themselves upon their father's death to serve as wives to *decuriones*. An illegitimate child once installed as (a wife to) a *decurion* was automatically legitimated, and was now entitled to inherit up to three-quarters of their father's estate, if there were no other heirs, the balance going to the state. This was a widely available means of legitimation, and could be used regardless of whether the father had other legitimate children. But this procedure was as much to the advantage of the state as to the child. It imposed heavy ongoing burdens on the child, defined his political position and upward mobility based on the status of his father, and imposed restrictions on the legitimated child's rights to inherit and later devise family property.[33]

A second method of legitimation was for a man to marry the mother of his illegitimate child. At the time of their intended marriage, both parties had to have the capacity (*conubium*) to marry each other. This latter requirement largely restricted this method of legitimation to "natural children" born of simple or premarital fornication, or children born of concubinage. It did not cover "spurious children" born of adultery, incest, or illicit unions. Adulterous paramours generally could not marry each other, even after they both became single; incestuous and illicit unions remained prohibited. Once a natural child was legitimated by this means, he or she was treated as a legitimately born child. If the man also had legitimate children by a prior marriage that was now ended, those legitimated children were equally entitled with others in the family to the father's support, protection, and inheritance.[34]

A third method was to have illegitimate children simply declared legitimate by an imperial order or rescript. This method was available to a man who could not marry his lover because she had died or was missing, had become deranged or of ill repute, had married another man, or had a *paterfamilias* or guardian who would not approve the match for fear of losing her property to him. Such a man, if he had no legitimate children, could have his natural illegitimate children legitimated by an imperial order. This would serve "to restore his offspring to nature and to their former

---

[33] JC 5.27.3, 4, 9; Nov. 89.3.   [34] JC 5.27.5–7, 10; Nov. 89, preface.

freedom and legal rights" and to "correct unnatural prejudices" against them.[35]

A fourth method was for a man to declare his natural children legitimate by his last will and testament, making them heirs to his estate. This was available to any man with "natural children" so long as he had no legitimate children. Spurious children, however, could not be so legitimated. Once the will was properly administered before an appropriate authority, these natural children received "the gift of legitimation" made available to them "from both nature and the law."[36]

Justinian offered these four methods of legitimation for natural children in place of the traditional remedy of adoption. This was an abrupt change. A decade before, in his *Institutes* and *Code,* Justinian had refined and defended the traditional rules of adoption and had enacted procedures to ensure that each adoption "was honorable and in the child's interest."[37] In his new law of 539, however, Justinian expressed reservations. The "adoption of natural children" into a new *familia* was "extremely absurd," he said, because it "inconsiderately places certain natural children in a superior class to those who are legitimate" in the adopting family.[38] The adoption of all other children is not "reprehensible," but it does "not pay sufficient regard to chastity."[39] Justinian's evident concern was that, under traditional rules, natural and spurious illegitimates alike could be adopted. This undercut his stern new rules just enacted against adultery, incest, and other illicit unions. Justinian repeated a law by his predecessor, Justin, that barred adoptions made to "benefit children born of a wicked or incestuous union" for such "unlawful lust will not be excused."[40]

It takes a bit of explanation of the Roman law of adoption to appreciate what Justinian was concerned about. Adoption was a

[35] Nov. 89.9.1.

[36] Nov. 89.10. See also Nov. 117.2 which makes provision for a declaration of legitimacy by a man and three witnesses during his lifetime. This is not an instance of legitimation, however, but of presumed proof of paternity in a disputed case. See Fred H. Blume, "Legitimation under the Roman Law," *Tulane Law Review* 5 (1931): 256–66, at 264–6. Medieval civilians would strengthen this into a separate form of legitimation. See below p. 68.

[37] Inst. 1.11.3. See also JC 8.48.1–11. [38] Nov. 89.7. See also Nov. 74.3.

[39] Nov. 89.11.2. [40] JC 5.27.7.

millennium-old institution in Rome, and it often had little to do with children or illegitimates. Roman law recognized two distinct forms of adoption. One form, called adrogation, involved the adoption of a new *paterfamilias* by an aging *paterfamilias* who had no heirs of his own to carry on the family property, lineage, and household religion. He could adopt an unrelated man as his son. The adopted son was to be an adult himself and emancipated in his own right. He would take over the adopting father's *familia* upon his adopted father's death. This would often lead to the dissolution of the adoptee's *familia* in favor of his adopted *familia*. This method, which featured a complex approval procedure by both religious and political officials, was a staple practice throughout Roman history.[41]

It was the second method of adoption, called arrogation, that evidently troubled Justinian, namely, the adoption of the child of another. This, too, was an ancient and enduring practice in Rome. Like adrogation, arrogation, too, often involved adults who agreed to come within the paternal authority of an adopting father and his *familia*. Minor children could also be so adopted and, upon reaching maturity, give their consent to the arrangement. A Roman father would adopt for all manner of reasons – charity, companionship, labor, commercial or strategic alliance, care and protection for his family, among others. But this type of adoption was an especially popular procedure to give childless men or couples a legitimate heir to take over their household.

This second form of adoption, however, yielded a fragile legal relationship. In many cases the adoption did not entirely sever the legal relationship between the biological father and child. Earlier emperors had sought to remedy this by contrasting simple arrogation (that preserved a child's legal ties with the biological father) and complete arrogation (that required the biological father to emancipate the child as part of the adoption process). But these reforms had evidently not prevailed, in part because the biological father was often not known or found at the time of the adoption but would appear on the scene later. The fragility of adoption was made worse because the adopting father had to support his adopted

---

[41] Gaius, 6.98–107, 134; *Rules of Ulpian*, 8.

child only during that father's lifetime. If he later had another legitimate heir, neither the adopting father nor his *familia* was required to leave his adopted child a legacy. The adopted child, however, could claim property if his adopting father died intestate or without legitimate issue, and he could also make claims on his biological father's estate if that father died intestate and without legitimate offspring.[42] The fragility and complexity of this traditional law of adoption may have been reason enough for Justinian to abolish it. But he may also have been concerned that spurious children could be adopted – even spurious children whom their father had given to another *familia*, but now wanted back in his custody or sought to favor with a gift or a legacy.[43]

Justinian's efforts to abolish adoption did not last. Succeeding emperors restored adoption and made it available effectively as a fifth form of legitimation. Emperor Leo III in the eighth century systematized the new rules governing adoption in an important law that came to be widely cited by Western jurists in medieval and early modern times. Adoption served the common good, Leo argued. It served "to diminish the sorrows of those who have no children" and "to acquire the appearance of a benefit that nature refuses." Adoption provided unwanted or needy children or adults with a home and with a *paterfamilias*. It provided adopting parents with an opportunity to replace children who had died and thereby provide themselves with "support in their old age," "relief of their misery," and various forms of "assistance which they could otherwise expect from their children." Even a wealthy widow, said Leo, will be advantaged by adopting a son "to manage her property," "share her burdens," and "procure for her a more peaceful and quiet life." Leo thus granted men and women alike the right to adopt, whether married or single, virgins or widows, eunuchs or virile adults. And he placed no conditions on the age, quality, or legitimacy of the children who were eligible for adoption and no restrictions on the adoptee's rights vis-à-vis other children or family members. "The benefit of the laws should be shared by everyone," Leo concluded.[44]

---

[42] See detailed study and relevant texts in Gardner, *Family and* Familia, 114–208.
[43] Weitnauer, *Die Legitimation*, 46–8.   [44] Nov. Leo 27.

MEDIEVAL CIVIL LAW

The Roman law of illegitimacy and legitimation came to its fullest juridical expression in the fifth and sixth centuries – just at the time when the Western Roman state was the least able to implement it effectively. Already in the fifth century, the Western empire gradually eroded in its power and reach, before ending with the death of the last Western emperor in 476. While Roman law lived on in the East, with its capital in Constantinople, in the West it became increasingly a legal relic.

Roman law, however, particularly in its later Christianized forms, would become the foundation of the later Western law of illegitimacy and legitimation (among many other legal subjects). While fragments of Roman law were preserved by Germanic courts and by occasional scholars in the last half of the first millennium,[45] the full texts of Justinian were preserved by the Muslims and Arabs of North Africa, the Middle East, and southern Spain. Through trade with Western Christians, these texts eventually came back into Western circulation in the later eleventh century and began to figure prominently in the law faculties of the new universities – among civil law and canon law jurists alike.[46]

The civil law jurists made active use of these inherited texts and helped slowly incorporate some of their teachings into the secular laws of the medieval political authorities.[47] Already in the later eleventh century, a small set of glossators, led by Azo and Accursius, began to add brief marginal comments to Justinian's *Corpus Iuris Civilis* and *Novellae,* including his texts on illegitimacy and legitimation. Then a growing number of commentators from the

---

[45] For Germanic laws on point, see Weitnauer, *Die Legitimation,* 49–103; Leineweber, *Die rechtliche Beziehung,* 34–44; Hans Hagn, *Illegitimität und Thronfolge: zur Thronfolgeproblematik illegitimiter Merowinger, Karolinger, und Ottonen* (Neureid: Ars Una, 2006). For a brief seventh-century summary of prevailing domestic categories, including illegitimacy, see *The Etymologies of Isidore of Seville,* trans. and ed. Stephen A. Barney *et al.* (Cambridge: Cambridge University Press, 2006), IX.iv.9–IX.vii.29.

[46] The canon law of illegitimacy is the subject of the next chapter.

[47] In a statistical analysis of medieval canon law and civil law texts, James Brundage shows that the civil law jurists dealt with issues of legitimacy and illegitimacy far more frequently than the canon law jurists – 7:1 in his sample. See James A. Brundage, *Sex, Law, and Marriage in the Middle Ages* (Aldershot: Variorum, 1993), v, 92.

twelfth to fifteenth centuries, most notably Bartolus and Baldus, brought these Roman law texts into greater thematic concordance as part of their writing on the laws of persons, marriage, and inheritance.[48] The commentators' efforts were further enhanced by the many legal humanists of the fifteenth and sixteenth centuries. Aided by the new printing press, these legal humanists developed critical new editions of a number of the ancient Roman legal texts, followed by detailed commentaries on each of them. They also prepared various legal collections that put side-by-side parallel Roman, canon, feudal, and other laws on various subjects, including illegitimacy, legitimation, and adoption. And these legal humanists developed a growing cache of textbooks on selected legal topics. Five short civil law texts on legitimacy and legitimation have survived from the fifteenth century.[49] Several more and lengthier texts from the sixteenth century have survived, written by Catholic and Protestant Roman law scholars alike (and without evident theological differences in their treatment of the Roman law of illegitimacy).[50] From the twelfth to the sixteenth centuries, this Roman law and legal learning also slowly soaked into the new legal codes, statutes, and cases of Continental cities, duchies, and territories as well as the laws of the Holy Roman Empire and emerging nation-states.[51]

---

[48] See generally Helmut Coing, ed., *Handbuch der Quellen und Literatur der neueren europäischen Privatrechtsgeschichte*, 3 vols. (Munich: Beck, 1973–88), I:129–261, 313–64. For analysis of the medieval glosses and early commentaries on the Roman texts on illegitimacy, see Leineweber, *Die rechtliche Beziehung*, 45–54; Thomas Kuehn, "A Medieval Conflict of Laws: Illegitimacy and Legitimation in *Ius Commune* and *Ius Proprium*," *Law and History Review* 15 (1997): 243–73.

[49] Mantua Bonauito Pataui, *Tractatus de legitima filiorum*, in *Tractatus universi iuris, duce, & auspice Gregorio XIII* (Venice, 1584), vol. VIII/1, 440a–445b; Benedecti de Barzis, *De filiis non legitimè natis*, in ibid., vol. VIII/2, 24a–29b; Ludovici a Sardis, *De naturalis liberis ac eorum successione*, in ibid., vol. VIII/2, 29b–45b; Antonii de Rosellis, *De legitimatione*, in ibid., vol. VIII/2, 75a–90a; Martinus Laudensis, *De Legitimatione*, in ibid., vol. VIII/2, 90b–98a.

[50] A good Protestant example is that of French Calvinist jurist François Hotman, *De spuriis et legitimatione*, appended to Barnabé Brisson, *De verteri ritu nuptiarum et jure connubiorum* (Amsterdam: Petrus le Grand, 1662), with further excerpts and discussion of Hotman's work in Christian Carpzov, *De legitima, quae vocantur ab Hotomano quarta legitima* (Wittenberg: Johannis Gormanni, 1631). A good Catholic example is Gabriele Paleotti, *De notis spuriisque* (Frankfurt am Main: Nicolai Bassaei, 1574), reprinted in *Tractatus universi juris*, vol. VIII/2: 45b–74b.

[51] Leineweber, *Die rechtliche Beziehung*, 101–54. For local case studies of illegitimacy, see L. Bischof, *"Die Rechtsstellung der ausserehelichen Kinder nach den zürcherischen Rechtsquellen"* (Dissertation, Zurich, 1931); G. Bückling, *Die Rechtstellung der unehelichen Kinder im*

Particularly the fifteenth and sixteenth centuries were known for their new "reception of Roman law" and legal learning.

While the medieval civil law jurists, called civilians, repeatedly discussed the inherited Roman teachings on illegitimacy, most made "no material legal changes concerning the Roman law of Justinian."[52] The civilians defined legitimate children as those born to or adopted by "a husband and wife capable of contracting matrimony and generating children while cohabiting together during the marriage."[53] They defined illegitimate children as those born "out of lawful wedlock," "outside of the power of their fathers," and beyond the responsibility of any relatives.[54] "Bastards have no kin" was a famous adage of the medieval civilians.[55]

Most civilians followed Justinian's method of dividing illegitimates into two main classes: (1) "natural illegitimates," born of concubinage, premarital fornication, or simple fornication; and (2) "spurious illegitimates," now often called "bastards" (*bastardi*),[56] born of adultery, incest, or other illicit unions (such as rape, prostitution, seduction of virgins, widows, or nuns, group sex, and various mixed-status unions).[57] All such illegitimates, the civilians noted, bore the "stain" (*macula*) of their "defective birth" (*defectus natilium*) caused by the "crimes of their parents" (*crimina paterna*.)[58] Natural legitimates could receive modest support from their mothers and sometimes their fathers during their lifetimes, but they were not

---

Mittelalter und in der heutigen Reformbewegung (Breslau: M. and H. Marcus, 1920); C. Etzensperger, "*Die Rechtsstellung des ausserehelichen Kinder nach den schaffhauserischen Rechtsquellen*" (Dissertation, Zurich, 1931); Thomas Kuehn, *Illegitimacy in Renaissance Florence* (Ann Arbor, MI: University of Michigan Press, 2002); Jean-François Poudret, *Coutumes et coutumiers: Histoire comparative des droits des pays romands du XIIIe à la fin du XVIe siècle*, 6 vols. (Berne: Staempfli, 1998), II:9–50; W. Strebi, "*Die Rechtsstellung der unehelichen Kinder in Kanton Luzern*" (Dissertation, Berne, 1928); Hermann Winterer, *Die rechtliche Stellung der Bastarden in Italien von 800 bis 1500* (Munich: Arbeo, 1978).

[52] Leineweber, *Die rechtliche Beziehung*, 53.

[53] Bartolo de Sassoferrato, *In primam ff. veteris commentaria* (Venice, 1585), fols. 24rb–va, using translation by Kuehne, *Illegitimacy*, 34.

[54] Ibid., 34–5 and further quotations in Leineweber, *Die rechtliche Beziehung*, 46–7, 70–73, 102–5, 121–4, 138–40.

[55] Beaùmanoir, *Coutumes des Beauvaisis*, no. 1697, quoted by Poudret, *Coutumes et coutumiers*, II:30.

[56] See Barziis, *De filiis*, 10–12.

[57] See esp. Sardis, *De naturalibus liberis*; Leineweber, *Die rechtliche Beziehung*, 46–7.

[58] Kuehne, *Illegitimacy*, 34–7; R. Génestal, *Histoire de la légitimation des enfants naturels en droit canonique* (Paris: Ernst Leroux, 1905), 4–44.

entitled to inherit from them unless one or both of their parents died intestate. Spurious illegitimates were generally foreclosed from any such parental support or inheritance. Absent legitimation, spurious illegitimates also faced firmer restrictions on their rights to property, inheritance, and contracts, their capacity to sue or testify in civil courts, and their rights to hold civil or political offices. Some civilians grounded these restrictions not only in the Roman law of Justinian, but also in the Bible. They quoted Sarah's denunciation of Ishmael, the spurious bastard, as a warrant for discriminating against the spurious illegitimates of their day: "Cast out this slave woman with her son; for the son of this slave woman shall not be heir with my son Isaac."[59]

The medieval civilians rehearsed Justinian's laws not only of illegitimacy, but also of legitimation. They offered modern variants on legitimation by oblation to the civil court, by imperial or princely rescript, by testamentary declaration of their fathers, or by subsequent marriage of their parents. Several civilians also argued that a good faith declaration by the father or mother of a child's legitimacy should be enough to remove the stigma of illegitimacy, particularly if the parents had witnesses to corroborate their claims. This corroborated declaration of legitimacy by a father or mother became a separate ground for legitimation in medieval civil law.[60] Similarly, some urged acceptance of the canon law argument that a putative marriage by a couple, innocently entered, which was later found to be invalid, was enough to render the child legitimate even if the marriage was later annulled.[61] Adoption, too, had the effect of rendering the adoptee the legitimate child of the adopter at civil law. But "adoption remained an exceptional event" in medieval and early modern Europe, though amply discussed by the jurists.[62]

---

[59] Jacobus Menochius [Giacomo Menochio], *De arbitrariis iudicium quaestionibus et causis libri II* (Venice, 1624) and Mercurialus Merlinus, *De legitima tractatus* (Venice, 1651), quoted and analyzed in Leineweber, *Die rechtliche Stellung,* 88. Leineweber, however, also points out that other later fifteenth- and sixteenth-century jurists relaxed these restrictions on spurious children. Ibid., 88–90, 98–100.

[60] Sardis, *De naturalis liberis,* 5.1–14.

[61] Ibid., 6.1–2. See further below p. 83 for the parallel canon law rules.

[62] Poudret, *Coutumes et coutumiers,* II:21; Jean Brissaud, *A History of French Private Law,* 2nd edn., trans. R. Howell (Boston: Little, Brown, and Company, 1912), 218. On the ample discussion of adoption among canonists, see Charles J. Reid, Jr. *Power over the Body, Equality*

The medieval civilians disputed endlessly whether these methods of legitimation could be extended from natural to spurious illegitimates, and whether legitimated children (*legitimati*) could be treated identically with legitimately born children (*legitimi*). The weight of opinion was to treat legitimately born children better than legitimated children, and to treat legitimated natural children more favorably than adopted children, particularly if they had been spurious before adoption. But the civilians also allowed spurious children to be more readily legitimated by other means than those available under classical Roman law rules; legitimation was not necessarily foreclosed to them, as Justinian had provided, just because their fathers had other natural children.[63] The medieval civilians also disputed endlessly whether legitimation and adoption should require full consent by the child and its mother, or involve only the consent of the father. The trend was to dispense with consent, since legitimation was regarded as a higher good and a child could later dissent from the arrangement if he or she chose to.[64]

Regardless of the exact reach and effect of these means of legitimation, the civilians regarded these procedures as a humane way of removing the stigma and stain of illegitimate birth and restoring a child to its natural rights. One late medieval commentator put it thus, echoing the sentiments of Justinian:

Strictly and properly speaking, he is called legitimated, who is brought back to said pristine state and right of descent and for whom all stain of birth is removed. So if the emperor or one having authority from him simply makes one legitimate, he therefore takes away all stain of simplicity, naturalness, and spuriousness, which are induced by means of written laws. For by nature all men were born free and legitimate; but wars introduced slavery; lust was the occasion of inordinate passion, of the system of naturalness, and of spuriousness; and so just as the laws introduced this so also laws, both legislated and unlegislated, can abolish the basis of this system.[65]

---

in the Family: Rights and Domestic Relations in Medieval Canon Law (Grand Rapids, MI: Wm. B. Eerdmans, 2004), 187–95. For a good summary of early modern civilian discussion of adoption, see Johannes Althusius, *Dicaeologicae libri tres, totum et universum Jus, quo utimur, methodice complectens* (Frankfurt am Main: Christophe Corvin, 1618), cap. 80.

[63] See esp. Barziis, *De filiis*, 41–57.

[64] See Kuehne, *Illegitimacy*, 49–66; Génestal, *Histoire de la légitimation*.

[65] Angelo degli Ubaldi, *Consilia* (Frankfurt am Main, 1575), fol. 12ra, using translation in Kuehne, *Illegitimacy*, 60–1. See above p. 60 for comparable quotation from Nov. 89 pr.

SUMMARY AND CONCLUSIONS

Historians of Roman law have long disputed to what extent the Christianization of the Roman empire led to a Christianization of the Roman law. No one contests the obvious Christian influences on the laws of religious establishment in the fourth through sixth centuries. After Rome established Trinitarian Christianity as the official religion of the empire in 380, the emperors defined in ever greater legal detail the orthodox Christian teachings on the Trinity, the sacraments, liturgy, holy days, the Sabbath Day, charity, education, sexual ethics, and more that were to be maintained in the empire. The Roman jurists built into the law a thick tangle of special new immunities, exemptions, and subsidies for Christian ministers, missionaries, and monastics. The Roman emperors and their delegates convoked many of the church councils and major synods. They appointed, disciplined, and removed the high clergy. They regulated many of the church's parishes, monasteries, and charities. They governed the acquisition, maintenance, and disposition of much church property. And the Roman law and legal authorities dealt harshly with pagans and heretics, brutally crushing Arians, Apollonarians, Manicheans, and other "enemies of Christ," as Emperor Justinian later called them, and subjecting Jews to severe new restrictions. On these subjects, evidence of the Christianization of the Roman law – and the Romanization of the Christian faith – is unmistakable.

The influence of Christianity proved more subtle and sporadic on various subjects of Roman private law, procedural law, criminal law, and the law of persons and associations.[66] On these legal subjects, Rome had a sophisticated body of law in place well before the arrival of Christianity, and later Christian influences on these laws were often more discrete and diffuse. As Don Browning put it, Christian theologians often accepted Roman laws and legal institutions and then slowly put "a complex spin or twist on them" in light of Gospel narratives and imperatives.[67] Roman officials, in

---

[66] These influences are summarized in John Witte, Jr. and Frank S. Alexander, eds., *Christianity and Law: An Introduction* (Cambridge: Cambridge University Press, 2008).

[67] Don S. Browning, "Family Law and Christian Jurisprudence," in *ibid.,* 163–83, at 163–4.

turn, as they accepted Christian teachings and practices, gradually reformed the laws in accordance with the new Christian morality.

The Roman law of illegitimacy and legitimation bears out Browning's keen insight. Rome had a sophisticated illegitimacy law in place well before the time of Christ. Children were legitimate if born into a lawful marriage. They were illegitimate if born outside of lawful marriage. If legitimate, children came within the power of their father. If illegitimate, they became the responsibility of their mother. Until the fourth century, the Roman law of illegitimacy was designed more to control commerce and society than to deter sex and immorality. The law of illegitimacy ensured that children born of unions between citizens and non-citizens, freemen and slaves, patrons and concubines, wives and paramours, soldiers and prostitutes did not become unwelcome burdens on the Roman *familia* or unworthy citizens in the Roman empire. Illegitimate children were not branded as bastards or foreclosed from political or social opportunities beyond paternal inheritance. Like unwanted legitimate children, unwanted illegitimates could be exposed on birth, sold into slavery, or put out for adoption. But they could just as well be raised in the homes of their mothers, fathers, adopters, or guardians, and upon adulthood achieve whatever office and opportunity was available to persons in their family's class. Their social class, not their birth status, defined their rights and opportunities.

The Christian emperors of the fourth through sixth century preserved much of this earlier Roman law of illegitimacy. But they coated and coded this inherited law with the thick Christian theology of lawful marriage and sexual immorality that we recounted in the last chapter. The Christian emperors retained the definition of illegitimacy as a child born out of lawful wedlock. But, applying patristic teachings on sexual immorality, they categorized and stigmatized illegitimate children according to the gravity of the sin that produced them. The graver the sexual sin of their parents, the lower these children fell in the eyes of the Roman law.

Two main classes of illegitimates emerged in the Roman law of the Christian emperors – natural and spurious illegitimates. Natural illegitimates were children born principally of simple fornication, premarital sex, and concubinage. These natural children could be legitimated by the testamentary declaration of their fathers, by the subsequent marriage of their parents, by adoption into new families, or by rescripts from or oblation to the state. They could also receive child support, inheritance, and various social and political positions. These methods of legitimation and support were forms of Christian charity designed to restore to natural children their natural rights and to redeem them from their parents' sin. Spurious illegitimates, by contrast, were children born of adultery, incest, interreligious marriage, and other serious sexual sins. These children became the outcasts of Christian Roman society. For the most part, they could not be legitimated, they could not be supported by their mothers or fathers, and they could not inherit property or title. They were foreclosed from many social and political positions and opportunities. While natural illegitimates were objects of Christian charity, spurious illegitimates were scapegoats of Christian retribution. While natural illegitimates could be redeemed and restored to their natural rights, spurious illegitimates were left as a permanent witness to the sins of their fathers.

CHAPTER 3

The wages of sin: Sex, marriage, and illegitimacy in medieval canon law

The medieval Catholic Church helped to bring the Western theology and law of illegitimacy into greater concordance. In the first millennium, the church's theology and the state's law of illegitimacy stood in sharp tension. The early Church Fathers, whom we encountered two chapters ago, denounced the doctrine of illegitimacy, even while preaching loudly against extramarital sex. They condemned the notion of visiting the sins of the fathers upon their children, though they punished those parents for their sexual sins with ever greater alacrity. Charity to all children, regardless of their birth status, was the overriding ethic. Adoption of the needy was a special form and application of Christian love and charity.

By contrast, the Christian Roman emperors, whom we encountered in the last chapter, combined the earlier Roman law of illegitimacy with the new Christian theology of sexual immorality. The more serious the sexual sin of the parents, the greater the punishment that the Christianized Roman law visited upon their children. Simple fornication, premarital sex, and concubinage produced natural children who could be legitimated and supported. But adultery, incest, interreligious marriage, and other serious offenses produced spurious children who were foreclosed from support and irredeemable. Rules for the legitimation and adoption of spurious illegitimates were tightened just as the rules defining spurious bastardy were clarified and the rights of the *spurii* were restricted.

While the medieval civilians perpetuated the classical Roman law of illegitimacy with few changes, medieval theologians and canonists harmonized these juxtaposed theological and legal teachings inherited from the first millennium. They developed a theology and

Figure 5 "Table Showing the Forbidden Degrees of Affinity"
(vellum) (Italian, fourteenth century).

law of sex and marriage that systematically explained how, why, and
when to visit the sexual sins of the parents upon their children.
Medieval theologians and canonists retained the Roman law definition of illegitimacy as a "child born out of lawful marriage" – a
product of adultery, incest, and other illicit and prohibited unions.
But they changed and deepened the understanding of what a
"lawful marriage" entailed and which other unions, besides adultery
and incest, were "prohibited" and thus yielded illegitimates. They
retained the traditional view that some illegitimate children could
be legitimated by their fathers (through testament or declaration),
by their parents (through subsequent marriage or adoption), or by
state officials (through curial oblations or princely rescripts). But
they added an important role for the church in legitimating children, too, through the laity's participation in various sacraments,
through the illegitimate's oblation to clerical or monastic life, and
through the clergy's newly claimed equitable powers of papal
rescript and dispensation.

The formative era for these changes in illegitimacy law was the
twelfth through fifteenth centuries, after the Catholic clergy had
thrown off their royal and civil rulers and established the Catholic
Church as an autonomous legal and political ruler of Western
Christendom. The church's theology of marriage was newly systematized by Hugh of St. Victor, Peter Lombard, Thomas Aquinas,
and scores of other commentators.[1] The church's canon law of
marriage was greatly expanded, first in the *Decretum Gratiani*
(*c.* 1140), then in a welter of later legal commentaries as well as in
the new papal and conciliar laws that eventually formed the *Corpus
Iuris Canonici* (*c.* 1586).[2] Both these theological and legal sources
included ample discussions of illegitimacy and legitimation. What
follows first is a summary of the new sacramental theology and
canon law of marriage and marital contracts in the High Middle
Ages. Thereafter, I turn to the hierarchies of legitimate and
illegitimate children that this new understanding of marriage
produced.

---

[1] See detailed sources in my *From Sacrament to Contract: Marriage, Religion, and Law in the Western Tradition* (Louisville, KY: Westminster John Knox Press, 1997), ch. 1.

[2] Emil Friedberg, *Corpus Iuris Canonici*, 2 vols. (Leipzig: Bernard Tauchnitz, 1879–81).

MARRIAGE, CELIBACY, AND ANNULMENT

It takes some explanation of the complex medieval doctrine of marriage to appreciate these changes to the church's canon law of illegitimacy and legitimation. Echoing and elaborating the teachings of the Church Fathers,[3] medieval theologians and canonists came to treat marriage at once as a natural, contractual, and sacramental union. First, they taught, marriage is a *natural association*, created by God to enable man and woman to "be fruitful and multiply" (Gen. 1:28) and to raise children in the service and love of God. Since the fall into sin, marriage has also become a remedy for lust, a channel to direct one's natural passion to the service of the community and the church. Second, marriage is a *contractual unit*, formed by the mutual consent of the parties. This contract prescribes for couples a life-long relation of love, service, and devotion to each other and proscribes unwarranted breach or relaxation of their connubial and parental duties. Third, marriage, when properly contracted between baptized Christians, is a *sacrament*. The temporal union of body, soul, and mind within the marital estate symbolizes the eternal union between Christ and his church. Participation in this sacrament confers sanctifying grace upon the couple and the community. Couples can perform this sacrament privately, provided they are capable of marriage and comply with the rules for marriage formation. Once they have performed this sacrament, the couple's marriage is rendered permanent, just as Christ's union with his church is permanent. This sacramental theology placed the institution of marriage squarely within the social hierarchy of the church.

The church did not regard marriage and the family as its most exalted estate, however. Though a sacrament and a sound way of Christian living, marriage was not considered to be especially spiritually edifying. Marriage was a remedy for sins of lust, not a recipe for righteousness. Marriage was considered subordinate to celibacy, propagation less virtuous than contemplation, marital love less wholesome than spiritual love. Marriage, Peter Lombard put it in 1142, "is a remedy not a reward; if anyone rejects it, he will deserve judgment of death. But an act which is allowed by

---

[3] See above pp. 27–36.

permission is voluntary, not necessary."[4] Clerics, monastics, and other ordained servants of the church were to forgo sex, marriage, and family life as a condition for ecclesiastical service. Those who could not were not worthy of the church's holy orders and offices.

This prohibition on sex and marriage, universally imposed on medieval clerics and monastics by the First Lateran Council of 1123, was defended with a whole arsenal of complex arguments. The most common arguments were based on St. Paul's statement on celibacy in 1 Corinthians 7:7 ("I wish all were celibate as I myself am"), which the Church Fathers had already heavily glossed.[5] These were buttressed by newly discovered classical Greek and Roman writings extolling celibacy for the contemplative as well as by the growing medieval celebration of the virginity of Mary as a model for pious Christian living. Mandatory clerical celibacy drew further support from new philosophical arguments that underscored the superiority of the celibate clergy to the married laity. It was a commonplace of medieval philosophy to describe God's creation as hierarchical in structure – a vast chain of being emanating from God and descending through various levels and layers of reality down to the smallest particulars. In this great chain of being, each creature found its place and its purpose. Each institution found its natural order and hierarchy. It was thus simply the nature of things that some persons and institutions were higher on this chain of being, some lower. It was the nature of things that some were closer and had more ready access to God, and some were further away and in need of mediation in their relationship with God. Through the sacrament of ordination or holy orders, medieval theologians argued, clergy were called to the higher spiritual activities in the realm of grace, while the laity were left to the lower temporal activities in the realm of nature. The clergy were thus distinct from the laity in their dress, in their language, and in their livings. They were exempt from earthly obligations, such as paying civil taxes or serving in the military. They were immune from the jurisdiction of civil courts or the prosecution of secular magistrates. And they were foreclosed

---

[4] Petrus Lombardus, *Libri IV sententiarum* [1150], 2nd rev. edn. (Florence: Collegii S. Bonaventurae, 1916), bk. 4, Dist. 26.3.

[5] See above p. 36.

from the natural activities of sex, marriage, and family life. These natural activities were literally beneath the clergy in ontological status. For a cleric or monastic to engage in "the outrageous behavior"[6] of marrying or having sex was thus, in a real sense, to act against nature (*contra naturam*).

The medieval church built upon this conceptual foundation a comprehensive canon law of sex, marriage, and family life. The medieval church claimed exclusive jurisdiction (the power to make law) over the many questions of marital formation, maintenance, and dissolution that were central to the sacrament of marriage. They also claimed jurisdiction over many aspects of child care and education, sexual sin and crime, inheritance and trusts that fell within the sacraments of baptism, penance, and extreme unction.[7] The church exercised this jurisdiction through its canon law, which was composed of the legal enactments of popes and bishops, councils and synods. This canon law was taught in the law faculties of all medieval Western universities and administered by the hierarchy of church courts and legal officials that ruled in every diocese. The canon law was the one universal law of marriage and family life that prevailed throughout the West. It was the exclusive law governing the papal territories and prince-bishoprics throughout Western Europe. It was the principal law governing the marriage and family life of the citizens of secular polities, too. The civil laws of marriage and family enacted by local temporal authorities were considered supplemental and subordinate to the canon law. They were focused on secular issues like marital property and inheritance, but not on the essentials of marital formation, maintenance, and dissolution.

Consistent with the natural perspective on marriage, the canon law privileged the natural kin relationships between parents and their children, and punished contraception, abortion, infanticide, and child abuse as violations of the natural marital functions of

---

[6] Second Lateran Council (1139), canon 7, in Norman P. Tanner, ed., *Decrees of the Ecumenical Councils* (Washington, DC: Georgetown University Press, 1990), vol. I. For detailed sources, see my *Law and Protestantism: The Legal Teachings of the Lutheran Reformation* (Cambridge: Cambridge University Press, 2002), 106–15.

[7] See Paul Wilpert, ed., *Lex et Sacramentum im Mittelalter* (Berlin: Walter de Gruyter, 1969); Peter Landau, "Sakramentalität und Jurisdiktion," in *Das Recht der Kirche*, ed. Gerhard Rau, Hans-Richard Reuter, and Klaus Schlaich, 4 vols. (Gütersloh: Chr. Kaiser, 1994–7), II:58–95.

propagation and childrearing. It prohibited unnatural relations such as incest and polygamy, unnatural acts such as bestiality and buggery, unnatural conduct such as wife abuse and desertion of one's family, and unnatural practices such as clerical marriage and sex. Consistent with the contractual perspective, the canon law prohibited marriages formed through mistake, duress, fraud, or coercion. It granted husband and wife alike equal rights to enforce conjugal debts that had been voluntarily assumed, and emphasized the importance of mutual love among the couple and their children. Consistent with the sacramental perspective, the church protected the sanctity and sanctifying purpose of marriage by declaring proper marital bonds to be indissoluble, and by prohibiting unions between Christians and non-Christians, believers and apostates.

These multiple perspectives on marriage came to concrete legal expression in the medieval canon law of marital contracts, impediments, and annulment. Medieval canonists distinguished between two types of contracts: contracts of engagement and contracts of marriage. An engagement contract or betrothal was a promise to be married in the future: "I, Jack, *promise to take you*, Jill, to be my wife." A marriage contract or espousal was a promise to marry here and now: "I, Jack, *now take you,* Jill, to be my lawfully wedded wife."

Neither contract required much formality to be valid and enforceable at medieval canon law. Parties were required simply to exchange these formulaic words – or if need be their symbolic equivalents. Parties could add much more to these contracts. They could attach conditions. We shall marry "so long as my parents agree"; "so long as we live in my hometown"; and the like. They could attach economic considerations, concerning dowries and dowers, marital gifts and properties. Medieval church councils, including the authoritative Fourth Lateran Council of 1215, repeatedly urged the parties to seek their parents' consent, to secure the testimony of witnesses, to publish banns of their pending nuptials, and to consecrate their marital vows "in the face [or view] of the church" (*in facie ecclesiae*) or at least "with the permission of the church" (*ex permissione ecclesiae*).[8] But none of this went to the

---

[8] Fourth Lateran Council (1215), canon 51, in H.J. Schroeder, *Disciplinary Decrees of the General Councils: Text, Translation, and Commentary* (London: Herder, 1937). The medieval canonists

essence of a valid marriage. A private voluntary exchange of promises between a man and woman of the age of consent and with capacity to marry was a valid and enforceable marriage at medieval canon law – and this was doubly true if the parties had consummated their vows and the woman was now pregnant. Clandestine or secret marriages, contracted without the church's blessing, were perennially frowned upon and periodically prohibited by severe canon laws and civil laws throughout the Middle Ages.[9] But they were generally considered to be valid marriages, with the marital promises implied and imputed to the parties. Concubinage was a more problematic category for canonists. While immoral and illegal, it was such a widespread practice that most canonists before the fifteenth century tended to view a man's longstanding cohabitation with a concubine that featured "marital affection" as a form of clandestine marriage that could be later ratified through a formal marriage ceremony. Here, too, marital contracts were imputed to the couple, and marital rights and duties attached.[10]

Not all parties were free and fit to make marital contracts, however, and not all marital promises were regarded as valid and enforceable, even if they had been consummated and yielded children. Certain relationships or experiences could disqualify the parties from engagement and marriage – altogether or at least with each other. Certain actions or conditions discovered after the exchange of promises could, and sometimes had to, lead to the dissolution of these promises. These disqualifying and disabling

were divided over whether the marriage had to take place in the church with a set religious liturgy, or whether the blessing of a priest at a private ceremony was sufficient to meet the requirement of "*in facie ecclesiae.*"

[9] See George Hayward Joyce, *Christian Marriage: An Historical and Doctrinal Study*, 2nd. rev. edn. (London: Sheed and Ward, 1948), 103–46.

[10] See the detailed discussion in James A. Brundage, *Law, Sex, and Christian Society in Medieval Europe* (Chicago: University of Chicago Press, 1987), 206–7, 225–6, 297–300, 341–3, 369–70, 441–7. But see below, p. 90, on the later prohibitions on concubinage. A variant on concubinage, closer to actual marriage, was the so-called "morganatic relationship" (later called a "left-hand marriage") between a nobleman and a common woman. This was viewed as an exclusive and permanent union, sometimes blessed by the church. The women were supported during the relationship and gained truncated inheritance rights. Children born of these unions were considered legitimate, and received support during their father's lifetime, but could not inherit from him. Gabriele Paleotti, *De notis spuriisque* (Frankfurt am Main: Nicolai Bassaei, 1574), cap. xvii.8, reprinted in *Tractatus universi iuris, duce, & auspice Gregorio XIII* (Venice, 1584), vol. VIII/2: 45b–74b.

factors were called impediments. Impediments provided either the man or the woman, and sometimes third parties as well, with grounds to seek annulment of the engagement or marriage contract. An annulment was an order by a church court or a qualified religious official that declared the contract to be null and void and the relationship between the parties dissolved. A declaration of annulment meant that the engagement or marriage never formally existed at law; it was never a legally binding union, however contrary to fact that might appear.

The canon law recognized several impediments to the marital contract. These were of two main types: prohibitive impediments and diriment (or absolute) impediments. *Prohibitive* impediments were less serious. They rendered the marriage contract voidable, but their violation did not necessarily render the marriage void, unless the innocent party insisted on pressing for an annulment. Seven prohibitive impediments were commonly recognized: (1) rape, the man's rape or violent abduction of a relative of his fiancée; (2) wife murder, the husband's (suspected) killing of his prior wife; (3) priest murder, either party's (suspected) killing of an ordained priest or monastic; (4) solemn penance, where either party had been assigned public penance for a mortal sin; (6) former monasticism, which precluded marriage to a former nun or monk who had renounced their vows; and (7) age, either too wide a disparity in age between the parties or a discovery that one or both of the parties was too young to give his or her consent to the union.

Discovery of any of these conditions after the couple had already been married gave the innocent spouse standing in a church court to press a case for annulment. An annulment suit based on one of these impediments was relatively easy to win if it was brought shortly after the marriage by a spouse who knew nothing of this impediment beforehand. It was harder, though not impossible, to win if a party had entered the marriage with full knowledge of this impediment and then had a change of heart, or learned of the impediment after the marriage but delayed long in suing for annulment on that basis. This case became doubly difficult to press if the woman was now pregnant or had given birth, since their child would be illegitimate.

Absolute (or diriment) impediments were more serious. They proscribed the contracting of marriage altogether and, upon discovery, rendered the marriage void regardless of what the parties wished. Two clusters of absolute impediments were commonly maintained. One set of impediments preserved the freedom of consent of both parties. Proof of extreme duress, fear, compulsion, or fraud to get married – by a parent, fiancé(e), or third party – impinged on consent and invalidated the marriage contract. Similarly, a mistake about the identity of the other party (think of Jacob's discovery of Leah, rather than Rachel under the bridal veil), or a mistake about the presumed virginity of the new wife was also a ground for annulment.

A second, larger set of absolute impediments defined which parties were free to give their consent to marriage. Clerics and monastics could not marry or have sex with anyone. Christians could not have sex or contract marriage with infidels, Jews, or pagans. Persons related by blood (consanguinity), by adoption, or by marriage (affinity) up to the fourth degree[11] could not marry each other. These impediments of consanguinity and affinity, as they were called, included the Mosaic law rules but also many other natural law rules not included in the Torah.[12] The rules of affinity applied also to the close relatives of parties who were related by engagement or even by sexual contact: this was the impediment of public honesty or public propriety, as it came to be called. (Notably, this impediment precluded a brother from marrying the widow or fiancée of his deceased brother – the impediment against levirate marriage that was at the heart of Henry VIII's dispute with the papacy over his marriage to Catherine of Aragon.)[13] Godparents could not marry their godchildren. Adulterers could not later marry their former paramours. Eunuchs and castrati could not marry anyone because they lacked the physical capacity for sex, nor could the insane, possessed, bewitched, or severely retarded or mentally incapacitated, because they lacked the mental capacity to consent. And those already engaged or married to one spouse could not betroth or marry another because of the impediment of precontract or polygamy.

[11] This was per the rules of the Fourth Lateran Council (1215), canon 50. Earlier canon laws had prohibited marriages up to six or seven degrees, a formidable barrier to marriage in a small town or isolated community.

[12] Paleotti, *De notis spuriisque*, caps. xvi–xix, xl–xliv.

[13] See my *From Sacrament to Contract*, 134–40.

Discovery of any of these absolute impediments could lead to a suit for annulment in a church court. The court's annulment not only broke the marriage, but could sometimes saddle the parties with serious criminal charges of sacrilege, incest, or polygamy. A church court judge, or a higher religious official, had power to dispense some of these absolute impediments in individual cases and allow the marriage to continue. But the spouses themselves had no corresponding right to forgive the impediment and continue the marriage without the church's approval. All children born of such improper marriages were presumptively illegitimate.

This thick canon law tangle of impediments to marriage – particularly the attenuated impediments of consanguinity, affinity, and public honesty that defined the expansive canon law crime of incestuous and other prohibited unions – sometimes left pious innocent couples and their children in a quandary. The couple had married out of love, had celebrated their wedding with the blessing of the church, and lived their lives together with their children as a Christian family. Now suddenly, because of an arcane and attenuated impediment understood only by lawyers or judges, the husband and wife were forced to separate and to face charges of sin and crime, and their children were declared illegitimate.[14] Charles Donahue has recently shown, after an exhaustive review of the records of several medieval church courts, that such involuntary dissolutions happened much less frequently than critics of the medieval canon law have supposed.[15] Yet such involuntary annulments did happen. To overcome this undue harshness, medieval canon lawyers introduced the concept of the "putative marriage." This was defined as an invalid marriage contracted in good faith, celebrated in a church wedding, and with at least one party ignorant of the impediment. Children born of a putative marriage were declared legitimate, even if their parents were ultimately forced to annul their marriage and to remain separated from each other thereafter.[16]

---

[14] For examples of the attenuated laws of incest in action, see Charles Donahue, *Law, Marriage, and Society in the Later Middle Ages: Arguments about Marriage in Five Courts* (Cambridge: Cambridge University Press, 2008), 562–98.

[15] See analysis and citations to authors who have concluded similarly in ibid., 563–4, 596–7.

[16] The precise origin of this rule in the twelfth century is disputed, but it was fully operative by the end of the twelfth century. See summary in McDevitt, *Legitimacy and Legitimation*,

LEGITIMACY, ILLEGITIMACY, AND LEGITIMATION[17]

This more complex understanding of marriage rendered the medieval canon law of illegitimacy more complex as well. In an important decretal of 1234, Pope Gregory IX summarized the prevailing canon law on marriage and annulment.[18] He then issued a separate decretal entitled: "Which Children Are Legitimate." The individual canons on legitimacy and illegitimacy in this decretal are as follows:

1. A natural child born to two unmarried individuals is legitimated by the parents' subsequent marriage, even for matters of inheritance.
2. When matrimony contracted before the Church is put asunder, children born or conceived before the decision are legitimate.
3. The word of a man or a woman who denies that someone is their child is to stand, unless the contrary is proved by legal process and witnesses.

23–9; and the sifting of ancient authorities on point in Paleotti, *De notis spuriisque,* cap. x.1–8.

[17] For primary sources, see First Lateran Council (1123), canons 7, 9, 21; Second Lateran Council (1139), canons 6–8, 17, 23; and Third Lateran Council (1179), canon 11, all in Tanner, ed., *Decrees,* vol. I; Fourth Lateran Council (1215), canons 14–16, 31, 50–2, in Schroeder, *Disciplinary Decrees.* Gratian, *Decretum,* Dist. 56; C. 27–32, 35–6, reprinted in Friedberg, *Corpus Iuris Canonici,* Part I; *Decretales,* X.4.1–21, reprinted in Friedberg, *Corpus Iuris Canonici,* Part II, with commentaries in Bernardus Papiensis, *Summa Decretalium,* repr. edn., ed. Theodore Laspeyres (Graz: Akademische Druck und Verlagsanstalt, 1956), 182–4; Henrici de Segusio [Hostiensis], *Summa aurea,* repr. edn. (Aalen: Scientia Verlag, 1962), esp. 215a–216b; Rufinus von Bologna (Master Rufinus), *Summa Decretorum,* ed. Henrich Singer, repr. edn. (Aalen: Scientia Verlag, 1963), 148–50, 429–536; Sinibaldus Fliscus [Innocent IV], *Commentaria Apparatus in V Libros Decretalium* [Frankfurt am Main, 1570], repr. edn. (Frankfurt am Main: Minerva, 1968), 478b–481b; Johannes Andreae, *Novella in Sextum* [Venice, 1499], repr. edn. (Graz: Scientia Verlag, 1963), esp. 166–8, 240–2. In the sixteenth century, Paleotti, *De notis spuriisque,* skillfully synthesized this canonical teaching and integrated it with Romanist teaching. Among numerous studies, see esp. R. Génestal, *Histoire de la légitimation des enfants naturels en droit canonique* (Paris: Ernst Leroux, 1905); H. Herrmann, *Die Stellung der unehelichen Kinder nach kanonischen Recht* (Amsterdam: Grüner, 1971); Anke Leineweber, *Die rechtliche Beziehung des nichtehelichen Kindes zu seinem Erzeuger in der Geschichte des Privatrechts* (Königstein: Peter Hanstein Verlag, 1978), 55–69; Laurent Mayali, "Note on the Legitimization by Subsequent Marriage from Alexander III to Innocent III," in *The Two Laws: Studies in Medieval Legal History Dedicated to Stephan Kuttner,* ed. Laurent Mayali and Stephanie A.J. Tibbets (Washington, DC: Catholic University of America Press, 1990), 55–75; Gilbert J. McDevitt, *Legitimacy and Legitimation: An Historical Synopsis and Commentary* (Washington, DC: Catholic University of America Press, 1941), 11–60; Ludwig Schmugge, *Kirche, Kinder, Karrieren: Päpstliche Dispense von der unehelichen Geburt in Spätmittelalter* (Zurich: Artemis & Winkler, 1995); Ludwig Schmugge, ed., *Illegitimät in Spätmittelalter* (Munich: R. Oldenbourg, 1994).

[18] *Decretales,* X.4.1–16.

4. An illegitimate child is one whom a wife conceives in adultery while her husband is alive, or by an adulterer or other man after her husband has died.

5. Actions on birth, when refused to one petitioning for an inheritance before a secular judge, are to be transferred to an ecclesiastical judge.

6. Natural children are legitimated by the parents' subsequent marriage, spurious children are not. Thus adhering to the literal text. This is a famous capitulum and is invoked daily in both forums.

7. The Church does not rule concerning civil cases between lay persons. But it will decide whether someone was born from a lawful marriage.

8. If a woman, separated by a judgment from her first husband, contracts with a second while the first is alive, the offspring she has by him are legitimate.

9. Children born from a clandestine marriage approved by the Church are legitimate.

10. Those born from matrimony contracted contrary to the impediment of public propriety are illegitimate and excluded from their parents' inheritance. It should be kept in mind that this often occurs through ignorance.

11. To prove a child illegitimate it is not sufficient to show there was an impediment to the marriage, if it was conducted before the Church.

12. The testimony of witnesses proving someone legitimate stands, even if local rumor and hearsay concerning the parents holds the contrary.

13. In the lands of the Church the pope can legitimize illegitimate children. In other lands, however, he does not, unless there are compelling reasons, or he does so only for spiritual matters. But in those cases, however, he is understood to legitimize, indirectly and consequently, for temporal matters as well. He should not act in these later cases without hesitation.

14. If a married man, not knowing his first wife is alive, contracts with a second before the Church, their offspring are legitimate.

15. Unbelievers' offspring who later convert are legitimate, even if the parents are related within a degree prohibited by canon law.[19]

---

[19] Ibid., X.4.17 (omitting the discussion and illustrative cases).

This decretal was a distillation of much prevailing canonical lore, a resolution of many disputed technical legal questions, and the starting point for a series of later medieval and early modern canonical discussions of legitimacy, illegitimacy, and legitimation.

The hierarchy of legitimates. As this list of canons illustrates, the medieval canonists recognized several categories of legitimate children, which the canonists arranged from the purest to the most suspect. The purest case of legitimacy was a child conceived and born after the contracting of a valid marriage, which the couple had properly celebrated in a church. A child adopted by a couple after they were married in a church was treated the same way.[20] So was a child born to a wife within a year of the death or disappearance of her husband – unless there was strong evidence of the woman's adultery.

The second kind of legitimacy was that of a child conceived and born after the contracting of a clandestine marriage. This was a valid marriage that had either been secretly entered into by the couple (without notification of church, state, or family members), or been celebrated publicly but not in the church or with a priestly blessing.[21] While the clandestine marriage itself "bore the stain of its imperfect formation," the canonists argued, "the child bore no stain" and was considered legitimate.[22] In the case of disputed

---

[20] Following Jack Goody, I had earlier mistakenly assumed that the medieval canonists did not recognize the institution of adoption. See John Witte, Jr., "Ishmael's Bane: The Sin and Crime of Illegitimacy Reconsidered," *Punishment and Society* 5 (2003): 327–45, at 333–4. Charles Reid has authoritatively refuted the Goody thesis, and shown all manner of medieval canon law texts that recognized adoption of children, even if the practice was not common. Reid, *Power over the Body*, 179–85 contra Jack Goody, *The Development of the Family and Marriage in Europe* (Cambridge: Cambridge University Press, 1983), 99ff. I am deeply grateful to Professor Reid for his criticisms of my work, and his fine scholarship on the medieval canon law of marriage and rights.

[21] According to some recent studies, "clandestine marriage" could sometimes also mean marriages between parties who married despite an absolute impediment (such as incest or polygamy/precontract) that they knew but kept secret. Some case studies in France and Germany suggest that secret marriage in this sense was heavily litigated in late medieval church courts. See Beatrice Gottlieb, "The Meaning of Clandestine Marriage," in Robert Wheaton and Tamara K. Hareven, eds., *Family and Sexuality in French History* (Philadelphia: University of Pennsylvania Press, 1980), 53; Reinhard Lettmann, *Die Diskussion über die klandestinen Ehen und die Einführung einer zur Gültigkeit verpflichtenden Eheschliessung auf dem Konzil von Trent* (Münster: Aschendorff, 1967).

[22] Hostiensis, *Summa aurea*, 216a.

paternity or of disciplinary procedures against the parents, however, the clandestine marriage had to be "ratified by the church" in order for the couple to secure the legitimacy of their children. The burden was then on the parties to prove that they had intended to enter into a valid marriage – that it was a true "marriage of conscience," not just a tryst that had led inadvertently to pregnancy and was now being held out as a valid marriage. If the couple could not make out their case of a valid clandestine marriage, it was safer for them to have a church wedding after the fact. This would remove any lingering doubt of their child's legitimacy.[23]

The third kind of legitimacy was that of a child who was conceived before the marriage but born after the wedding day. In most of these cases of premarital conception, the child was presumed to be the couple's own, unless there was strong evidence of alternative paternity (in which case the child was treated as an adulterine bastard).[24] The premarital fornication and conception were considered less serious if the couple had already been engaged; the engagement contract lessened the immorality of their fornication, though it did not eliminate it altogether. It was also better that the man and his pregnant wife-to-be marry in a church wedding after doing penance for their fornication; a clandestine marriage would only compound their sin of premarital fornication. While this child bore the taint of its illicit premarital conception, it was rendered legitimate by its parents' later participation in the sacrament of marriage. This followed naturally from the familiar doctrine of legitimation of natural children by subsequent marriage, which the canonists took over from the Roman law. Since the marriage of a couple served to legitimate their already born natural child, the marriage had to legitimate their natural child still in the womb, too.

A fourth kind of legitimacy was that of a child who was born of an invalid marriage between non-Christians but was baptized as an infant or later baptized as an adult after conversion to the faith. The non-believer's baptism, the canonists argued, washed away any stain of illegitimacy. This was true even if the child was born to non-Christian parents who lived in a blatantly adulterous, incestuous, or polygamous union. The sexual unions of non-believers, Pope

---

[23] *Decretales Gregorii*, X.4.17.9. [24] Ibid., X.4.17.3, 12.

Gregory IX declared, are "not bound by canonical enactments" or "subject to the canonical discipline" that governs the marriage of Christians, and thus their seeming illegality is irrelevant to the status of their child upon baptism. The "waters of baptism" cleanse the child from both the pagan practices and the sexual sins of its parents.[25]

A fifth kind of legitimacy was that of a child born of an innocently contracted putative marriage that was later annulled. The annulment could be the result of a prohibitive impediment that the innocent spouse wanted to have enforced or an absolute impediment that had to be enforced regardless of what the parties wanted. The canon law decreed that children born "before the annulment and those conceived before the sentence [of annulment] is passed should not be considered less than legitimate. They should have the right to succeed by inheritance to paternal goods and be supported by their parents' resources."[26] The canonists made clear that a putative marriage would be found only if the husband and/or wife had remained ignorant of the absolute impediment and only if the parties had demonstrated their faith by getting married before the church. If both had known of the defect but kept it hidden, or if they had married secretly outside of the church regardless of what they knew, no putative marriage would be found and their children were illegitimate.[27]

These medieval canon law provisions formed a longer and more nuanced list of legitimates than that maintained in the classical Roman law and medieval civil law. Roman law made no distinction between children born of church weddings versus clandestine marriages, and they had no theory to explain why a pregnant single woman could produce a legitimate child if she married her lover before giving birth. Moreover, Roman law had no developed concept of legitimation by baptism, and no concept at all of a putative marriage that could legitimate the children of incestuous or other illegal unions entered innocently.

---

[25] Ibid., X.4.17.15; see also ibid., X.4.19.8. Why these same "waters of baptism" could not cleanse the sexual sins of parents who were Christian is not explained. See later critical queries about this below on p. 112.

[26] Ibid., X.4.17.3.

[27] Lombard, *Sent.* IV, Dist. 41.3–4; see also *Decretales Gregorii*, X.4.17.2; X.4.17.11.

The medieval canonists added these categories of legitimacy as equitable rewards for pious acts. Each of these new categories of legitimacy depended on a sacramental act of faith – dedicating oneself or one's child to the faith through the sacrament of baptism, confessing one's sins of fornication in the sacrament of penance, or celebrating the sacrament of marriage with the blessing of an ordained priest. Each of these sacramental acts, a late medieval canonist put it, "cancels the sins of the parents, whether sins of omission or commission, and keeps these sins from being visited upon the children." The sacrament of baptism cancels the original sin of children who "were conceived and born in sin." The sacrament of penance cancels the actual sin of fornication and its odious effects on others, including children born of this act. And the sacrament of marriage cancels the inherent sinfulness of sexual intercourse, transforming it into a licit act of natural creation of a new child of God. Even an invalid marriage, celebrated by an innocent faithful party in the church and consecrated mistakenly by the presiding cleric, will thus produce legitimate children.[28]

The hierarchy of illegitimates. But even the faith of the parents and the sacraments of the church could not spare every child born out of wedlock from the stain of illegitimacy. The medieval canonists kept an ample roll of illegitimates, some drawn from the Roman law, some products of the new theology of marriage. They retained the Roman law forms of civil legitimation (by fathers, parents, or civil officials) for natural illegitimates, and added new forms of (partial) spiritual legitimation for children born of more serious sexual sins.[29]

The canonists divided illegitimate children into five main classes, arranged in order of the severity of the sexual sin of their parents. The first and least stigmatized class was made up of the "natural illegitimates" who were born to couples capable of marriage with each other. Every canonist included in this category children born of simple fornication between single parties or premarital fornication

---

[28] Paleotti, *De notis spuriisque,* caps. xxxi, xlvii, liii and more generally Eugen Wohlhaupter, *Aequitas canonica. Eine Studie aus dem kanonischen Recht* (Paderborn: F. Schöning, 1931).
[29] Rosellis, *De legitimatione,* passim.

between fiancés. Some medieval canonists added children of concubinage, too, especially if it could be shown that this was a relation of "marital affection" like clandestine marriage. The legal status of (the children of) concubinage remained a perennially disputed issue, however, and the canonists gradually moved against the institution. The Fifth Lateran Council (1514) finally and firmly outlawed concubinage and called for all who practiced or condoned this "evil custom" to be "punished severely" and for all children born of such unions to be declared illegitimate.[30]

As in Roman law, so in medieval canon law, "natural illegitimates" could be legitimated by the declarations or testaments of their fathers, by the subsequent marriage of their parents, by adoption into a new family, by oblation to or marriage into the civil court, or by rescripts issued by the emperor or other authorized secular official. The canonists added little to these traditional methods of legitimation, regarding most of them as matters for the secular courts to administer.[31] But the canonists underscored the traditional rule that, before the church, legitimation by subsequent marriage of the parents was reserved only to natural illegitimates, not spurious children.[32] Once legitimated by any one of these means, the canonists argued, natural children could enjoy full rights (*plenissimo iura*) both under the civil law and the canon law.

A second, more serious class was composed of illegitimates born to parents whose unions violated the positive laws of the church, though not necessarily the laws of nature. These were children born of unions that violated the technical impediments of age, solemn penance, former crimes, rape, abduction, seduction, and various other forms of coerced sex or marriage. They were also children born of prohibited unions between relatives with more attenuated spiritual, family, or blood ties, or born to the insane, possessed, bewitched, or severely retarded, who could not be married because they lacked the capacity to consent to marriage. If these impediments

---

[30] Fifth Lateran Council (1514), session 9 (5 May 14), in Schroeder, *Disciplinary Decrees*. See Brundage, *Law, Sex, and Christian Society*, 514–17.

[31] Leineweber, *Die rechtliche Beziehung*, 64–9.

[32] *Decretales Gregorii*, X.4.17.6. For analysis of this restriction at canon law, and how it changed more permissive earlier views, see Mayali, "Note on the Legitimization by Subsequent Marriage."

were not waived by the innocent party (in the case of prohibitive impediments) or dispensed by the church court (on finding a putative marriage), the children born of such unions were illegitimate.

These children were usually called "merely spurious bastards," however. Since their illegitimacy was a product of the church's canon law, these children could not be legitimated by traditional Roman law methods that were administered by the laity, whether fathers, parents, or state officials. But the merely spurious illegitimates could be legitimated by the church itself. Since the church made the positive laws that illegitimated these children, the canonists argued, the church could dispense with these laws as well. Medieval popes accordingly claimed the power to issue rescripts of legitimation in emulation of the imperial rescripts used by the secular authorities. These papal rescripts were a staple part of the canon law by the thirteenth century. A papal rescript could either legitimize these children directly, or legitimize them indirectly by validating the defective marriages from which they were born – what was sometimes called "radical sanation of the marriage" (*sanatio matrimonii in radice*). Either way the child was now viewed as legitimate. Legitimation by papal rescript was a costly and cumbersome procedure, however, and generally reserved to the highborn, who could get a papal hearing. But it provided some recourse for children whose legitimacy proved especially important – say, in order for them to enter a diplomatically expedient marriage, or to accede to a coveted political or ecclesiastical position foreclosed to bastards.

It remained a highly contested issue throughout the Middle Ages and beyond whether a child legitimated by papal rescript could enjoy plenary rights in all spheres of life. Obviously, the church's order of legitimation gave the child full spiritual rights (*iura ad sacra*) under the canon law. In papal territories and in ecclesiastical principalities, where only the canon law governed, this was enough. It was also enough for those who became clerics or monastics and now lived under the exclusive rule of the canon law. It was less obvious, however, that a papal rescript ordering legitimation was also effective in the secular sphere. Could an order of legitimation by papal rescript give the merely spurious child full secular rights (*iura ad temporalia*), including the important rights to parental support and paternal inheritance under secular law?[33] The popes and canonists believed it did, especially given that canon law was the preemptory law of Western Christendom, and that the church held a spiritual sword that was superior to any temporal sword. "The Apostolic See does have full power to . . . legitimize for secular acts," Pope Gregory IX put it in 1234. But to maintain comity and balance between the spiritual and secular powers, Gregory continued, the pope should not exercise this power of dispensation "unless there are compelling reasons," and even then "not without hesitation."[34]

The third category of illegitimacy was made up of children born of unions "not only against the positive law, but also against the express natural law," which was written on the hearts and mind of men (Rom. 2:14–15), and rewritten in the pages of Scripture.[35] These were called "infamous bastards" (*infami spurii*), "the bitter fruits" of "damned sexual intercourse" (*ex damnato coitu*). The canonists included in this category children born of polygamy, of adultery, and of blatant fornication, promiscuity, or prostitution which were tantamount to adultery. Both "the Mosaic and canon laws detest those born from adultery," one decretal put it. "The Lord says that those who are bastards or spurious may not enter the assembly until the tenth generation, the canon law forbids their advancement to holy orders, and secular laws bar them from succession to their parents, denying them any support."[36] The canonists also labelled "infamous" children born of incest – now a potentially very large category, given the sweeping canonical impediments of consanguinity and affinity. The church "condemns" children of incest, the First Lateran Council (1123) explained, "because both the divine and secular laws prohibit them. For the divine laws not only cast out those doing this and their progeny but also call them accursed; the

---

[33] See Reid, *Power over the Body*, 200–10; Pataui, *Tractatus de legitima filiorium*, 440a–445b.

[34] *Decretales Gregorii*, X.4.17.13; Innocent IV, *Commentaria*, 479a–480b. See detailed discussion in Génestal, *Histoire de la légitimation*, 91–180; Schmugge, *Kirche, Kinder, Karrieren*, passim. See the struggle over this issue in medieval England at the Council of Merton (1234), discussed below pp. 105–6.

[35] Thomas Aquinas, *The Summa Theologica*, trans. English Dominican Fathers, repr. edn. (New York: Benzinger Brothers, 1948), Supp. Q. 68, art. 1 (hereafter "ST"). This Supplement was adapted from Thomas's early Commentary on Peter Lombard's *Book of Sentences*.

[36] *Decretales Gregorii*, X.4.17.13.

secular laws call such people disreputable and deprive them of inheritance. We, therefore, following our fathers, mark them with infamy and judge them to be infamous."[37]

More "infamous" still were children born of sacrilegious unions that offended not only the positive law and the natural law but also the spiritual law of the sacraments. This included children born of forbidden unions between godparents and godchildren (an affront to the sacrament of baptism) or between Christians and non-Christians (an affront to the sacrament of marriage). Interreligious unions and marriages were a particular concern for the medieval church, given that marriage was now regarded as a sacrament. The church generally recognized marriages of Catholics with baptized Eastern Orthodox Christians (and, later, with baptized Protestants), and viewed their children as legitimate, at least once they were baptized or confirmed in the Catholic faith. But they did not recognize as sacramental marriages the unions of Christians with Jews, Muslims, pagans, or heretics, all of whom lacked the threshold requirement of baptism. Children born of these latter unions were thus illegitimate. The canonists made clear that the couple's disparity of religion had to be judged at the time of the marriage, not at the time of conception or birth of the child. The children were legitimate if both parties were baptized believers at the time of their marriage, even if one party subsequently lapsed from the faith, or was excommunicated. That was grounds for separation or even annulment of the marriage, but not for the illegitimation of their children. Conversely, if both parties were non-believers at the time of their marriage, and then "one of the two unbelieving spouses converts to the faith, and the other refuses, . . . the marriage is dissolved and the children are automatically legitimated" and put in the custody of the Christian convert.[38]

The most infamous sacrilegious unions of all were children born to monastics or clerics (*filii presbyterorum*), whose birth was an affront to the sacrament of holy orders and to the vows of celibacy or chastity. The birth of these children was regarded as "the worst of corruptions,"[39] and it was a topic of voluminous commentary

---

[37] First Lateran Council (1123), Canon 9.   [38] *Decretales Gregorii*, X.4.18.7.
[39] Fourth Lateran Council (1215), Canon 31.

among medieval canonists, beginning with Gratian.[40] The medieval church councils came down hard on clerical sex and marriage, and any children produced from the same. Reviving earlier rules, the First Lateran Council (1123) forbad any ordained cleric and monastic from sex and marriage with anyone, or cohabitation with any women who were not themselves celibate or close relatives of the cleric.[41] The Second Lateran Council (1139) ordered that clergy who violated these rules "be deprived of their position and ecclesiastical benefice. For since they ought to be, in fact and in name, temples of God, vessels of the Lord, and sanctuaries of the Holy Spirit, it is unbecoming that they give themselves up to marriage and impurity."[42] The Third Lateran Council (1179) sought to stamp out the continued practice of clerical concubinage as well: "Let all who are found guilty of that unnatural vice for which the wrath of God came down upon the sons of disobedience and destroyed the five cities with fire, if they are clerics be expelled from the clergy or confined in monasteries to do penance."[43] The Fourth Lateran Council (1215) became even more severe, calling for all prohibitions on clerical sex "to be strictly and rigorously observed, so that he whom divine fear does not restrain from evil, may at least be withheld from sin by a temporal penalty." Clerics who repeated their sexual offenses after being convicted once, or who administered the sacraments while under discipline for committing sexual sins, were to be defrocked and excommunicated, along with the "prelates who dare support such in their iniquities, especially in view of money or other temporal advantages."[44]

Children born of infamy or sacrilege were the most stigmatized bastards at medieval canon law. Their parents could never marry, and thus even the fiction of marriage through papal rescripts or radical sanation was not available to them. Parents guilty of polygamy and adultery could not marry because of the prior indissoluble marriage contract that their actions had betrayed.

---

[40] Gratian, *Decretum,* Dist. 56; Rufinus, *Summa Decretorum,* 148–50 with discussion of other medieval canonists in Génestal, *Histoire de la légitimation,* 25–44.

[41] Canon 9.   [42] Canon 6.   [43] Canon 11.

[44] Canon 14. See further sources in John Boswell, *The Kindness of Strangers: The Abandonment of Children in Western Europe from Late Antiquity to the Renaissance* (New York: Pantheon Books, 1988), 341–5.

Parents guilty of serious incest could not marry because the law of God against such unions was eternal. Parents guilty of sacrilege could not marry because they had breached the permanent vows of chastity or celibacy they had sworn on taking the sacrament. The children born of such sins were thus generally viewed as irredeemable. As Pope Innocent IV put it, it was on account of these spurious bastards that the Bible had uttered the "perilous admonition" that "the sins of the fathers shall be visited upon their children."[45]

Children born of infamy or sacrilege were to suffer all the disabilities on their rights to property, inheritance, contracts, court testimony, office holding, and more imposed by the civil law. They would find no relief from such secular strictures in the church courts. These children were to suffer further disabilities imposed by the canon law – most notably being barred from holding clerical office or entering religious orders, unless they received the rare prize of a papal dispensation. The canonists described this rule as a direct and necessary application of the law of Deuteronomy 23:2 ("No bastard shall enter the assembly of the Lord") and of the many rules of priestly and clerical purity set out in both the Old and New Testaments. Clerics, the Second Lateran Council (1139) put it, were to be pure "temples of God, vessels of the Lord, and sanctuaries of the Holy Spirit."[46]

Illegitimates were too impure to uphold the necessary dignity and sanctity of the clerical office, Thomas Aquinas explained: "They who are ordained are placed in a position of dignity over others. Hence . . . they should be of good repute, bedecked with a virtuous life and not publicly penitent. And since a man's good name is bedimmed by a sinful origin, therefore those also who are born of an unlawful union are debarred from receiving orders, unless they receive a dispensation; and this is the more difficult to obtain, according as their origin is the more discreditable."[47]

A few canonists extended this logic of purity to bar infamous and sacrilegious bastards not only from the sacrament of holy orders,

---

[45] Innocent IV, *Commentaria,* 481. See texts and discussion in Génestal, *Histoire de la légitimation,* 50.
[46] Canon 6.   [47] ST, Supp. Q. 39, art. 5.

but also from the sacrament of marriage. "Scripture had good reason to say that children of adulterers and other grave sinners must not mature, but perish," the fourteenth-century canonist Johannes Andreae wrote, citing the Book of Wisdom. Children born of grave sexual sins "will imitate their parents when they mature," bringing even "greater sin and harm to the church in the next generations."[48] "[B]astards are commonly infected with the leprosy of their sire's disease," wrote another authority: "and being encouraged with the example and pattern of their father's filthiness, they are not only prone to follow their sinful steps, but do sometimes exceed both them and others in all kinds of wickedness."[49] Illegitimates must, of course, not be killed in the womb or after birth, for that is homicide. But they must be "cast out" of the home like Ishmael, and their "bastard seed" must be left to "die out," in accordance with the Scripture. It cannot be "cultivated" or blessed by allowing illegitimates to participate in the sacrament of marriage.[50]

Medieval theologians and canonists were well aware of the biblical and patristic passages that counseled against imposing vicarious liability on innocent children for the sexual sins of their parents. But "the general conclusion of the law on this matter was that the children of irregular unions ought indeed to be discriminated against by the law" – just as Abraham had done with Ishmael in casting him out of his home.[51] Some writers, Aquinas reported, objected "that children ought not to suffer any loss through being illegitimate. For a child should not be punished on account of his father's sin," according to Deuteronomy 24:16, Ezekiel 18:20, and other biblical passages. "[I]t is not his own but his father's fault that he is born of an unlawful union. Therefore, he should not incur a loss on this account." To this objection Aquinas responded with word play: "To incur a loss in this way is not a punishment. Hence

---

[48] Andreae, *Novella,* 240. See further Shulamith Shahar, *Childhood in the Middle Ages* (London/New York: Routledge, 1990), 127–44.

[49] Henry Swinburne, *A Briefe Treatise of Testaments and Last Willes* (London: John Windet, 1590), 201a (citing an array of late medieval canonical authorities).

[50] Swinburne, *A Briefe Treatise,* 201a–b. See the biblical passages above pp. 13–16.

[51] Vern L. Bullough and James A. Brundage, *Sexual Practices and the Medieval Church* (Buffalo, NY: Prometheus Books, 1982), 134.

we do not say that person is punished by not succeeding to the throne through not being the king's son. In like manner, it is no punishment to an illegitimate child that he has no right to that which belongs to legitimate children."[52] A second objection taken up by Aquinas read thus: "[H]uman justice is copied from divine. Now God confers natural goods equally on legitimate and illegitimate children. Therefore illegitimate should be equaled to legitimate according to human laws." This argument conflates divine power and human will, said Aquinas. "Illegitimate intercourse is contrary to the law, not as an act of the generative power, but as proceeding from a wicked will. Hence an illegitimate son incurs a loss, not in those things which come to him by natural origin, but in those things which are dependent on the will for being done or possessed."[53] The upshot of Aquinas' arguments was that a child's illegitimate state, and the restrictions it imposed upon him or her in life, were much like a natural handicap such as blindness or lameness. A child had to learn to live within these natural limits and not think it unjust or unfair that other children could see or run. It made no difference that a child was born with these defects, or they were caused by the willful acts of his or her parents. Either way, he now faced natural limits.

It was no answer to these arguments, various other commentators argued, that biblical titans like Abraham, Jacob, Judah, and David had committed grave sexual sins of adultery, incest, concubinage, and polygamy and yet their children became heroes of the faith. Abraham, Jacob, and Judah did not have the full light of the Mosaic law, only the natural light that had been dimmed by sin, Gratian's *Decretum* argued. "A penalty for a crime takes effect when a law is enacted to prohibit the crime. Before the law, the guilty are not punished, but only after the law."[54] David's adultery with Bathsheba was, indeed, a serious violation of the Mosaic law. But God forgave him for his offense for the higher purposes of the kingdom. What is important about these ancient biblical stories is not their moral instruction to the faithful today but "their symbolic reality" in the history of salvation. God allows in his grace that "through good people, both evil and good will be born into the faith, and

---

[52] ST, Supp. Q. 68, art. 2. [53] Ibid. [54] Gratian, *Decretum*, C. 32, q. 4, c. 3.

that, through evil people, both good and evil will be drawn to the faith."[55] But while God has power to forgive violations of his divine and natural law, all the church can do is to abide by God's law, and exercise God's mercy so much as possible for those who violate it.

In that spirit, the church did hold out three remedies to mitigate the plight of infamous and sacrilegious illegitimates. First, the church gave these children, along with other illegitimates, standing in church courts to sue their fathers and mothers for support during their lifetimes. This was an important remedy not available at Roman law and not much recognized by medieval civilians. It especially helped illegitimates born from well-to-do parents. But even some less well-off parents could provide the child with sufficient support to avert chronic poverty. The canonists made clear, however, that children could not sue parents who were clerics or monastics. Such sacrilegious children could avail themselves of the church's general diaconal care and poor relief programs.[56] But they had no special claim on the church just because they had been born of the sexual offenses of a church officer.

Second, the church allowed infamous and sacrilegious bastards to enter into a monastic order and "live a life of mortification and prayer" in order "to remedy their previous ignoble status."[57] This was the medieval church's rough equivalent to the Roman law method of legitimation by oblation to the secular court. The oblation was now to the church's monastery or cloister, and it served to legitimize the person at least in the spiritual sphere. Like the curial oblation in the state, monastic oblation in the church was an onerous arrangement that imposed severe restrictions on the life of the oblate. But it at least provided a living, a community, and some social standing. Moreover, monasteries and cloisters took in some of these illegitimates already as infants, or accepted them as foundlings abandoned on their

---

[55] Ibid., C. 32, q. 4, c. 1. See also ST, Supp. Q. 65 using the same argument against drawing any moral license for concubinage from the story of Abraham and Hagar: "Intercourse with a woman outside wedlock is an action improportionate to the good of the offspring which is the principal end of marriage: and consequently it is against the first precepts of the natural law which admit of no dispensation."

[56] See Brian Tierney, *Medieval Poor Law* (Berkeley: University of California Press, 1959); Gilles Couvreur, *Les pauvres on-ils des droits?* (Rome: Libraria editrice dell'Universita Gregoriana, 1961), esp. 37ff.

[57] Quoted and discussed in McDevitt, *Legitimacy and Legitimation*, 56–8.

doorsteps. The monasteries reared and educated these children at their own expense, until the children were mature enough to decide to oblate themselves or to leave. In all cases of oblation, however, children of clerics and monastics could not advance to a bishopric or other ecclesiastical position absent special papal dispensation.[58]

Papal dispensation from the defect of birth (*ex defectu natalium*) was the third partial remedy that the church held out to all illegitimates, including infamous or sacrilegious illegitimates. This form of equitable power allowed illegitimates to be legitimated for purposes of entering monastic orders or clerical offices. Popes and bishops routinely granted these dispensations to all manner of illegitimates for lower clerical or monastic positions. Popes alone could grant illegitimates dispensations for higher clerical and monastic offices, and for clerical benefices (that is, paid clerical livings). The graver the form of the illegitimacy and the higher the clerical office sought by the illegitimate child, the harder it was to acquire the dispensation. Only the truly pious illegitimates could be rewarded by these dispensations, and evidently they were rarely given. And even so, illegitimate sons of priests were permanently foreclosed from inheriting their father's office or benefice, a restriction reiterated by the Council of Trent in 1563.[59]

SUMMARY AND CONCLUSIONS

The medieval church helped to bring the Western theology and law of illegitimacy into greater concordance. Marriage, the church taught, was the natural and proper place for a Christian to pursue sex and procreation. Sexual intercourse outside of marriage was a serious crime and sin. The natural father and mother were best suited by nature to care for their own children. Unnatural relations between parents and children could not be countenanced or perpetuated. Marriage was a sacrament that sanctified the sexual act and purified the couple, the children, and the church. Extramarital

---

[58] Boswell, *The Kindness of Strangers*, 139–41, 340–6, 403–27.

[59] Génestal, *Histoire de la légitimation*, 33–90. Fourth Lateran Council (1215), canon 31; See also H.J. Schroeder, *Councils and Decrees of the Council of Trent* (St. Louis, MO: B. Herder Book Co., 1941), "Doctrine of the Sacrament of Matrimony," Twenty-Fourth Session (November 11, 1563), chap. xv, at p. 180.

sex was a perversion that stained the couple, their children, and the church. Some sexual unions, even if imperfectly formed, could be raised to the dignity of a marital sacrament by the pious acts of the faithful. But other sexual unions, even if innocently entered, could only be condemned if they violated God's express laws. Natural illegitimates could be rescued from their plight if their parents were subsequently married. But unnatural illegitimates could never be legitimated, because their parents could never marry. The church could ease the plight of the permanent bastard by ordering their fathers and mothers to support them and by opening their orders and offices to receive them. But the stain and stigma of illegitimacy could never be removed. A child's illegitimate status was recorded on the birth certificates and death certificates kept by the church, rendering the child a permanent witness to the sins of the parents.

The medieval church's appetite for hierarchy and order gave the canonists more refined grids than the civilians had to calibrate the purity of the legitimate and the impurity of the illegitimate. The purity of the legitimate turned on the quality of their parents' marriage. The purest were children born after a church wedding. Then, in turn, came children born after a secret marriage, then children conceived before marriage but born afterward, then children who were born of improperly joined pagans but who were later baptized, and finally children born of illicit unions innocently entered and mistakenly consecrated. The impurity of the illegitimate turned on the nature of the law that their parents had violated. The least impure were children of simple fornication, whose parents' subsequent confession and marriage covered their sin. Then, in turn, came children born in violation of the church's canon law, then children born in violation of canon law and natural law together, and finally children born in violation of canon law, natural law, and spiritual law at once. Laity and clergy alike could legitimate children of simple fornication. Only clergy could legitimize children whose parents violated the canon law. But only God could legitimate children born of violation of his natural and spiritual law; the church could only offer them some comfort and mercy through dispensations in the spiritual sphere.

This elaborate legal system rested not only on a refined philosophy of hierarchy but also on a complex economy of sin and grace. Particularly in expounding the sacrament of penance in their confessional manuals, medieval theologians arranged sins in a vast order – from the most venial to the most mortal. They also assigned works of purgation in a corresponding order – from short and easy tasks to purge the lightest venial sins to heavy and lengthy burdens to offset the gravest mortal sins. Third parties could contribute to the purgation of the sins of their family members or friends – even after those family members or friends had passed away – through acts of charity, gift-giving, and sacrifice, payments of mortuaries, indulgences, and more. With such an understanding of sin and grace, it was easy enough for the medieval mind to understand the hierarchies of purity and impurity at work in the doctrine of illegitimacy and legitimation. It was also easy enough to understand how third parties, even innocent children, could find themselves paying for the sins of their parents.

The medieval law of illegitimacy and legitimation, built on classical Roman foundations, dominated much of the West until the nineteenth century.[60] The Catholic Church confirmed and extended its canon law teachings, first in the decrees of the Council of Trent (1563), then in the writings of the early modern Catholic naturalists and manualists. The Catholic Church implemented these laws not only through the pulpit, catechism, and confessional, but also through the work of its early modern schools, hospitals, and charities that kept a discriminating eye on the pedigree of the children under their watch.[61] The 1917 Code of Canon Law repeated many of the medieval canon law provisions on illegitimacy and legitimation for the maintenance of ecclesiastical and clerical discipline within the church.[62]

Early modern Catholic nations and their colonies ultimately merged the canon law and civil law teachings on illegitimacy, as the church lost much of its property and power to rule as an independent sovereign in the West. This merged *ius commune* of the sixteenth to nineteenth centuries was enforced by the secular authorities. It featured a slightly more refined differentiation of

---

[60] John C. Ayer, Jr., "Legitimacy and Marriage," *Harvard Law Review* 16 (1902–3): 22–42.
[61] Jeffrey R. Watt, "The Impact of the Reformation and Counter-Reformation," in *Family Life in Early Modern Times, 1500–1789,* ed. David I. Kertzer and Marzio Barbagli (New Haven, CT: Yale University Press, 2001), 125–54.
[62] *The 1917 or Pio-Benedictine Code of Canon Law in English Translation,* ed. and trans. Edward N. Peters (San Francisco: Ignatius Press, 2001), Canons 1051, 1114–17, with further analysis in McDevitt, *Legitimacy and Legitimation,* 61–222.

bastardy than prevailed at Roman law, a modest expansion of the traditional laws of legitimation and adoption, and a greater accommodation by civil courts of a bastard's claims for support both from the parents and from their broader families. Various natural law reformers – notably Hugo Grotius, Samuel von Pufendorf, and Christian Wolff – criticized the legal concept of illegitimacy as a violation of emerging theories of the natural liberty and natural equality of all. But the basic civil law on the subject remained largely unchanged.[63] Even the great legal codes of the Enlightenment – the Prussian Code of King Frederick (1791) and the French Civil Code of Napoleon (1804) – though bristling with revolutionary new teachings on liberty, equality, and fraternity, retained much of the legal structure of illegitimacy and legitimation taught by the medieval *ius commune*.[64]

Early modern Protestant lands on the Continent remained more faithful to the classical Roman law of illegitimacy, and dropped several of the medieval canon law reforms. Because they rejected the notion of sacramental marriage and clerical celibacy, Protestant lands rejected the canon law category of illegitimacy born of sacrilege. Because they truncated the impediments of blood and affinity and rejected the impediment of public honesty, most Protestant legal codes reduced the canon law category of incest to its Roman law core. And because they rejected the legal authority of the pope, Protestant lands did not recognize legitimation by papal rescript or dispensation.[65] But early modern Protestants were, if

[63] See Leineweber, *Die rechtliche Beziehung*, 208–26.
[64] *The Frederician Code*, 2 vols. (Edinburgh: A. Donaldson and J. Reid, 1791), pt. I, bk. 2, tit. 3.1, 3.3, 4.1.37, 5.1–10, 6.1–8. 7.1–5; *Code Napoleon, or The French Civil Code*, trans. George Spence (London: William Benning, 1827), bk. 1, tit. 2.2.58, 61; tit. 5.1.158–9, tit. 5.4.197, 201–2; tit. 7 passim; tit. 8.1 passim. See analysis in Beate Harms-Ziegler, *Illegitimität und Ehe: Illegitimität als Reflex des Ehediskurses in Preussen im 18. und 19. Jahrhundert* (Berlin: Duncker & Humblot, 1991); Jean Brissaud, *A History of French Private Law*, 2nd edn., trans. R. Howell (Boston: Little, Brown, and Company, 1912), 202–16; Crane Brinton, *The French Revolutionary Legislation on Illegitimacy* (Cambridge, MA: Harvard University Press, 1936). The changes that were made respecting paternity claims and paternal succession are recounted in Suzanne Desan, *The Family on Trial in Revolutionary France* (Berkeley: University of California Press, 2004); John Eekelaar, *Family Life and Personal Life* (Oxford: Oxford University Press, 2006), 59ff.
[65] For an overview of the Protestant reforms of the canon law of marriage, see Witte, *From Sacrament to Contract*, 42–193.

anything, harsher than Catholics in punishing extramarital sex, and they accordingly enforced their truncated laws of illegitimacy with fresh vigor. Moreover, the dissolution of the monasteries in many Protestant lands, together with many of the hospitals, charities, and orphanages run by the monastic orders, removed a critical support system available to illegitimates before the Reformation. It also foreclosed an important avenue of legitimation – the oblation of an illegitimate child into a monastery or cloister. Infanticide and child abandonment rates spiked as a consequence, notwithstanding a fresh wave of firm new criminal laws against them.[66] "The most notable feature" of the law of early modern Protestant lands, Anke Leineweber concludes after an exhaustive study, "is its conservative attitude and its indifference in general to the problems that illegitimacy brought forth. No new legal ideas were developed to improve the situation of the illegitimate child" – whether in the laws of marriage and family, inheritance and trusts, or social welfare and poor relief.[67] It is a telling anecdote that when the innovative Calvinist jurist François Hotman sat down in the 1560s to write a new Protestant law *On Illegitimacy and Legitimacy,* he simply rehearsed the laws of the Christian Roman emperors on point, and concluded: "that which has not been rescinded by the old [Roman] law, I think, should probably remain established."[68]

---

[66] See analysis and literature in Mark Jackson, *New-Born Child Murder: Women, Illegitimacy, and the Courts in Eighteenth-Century England* (Manchester: Manchester University Press, 1996); Lionel Rose, *The Massacre of the Innocents: Infanticide in Britain, 1800–1939* (London/Boston: Routledge & Kegan-Paul, 1986); Katharina Schrader, *et al.*, *Vorehelich, ausserehelichen, uneheliche – wegen der grossen Schande: Kindestötung im 17. und 18. Jahrhundert* (Hildesheim: Gerstenberg, 2006). See further below, pp. 128–30.

[67] Leineweber, *Die rechtliche Beziehung*, 154. While Leineweber is referring principally to the law of Lutheran Germany, the same is true in Calvinist communities. See sources and analysis in Jeffrey R. Watt, *The Making of Modern Marriage: Matrimonial Control and the Rise of Sentiment in Neuchâtel, 1550–1800* (Ithaca, NY: Cornell University Press, 1992), esp. 99–108, 178–94; Leah Leneman and Rosalind Mitchinson, *Sin in the City: Sexuality and Social Control in Urban Scotland, 1660–1780* (Edinburgh: Scottish Cultural Press, 1998); Karen E. Spierling, *Infant Baptism in Reformation Geneva: The Shaping of a Community, 1536–1564* (Aldershot: Ashgate, 2005); John Witte, Jr. and Robert M. Kingdon, *Sex, Marriage and Family in John Calvin's Geneva*, 3 vols. (Grand Rapids, MI: Wm B. Eerdmans, 2005).

[68] Franciscus Hotmanus, J.C., *De spuriis et legitimatione* [c. 1568], IV.E., appended to Barnabé Brisson, *De verteri ritu nuptiarum et jure connubiorum* (Amsterdam: Petrus le Grand, 1662).

Figure 6 *Hereward the Wake Submits to William the Conqueror*, 1072.

CHAPTER 4

Heir of no one: The English common law of illegitimacy and its reform

This chapter focuses on the development of illegitimacy in the English common law. I focus on this common law development, in part to render the continued story more manageable in size and more immediate to the experience of Anglo-American readers.[1] The Anglo-American common law of illegitimacy also presents interesting tensions with the *ius commune* on the Continent, and an alternative logic of illegitimacy focused more on property than morality. The English common law was not based directly on the classical Roman law texts but on English statutes and cases, a few of which went back to Anglo-Saxon times. While medieval civil law and Catholic canon law certainly had a place in English jurisprudence,[2] on some topics English judges and jurists went their own legal way in opposition to the Catholic Church and its canon law – doubly so after the Protestant Reformation in England in the 1530s.[3]

Indeed, it was the canon law of illegitimacy and legitimation that sparked one of the great encounters between church and state in medieval England at the Council of Merton in 1234. The bishops gathered at the council asked the king and lords to accept the old Roman law rule, taken over by the medieval canonists, that allowed

---

[1] The continued Continental story is well told in Anke Leineweber, *Die rechtliche Beziehung des nichtehelichen Kindes zu seinem Erzeuger in der Geschichte des Privatrechts* (Königstein: Peter Hanstein Verlag, 1978), 155–279.

[2] See R.H. Helmholz, *Roman Canon Law in Reformation England* (Cambridge: Cambridge University Press, 1990), 121–95.

[3] R.H. Helmholz, *The Oxford History of the Laws of England, vol. I, The Canon Law and Ecclesiastical Jurisdiction, 597 to the 1640s* (Oxford: Oxford University Press, 2004), 237–310; Martin Ingram, *Church Courts, Sex and Marriage in England, 1570–1640* (Cambridge: Cambridge University Press, 1987); Eric Josef Carlson, *Marriage and the English Reformation* (Oxford: Blackwell, 1994).

natural children to be legitimated by the subsequent marriage of their parents. Most civil law countries had adopted this rule by the thirteenth century. England was holding out. The bishops sought to make this a universal rule of Western Christendom, evidently as part of their effort to consolidate the church's governance of marriage and family law. The secular rulers gathered at Merton would have none of it. As the early common law authority Henry Bracton reported: "All the earls and the barons, as many as there were, answered with one voice that they did not wish to change the laws of England, which had hitherto been used and approved."[4] The English common law of illegitimacy has never had "any dependency upon any foreign law whatsoever, no not upon the civil or canon law," Sir Edward Coke announced proudly four centuries later.[5]

This was a deliberate overstatement, but it underscored the reality that the English law of legitimacy and legitimation proceeded on two tracks in the Middle Ages. The church's canon law dealt with spiritual sanctions for the parents' sexual sins and the pastoral care and control of illegitimate children. The common law dealt with the civil status of illegitimate children and their eligibility to inherit. The church's declarations of illegitimacy and legitimation were considered binding in the spiritual sphere, with the rights and duties of parent and child enforceable within the church courts. The secular courts maintained their own laws of illegitimacy and legitimation that governed secular cases of property, inheritance, and contract. The canon law and common law of illegitimacy did overlap, and if there was no conflict of laws, church and state authorities would cooperate. The secular courts would send cases to the church court to answer the factual question of whether a person was illegitimate. The secular courts would then use this answer to judge the case before them – say, whether a party could hold or inherit land or a title, or whether a defendant had committed slander

---

[4] *Bracton on the Laws and Customs of England,* trans. Samuel E. Thorne, 4 vols. (Cambridge, Mass: Harvard University Press, 1968), IV:296. See further editorial notes in ibid., III:xv–xvii; R.H. Helmholz, "Bastardy Litigation in Medieval England," *American Journal of Legal History* 13 (1969): 361–83; J.D. White, "Legitimation by Subsequent Marriage," *Law Quarterly Review* 36 (1920): 255–67.

[5] Sir Edward Coke, *The Second Part of the Institutes of the Laws of England,* repr. of the 1797 edn., 4 vols. (Buffalo, NY: William S. Hein, 1986), II:96–8.

or defamation by calling another a "bastard." But, if the canon and common laws conflicted, the secular courts insisted on deciding both the fact and the consequences of illegitimacy, sometimes by jury trial, which was a coveted procedural right at common law.[6]

After the Protestant Reformation in England in the 1530s, these two laws of illegitimacy were merged. Some of the canon law definitions of illegitimacy were dropped in expression of the new Protestant teachings. Some of the church's traditional pastoral and parental care of illegitimates shifted to the justices of the peace who administered the state's poor laws. The church courts of England were given exclusive jurisdiction to determine the factual question whether a person was illegitimate, while various secular courts determined the legal consequences of their findings. But the definition of illegitimacy that the church courts now applied was set by Parliament, not by the pope. It was this merged English law of illegitimacy and legitimation that came to prevail, with endless local variations, in the American colonies and states of the seventeenth to nineteenth centuries. What follows is a brief analysis of the late medieval and early modern English common law of illegitimacy, with emphasis on the differences with the prevailing *ius commune* of the Continent both before and after the Reformation. Some of these common law differences, we shall see, were more favorable to illegitimate children, some imposed greater hardship.

THE CONTOURS AND CONTRASTS OF COMMON LAW ILLEGITIMACY[7]

Like the medieval civil law and canon law, the medieval common law of England defined illegitimates as children "born out of

---

[6] *Bracton*, IV:294–308; Richard Burn, *Ecclesiastical Law,* 6th edn., 4 vols. (Philadelphia: 1787), I:242ff.; John Godolphin, *Repertorium Canonicum,* 3rd edn. (London: Assigns of R. & E. Atkins, 1687), 480ff.; Helmholz, "Bastardy Litigation"; Helmholz, *Oxford History,* 144–5, 565–98; Michael M. Sheehan, "Illegitimacy in Late Medieval England," in Ludwig Schmugge *et al.,* eds., *Illegitimität im Spätmittelalter* (Munich: R. Oldenbourg Verlag, 1994), 115–22, at 116–17.

[7] Within the vast literature, see among primary sources beyond those already cited: *Bracton*, II:31–5, 75–81, 185–8; IV:294–310; William Clerke, *The Triall of Bastardie* (London: Adam Islip, 1594); John Selden, *De successionibus ad leges Ebraeorum in bona defunctorum,* new edn. (Frankfurt an der Oder: 1673), cap. 3, pp. 9–17; id., *De iure naturali et gentium, juxta*

rightful and lawful wedlock."[8] These were generally children born of fornication, concubinage, prostitution, incest, adultery, polygamy, and other unions prohibited by various marital impediments. Some common lawyers took pains to label these illegitimates with the Latin titles used by the canonists and civilians: *naturales, spurii, incestui, nothi, adulterini, infamii,* among others.[9] A few other common lawyers, who had been trained in civil law and canon law, took pains to arrange these illegitimates in the order of severity of the sexual sins of their parents. Bracton's thirteenth-century list, for example, could have come straight from the texts of his civil law teacher, Azo:

> Some children . . . are natural and legitimate, those born in lawful wedlock and of a lawful wife. Some are natural only, and not legitimate, as those born of a legitimate concubine, with whom a marriage was possible at the time of procreation, as between an unmarried man and an unmarried woman. Some are neither legitimate nor natural, as those born of prohibited intercourse, of persons for whom no marriage was possible at the time of procreation; such children are *spurii* who are fit for nothing.[10]

Most common lawyers, however, in devising the common law of illegitimacy, were not so concerned about the gravity of the parents' sexual sin, or about the escalating scale of deprivations that should befall their illegitimate children. Nor were they so concerned about the sanctity of marriage, and to what extent it had been impugned by the extramarital sex. These were spiritual and moral matters for

disciplinam Ebraeorum libri septem (London, 1640), 5.16; John Brydall, *Lex Spuriorum: Or the Law Relating to Bastardy* (London: Assigns of R. & E. Atkins, 1703); *A Translation of Glanville,* trans. John Beames, repr. edn. (Littleton, CO: Fred B. Rothman & Co., 1980), 180–2; William Nelson, *Lex Testamentaria* (London: J. Nutt, 1714), 98–101, 331; Henry Swinburne, *A Briefe Treatise on Testaments and Last Willes* (London: John Windet, 1590), 198a–201b; Sir Henry Finch, *Law or a Discourse Thereof* (London: Henry Lintot, 1759), 117–19; Christopher Saint Germain, *Doctor and Student,* rev. edn., corrected by William Muchall (Cincinnati, OH: Robert Clarke & Co., 1874), 20–1, 116–17, 247ff.; William Blackstone, *Commentaries on the Laws of England* (Oxford: Clarendon Press, 1765), bk. I, ch. 16.2; Henry John Stephen, *New Commentaries on the Laws of England (Partly Founded on Blackstone),* 4 vols. (London: Henry Butterworth, 1842), IV:314–30; Matthew Bacon, *A New Abridgement of the Law* (London: A. Strahan, 1798). s.v. "Bastardy"; Harris Nicolas, *Treatise on the Law of Adulterine Bastardy* (London: W. Pickering, 1836); Wilfrid Hooper, *The Law of Illegitimacy* (London: Sweet & Maxwell, Ltd., 1911).

[8] *Bracton,* II:31, 34; Blackstone, *Commentaries,* bk. I, ch. 16.2.
[9] Brydall, *Lex Spuriorum,* 4–14.
[10] *Bracton,* II:187; see also Swinburne, *Testaments and Last Willes,* 198b–203b.

the church courts to sort out. "The holiness of the matrimonial state is left entirely to the ecclesiastical law; the temporal courts not having jurisdiction to consider unlawful marriages as a sin, but merely as a civil inconvenience."[11]

The common lawyers' concerns on the subject of illegitimacy were more material than moral. They were concerned with title to the family's property, not purity of the child's pedigree. They wanted a bright-line rule to determine which parents took care of the child in its early years, and which child stood to inherit from its parents after caring for them in their later years. Birth within marriage provided them with that bright-line test. If a child was born within marriage, the child was legitimate. If the child was born outside of marriage, it was illegitimate. Legitimate children could inherit. Illegitimate children could not. Legitimate children had to care for their parents. Illegitimate children did not. Nothing could change that reality. So there was little point in differentiating among bastards based on their parents' sinfulness. As far as we are concerned, Coke wrote in summary of the medieval common law, "we term all that be born out of lawful marriage by the name of bastards," and we "treat them all the same way."[12]

Many common lawyers thought this bright-line rule better than the tangled loopholes and fictions that the medieval canonists and civilians had spun into their laws of illegitimacy and legitimation. As William Blackstone later put it in defense of the traditional common law:

English law is surely much superior to that of the Roman, if we consider the principal end and design of establishing the contract of marriage, taken in a civil light: abstractedly, from any religious view, which has nothing to do with the legitimacy or illegitimacy of the children. The main end and design of marriage therefore being to ascertain and fix upon some certain person, to whom the care, the protection, the maintenance, and the education of the children should belong.[13]

---

[11] Blackstone, *Commentaries,* bk. I, ch. 5.1. See also John Selden, *Table Talk,* in John Selden, *Opera Omnia tam edita quam inedita in tribus voluminibus,* 3 vols. (London: Guil. Bowyer, 1726), III:2044: "1. Of all actions of a man's life, his marriage does least concern other people; yet of all activities of our life, 'tis most meddled with by other people. 2. Marriage is nothing but a civil contract. 'Tis true 'tis an ordinance of God; so is every other contract; God commands me to keep it, when I have made it."
[12] Coke, *Institutes,* I:244a. [13] Blackstone, *Commentaries, bk.* I., ch. 16.2.

The English jurist John Brydall argued further that connecting marriage, legitimacy, and inheritance was the whole point of the biblical story of Ishmael that the Christian nation of England should seek to emulate:

[I]t is not only human laws which say that none can inherit that are not born in matrimony, but God calls Isaac, Abraham's only son, though at the same time Abraham had his son Ishmael by Hagar, his handmaid or concubine. "And Abraham gave all he had to Isaac: but to the sons of the concubine, which Abraham had, he gave gifts, and sent them away from Isaac his son (while he yet lived) eastward, to the east country" (Gen. 25:5–6). So though Ishmael was Isaac's elder brother, yet in comparison to Isaac born in wedlock, God himself did not account him Abraham's son. Nor can one instance be given, that ever, either by God's command or permission, any born out of marriage did inherit. By the law therefore of God, as well as man's law, none can inherit that are born out of matrimony.[14]

Abraham's dismissal of Ishmael, Henry Swinburne argued still further, is a moral example for all of us. It underscores the wisdom of the rule that only legitimate children born within marriage may and should inherit, and that children of an adulteress, harlot, or concubine must be dismissed from the household, and their debauched mothers with them. Any other rule, said Swinburne, with a rhetorical flourish,

cannot but redound to the great prejudice of right heirs, considering the danger whereunto children are subject, and which they do many times sustain, through forcible flatteries of vile dissembling harlots, no less void of all modesty, than full of all a kind of subtlety with whose sweet poison and pleasant sting, many men are so charmed and enchanted that they have neither power to hearken to just petitions of a virtuous wife, praying and craving for her children, and a shameless whore, prating and grating for her bastards: never remembering that when Sarah said to Abraham, "Cast out this bond woman and her son, for the son of his bond woman shall not be heir with my son Isaac," Abraham by the commandment of God, hearkened to the voice of Sarah.[15]

This bright-line common-law rule – that children born to a married woman are legitimate and heritable, and children born to an unmarried woman are not and can never be – introduced some

---

[14] Brydall, *Lex Spuriorum,* 4–5.   [15] Swinburne, *Testaments and Last Willes,* 200b–201a.

striking departures from the medieval canon and civil law. Some of these common law changes exacerbated the plight of illegitimate children, some eased it.

First, the common law rejected the canon law rule of putative marriages, innocently contracted in violation of an absolute impediment of incest or precontract. At canon law, so long as at least one of the two parties was ignorant of the impediment, and so long as both of them had celebrated their wedding in the church, their children would remain legitimate and heritable, even if their parents were forced to separate.[16] The common lawyers would have none of this. They did not countenance polygamy or incest any more than the canonists did. But for them a polygamous or incestuous union was simply not a marriage, regardless of what the parties knew or where the marriage had been celebrated. Thus any children born to the couple were by definition illegitimate. The canon law rule of putative marriage, the common lawyers argued, introduced unnecessary uncertainty by separating marriage, legitimacy, and heritability. It further left children without the custody and support of both parents. It left parents torn between children of putative marriages and those of later proper marriages. And it left heirs uncertain of their inheritance. Moreover, the canon law rule of putative marriage defied another elementary common law rule: that ignorance of the law and mistake of fact were not defenses to criminal or immoral conduct.

Second, the common law rejected the canon law rule that subsequent marriage of the parents automatically legitimated their "natural children" and rendered them heritable. This was the issue that had divided church and state at the Council of Merton. At common law, a child born before his or her mother married remained illegitimate even if the parents subsequently married. "Shotgun weddings" (as they were later called) between conception and birth legitimated the child, but post-birth weddings were of no avail. It made no difference that the pregnant couple had become engaged by the time of the birth, or that the child arrived prematurely. If the child was born before the couple exchanged their

---

[16] See above p. 83.

marital vows, it was illegitimate and would remain so. This presumptive nine-month window gives "sufficient allowance to the frailties of human nature," Blackstone wrote, in defending the English rule that would last until 1926. "For if the child be begotten while the parents are single, and they will endeavor to make an early reparation for the offense, by marrying within a few months after, our law is so indulgent as not to bastardize the child" but rather have it "born within the rules of honor and civil society."[17]

But accommodating human frailty could not come at the cost of corrupting the rule that only children born within marriage are legitimate heirs, Blackstone continued. Allowing legitimation by subsequent marriage of the parents just confuses matters. How can canonists allow only the parents' natural children to be legitimated but not their spurious children? If the sacrament of marriage purifies some sexual sins and their illicit fruit, why can't it purify them all? Is God's abundant sacramental grace really so parsimonious and selective? Moreover, how can we be certain that all children brought into the subsequent marriage were "really begotten by the same man"? How can we let a man ignore his responsibilities to his illegitimate children all his life, and then have them declared legitimate by his late-life marriage to their mother? This "totally frustrates . . . the main end of marriage, the protection of infants." Even worse, how can we let legitimate children, whom we saddle with duties to care for their parents in their old age, dangle with such uncertainty about their inheritance and eventual reward? "[T]he Roman [and canon] law admits of no limitations as to the time, or number, of bastards so to be legitimated; but a dozen of them may, twenty years after their birth, by the subsequent marriage of their parents, be admitted to all the privileges of legitimate children. This is plainly a great discouragement to the matrimonial state; to which one main inducement is usually not only the desire of having *children,* but procreating lawful *heirs.*"[18]

---

[17] Blackstone, *Commentaries,* bk. I, ch. 16.3.

[18] Ibid., bk. I, ch. 16.1.3; 16.2.1 (emphasis in original). Some of these views were articulated by John Locke in his discussion of the procreative end of the marriage contract. See John Locke, *Two Treatises of Government,* ed. Peter Laslett (Cambridge: Cambridge University Press, 1960), II.77–83.

Third, the common law rejected adoption and other forms of legitimation of illegitimate children.[19] Medieval civil law and canon law together allowed a child to be legitimated by various means – by the father's declaration, by the parents' marriage, by another family's adoption, by oblation to the church or state, or by rescripts and dispensations issued by popes or kings and their delegates. Legitimation by any one of these means allowed natural children to become full siblings and heirs with legitimate children, and it enhanced somewhat the standing and opportunities of spurious children. While the *ius commune* "reckoned the bastard among the 'rightless'" by nature, one common lawyer wrote, it preserved their right to "legitimation in imitation of nature."[20]

The common lawyers wanted little to do with such a "base imitation of nature."[21] For them, these artificial methods of legitimation only served to fracture domestic households, cloud property titles, and unsettle the family's inheritance. Thus all these "means to make children lawful heirs, except marriage, we have no use [of] here in England." If a propertied person is left childless, Sir Edward Coke declared, "the surest adoption of an heir" is not to create fictitious children on paper, but to draw up a last will and testament under the "learned advice" of legal counsel who could "make good assurance of the land, etc." It is too "dangerous . . . to change an ancient maxim of the common law" that only legitimately born children of marriage can inherit.[22]

Some medieval common lawyers did tinker a bit with the idea of legitimation, though to no lasting effect. In the thirteenth century, for example, Bracton suggested that England had something close to adoption, since it allowed a husband to claim as his own a child whom his wife had conceived with another man. But Coke and other later jurists made clear that this was a far cry from adoption of

[19] For later reforms, see T.E. James, "The Illegitimate and Deprived Child," in *A Century of Family Law*, ed. R.H. Graveson and F.R. Crane (London: Sweet & Mawell, Ltd., 1957), 39–55; J.M. Eekelaar, "Reforming the English Law Concerning Illegitimate Persons," *Family Law Quarterly* 14 (1980): 41–58.

[20] Sir Frederick Pollock and F.W. Maitland, *The History of English Law before the Time of Edward I*, 2nd edn. by S.F.C. Milsom, 2 vols. (Cambridge: Cambridge University Press, 1968), II:397, quoting in part from the French jurist, Beaumanoir.

[21] Clerke, *The Triall of Bastardie*, fol. 39.

[22] Coke, *Institutes*, II:96–7; Brydall, *Lex Spuriorum*, 42–3.

a stranger as one's own child. Bracton, they insisted, was merely repeating the common law's "very strong presumption of paternity ... which absolves the court from difficult inquiries" into the intimacies of bed and board. "[W]e have no adoption in England."[23] In the later Middle Ages, Parliament occasionally did issue a special act legitimating the children of a favored family of the realm, a practice that continued haltingly until modern times. But such acts were rarely granted privileges reserved for the very well-connected who found themselves in extreme need. And while it conferred some rights and dignities, this private act of Parliament did not give a bastard son the right to succeed to his father's political (or clerical) office.

Henry VIII – and the whole English nation with him – found this out the hard way in the 1520s. Unable to sire a male heir with his wife, Catherine of Aragon, Henry sought to legitimate his bastard son, Henry Fitzroy, who had been born of his concubine Mary Boleyn (sister of Anne Boleyn). A male heir to the English throne, Henry believed, would be better than Princess Mary, whom his wife Catherine had produced for him. After all, England had fought the bloody Wars of the Roses over royal succession, and Henry thought it best to have a strong prince ready to succeed him when the time came. His legal advisors talked him out of it. They made clear that a private Act of Parliament might legitimate young Fitzroy for some purposes, but it could not entitle him to the throne, even if England had to risk another war of succession as a result. Lacking other means of securing a male heir, Henry embarked on his famous and tawdry six-year dispute with the papacy to annul his marriage to Catherine and to have a son by another wife – a dispute that ultimately yielded the English Reformation. Six wives and two daughters later, Henry finally sired a sickly son, Edward, to succeed him as his legitimate heir to the English throne.[24]

---

[23] Pollock and Maitland, *History of English Law*, II:399, citing Coke, *Institutes*, II:97. See further Stephen B. Presser, "The Historical Background of the American Law of Adoption," *Journal of Family Law* 11 (1972): 443–516, at 450.

[24] Henry Ansgar Kelly, *The Matrimonial Trials of Henry VIII* (Stanford: Stanford University Press, 1976).

Fourth, the common law treated as legitimate and heritable any child born to a married woman – even if the child was conceived by another man. This rule covered children born to a woman who had premarital sex with a third party either before her engagement or before her wedding day. Even "if a child was born but an hour after the solemnization of marriage, it shall be the husband's, though it were begotten by another man," John Godolphin wrote. "He is not reputed as a bastard," and he "may be the heir of him who married the mother."[25] This rule also covered a child conceived by a wife and her lover after her marriage. So long as the child was born to the married couple, the very strong presumption was that the child was theirs and that the husband was its father. This was true even if the husband was impotent, or had been away for a time, or if the woman was a notorious bed-hopper. "Whoso bulleth my cow, the calf is mine," was the old farming adage used to express the presumptive paternity of the husband and the legitimacy of the child.[26] The only way to defeat this presumption was to show that the husband was completely incapable of sexual intercourse, say, because of castration or an injury. Or one had to give absolute proof that the husband and wife had not had any contact within the prior two years – that the husband was far away "beyond the four seas" with no opportunity to get home. But if he was merely stationed across the country or across the Channel, the mere possibility, however far-fetched, that he could slip home for a single moment of romance with his wife was enough to defeat the presumption. And even if his paternity was impossible, if the husband accepted the child born to his wife as his own, the common law courts would usually inquire no further, and declare that child to be his legitimate heir.[27]

This same rule of presumptive legitimacy applied to a child born to a new widow. Any child born to a woman within roughly ten months of the death of her husband was still considered to be the

[25] Godolphin, *Repertorium Canonicum,* 482.

[26] Quoted in Helmholz, "Bastardy Litigation," 370, from the fourteenth-century yearbooks.

[27] Coke, *Institutes,* I:244a; Nicholas, *Treatise,* passim; Hooper, *Illegitimacy,* 13–19. The "four seas" doctrine was finally rejected in 1732, but the strong presumption of the husband's paternity and the child's legitimacy remained in place. See Helmholz, "Bastardy Litigation," 370.

legitimate heir of the deceased father. This was true even if the widow was notorious for her philandering during and after husband's lifetime, or if the couple had been estranged. It was also true if the pregnant widow remarried within nine months. The child was considered the first husband's heir if she was well along in her pregnancy on her wedding day. It was the second husband's heir if she was not yet showing. Either way, her child was legitimate.

This was a marked departure from the canon law, which regarded all such children as illegitimate. The children's status at canon law turned on the gravity of their mother's sin. Mere fornication of a single woman before any engagement was bad enough, though her children could be legitimated (so long as the father was not himself a married man or a cleric). But adultery of a woman in violation of her engagement contract, or even worse in breach of her own marital contract, was more serious. Her adulterine children usually faced permanent illegitimacy, unless they received a rare rescript or dispensation, which gave them a modest career within the church. Because of these striking differences between the canon law and common law, the secular courts kept these cases away from the church courts. The secular courts certainly punished the woman for her sexual crimes – usually more severely than they punished husbands who strayed. And they allowed the husband to separate from his adulterous wife, and withhold from her the dower, child support, alimony (introduced in the later sixteenth century), and other property claims she might otherwise have against her husband.[28] But at common law "the mother's sin was not visited on the child."[29] The child remained legitimate.

Fifth, after the Reformation, the common law rejected mandatory clerical celibacy and the illegitimacy of all children born to clerics. Clerical sex, concubinage, and marriage had been touchy topics throughout the Middle Ages. From 1123 onward, the Catholic Church authorities issued increasingly stern prohibitions on all clerical sex. The church also denounced clerical children as the bitterest fruits of sacrilege, and pronounced that these bastards in particular could not hold even a minor clerical office without a papal dispensation.[30] Some English clergy, however, continued to

---

[28] Nicolas, *Treatise.*   [29] Hooper, *Illegitimacy,* 9–10.   [30] See above pp. 93–9.

produce children and to live in secret concubinage, if not marriage. A few indulging bishops allowed learned sons of the clergy to succeed to their father's benefices, particularly if the clerics held them out as their nephews. A few common law courts regarded as legitimate those children born to clergy below the order of sub-deacons who were secretly married. Clerical sex, marriage, and children remained a subject of perennial controversy between and among church and state officials in England (and elsewhere) until the Reformation. To settle matters once and for all, the Catholic Council of Trent in 1563 declared anathema on any Catholic cleric who deviated from its canonical rules on mandatory celibacy and chastity. But, by then, the church in England had severed its ties with Rome and become the Church of England.

Clerical marriage was one of the hallmarks of the early Protestant Reformation. Indeed, the early English reformers held up the 1525 marriage of ex-monk Martin Luther with ex-nun Katherine von Bora as an iconic act of liberation. English church and state officials thus embraced the new clerical freedom to marry soon after England's formal break with Rome in 1533/4. But clerical marriage remained controversial in the minds of the Tudor monarchs, and their Parliaments intermittently banned the practice. A 1603 statute finally declared clerical marriage legal in the church and commonwealth of England. English clergy at all levels were now free to marry, and their children were deemed legitimate and heritable.

Similarly, the canonical prohibition on illegitimate sons serving in clerical office fell away in the seventeenth century, as it had in other Protestant lands.[31] In the sixteenth century, the English crown had given the Archbishop of Canterbury the power to grant bastards dispensations to serve in clerical office.[32] The archbishop, operating through an Office of Faculties, had occasionally used this power to clear clerical candidates of doubtful origin. But this practice of dispensing bastards for clerical office was eventually discarded as "too redolent of Catholicism," in the words of seventeenth-century

---

[31] Hooper, *Illegitimacy*, 89–100; F.W. Maitland, *Roman Canon Law in the Church of England: Six Essays* (London: Methuen, 1898), 54ff.

[32] 25 Hen. VIII, c. 21, 1524; 28 Hen. VIII, c. 16, 1536, with discussion in Helmholz, *Oxford History*, 211–12.

jurist John Selden. A cleric's eligibility for office should turn on his character and learning, not on his pedigree and birth status. Anyone who harbored doubts whether the Bible allowed bastards to serve in clerical office could turn to Selden's learned exegesis of Deuteronomy 23:2 ("No bastard shall enter the congregation of the Lord, even to the tenth generation"). Drawing on his extensive knowledge of Jewish law, Selden showed that this verse had nothing to do with the birth status of priests and other religious officials. Properly understood, Selden concluded, "the meaning of the phrase is, he shall not marry a Jewish woman." To use this text to bar bastards from the priesthood is "grossly mistaken."[33]

Sixth, after the Reformation, the common law also rejected the canon law teaching that marriage was a sacrament and that children born of interreligious marriages were illegitimate. This was a marked departure from medieval rules. At medieval canon law, only baptized Christians in good standing with the church could be sacramentally married. Marriages that joined Christians with Jews, Muslims, heretics, or excommunicants were invalid, and their children were regarded as illegitimate.[34] The medieval secular courts in England were, if anything, harder than the church courts on mixed marriages, particularly those involving Christians and Jews. After the formal expulsion of the Jews from England in the thirteenth century, Christian–Jewish unions became capital offenses, and children born to these couples were routinely expelled from the land, if not killed upon birth.[35]

After the Reformation, the Church of England gradually came to reject the concept of marriage as a canonical sacrament. And with that reform, the rationale for the prohibitions on interreligious marriage and illegitimation of their children slowly dissolved. Marriage was no longer a sacrament, and baptism was no longer a prerequisite to its validity. The traditional prohibition on interreligious marriage simply melted away in the seventeenth century,

---

[33] Selden, *Opera Omnia*, III:2009, I:576–79. See above p. 21 on Jewish interpretations.

[34] See above pp. 87–8, 93.

[35] Selden, *Opera Omnia*, III:1459ff.; James Parkes, *The Jew in the Medieval Community: A Study of His Political and Economic Situation*, 2nd edn. (New York: Hermon Press, 1976), 101–36; Solomon Grayzel, *The Church and the Jews in the XIIIth Century* (Philadelphia: Dropsie College, 1933), 49–59, 72–82.

evidently without formal announcement. Even if legally valid, however, interreligious marriages remained culturally suspect. Marriages between Anglicans and other Protestants became more acceptable after the Toleration Act in 1689 lifted some of the sanctions on non-Anglican Protestants. But the occasional Protestant marriages with Catholics and Jews remained stigmatized until the Catholic and Jewish Emancipation Acts of 1829 and 1833. And, even then, these mixed marriages often proved unwelcome to either side, particularly if the parties sought to celebrate their nuptials in the established Anglican Church. The *Book of Common Prayer,* used in these services, had no contemplation or liturgy for interreligious marriages, and no Anglican priest could properly preside over such a wedding under Anglican ordination rules of the day.[36]

Whatever legal rationale may have still remained for the prohibition on interreligious marriages evaporated altogether as England faced a fresh wave of clandestine marriages in the seventeenth and eighteenth centuries. As in the Middle Ages, so in early modern times English common law courts recognized marriages to be valid, even if they were contracted without the necessary consent of parents, testimony of witnesses, publication of banns, or celebration in church. A consensual union between a man and woman willing and able to marry was a marriage, especially if it had been consummated. A 1604 canon confirmed the traditional requirements of parental consent, public banns, and church consecration for a valid marriage. But this same law also confirmed the traditional licensing exception to these publicity requirements. "Licensed marriages" were initially conceived as narrow exceptions to the usual rules, reserved for instances where necessity, such as imminent travel or military service, demanded an abridged engagement and marriage ceremony. The 1604 canon stipulated that only the archbishop and his clerical delegates could grant a license.[37] In the course of the seventeenth century, however, this licensing exception came to be treated as an attractive alternative method of marrying without the

---

[36] See John Witte, Jr., *From Sacrament to Contract: Marriage, Religion, and Law in the Western Tradition* (Louisville, KY: Westminster John Knox Press, 1997), 140–79, 233–63.

[37] Acts and Proceedings of Convocation (1604), in Edward Cardwell, ed., *Synodalia: A Collection of Articles of Religion, Canons, and Proceedings of Convocations in the Province of Canterbury* (Oxford: University Press, 1842), Canons 101–4.

involvement of church, family, or community. Licensing officials proliferated, licensing requirements eroded, and false licenses abounded. Couples who sought to marry secretly could easily steal away to a remote parish to be married, or make their way to one of the many licensing booths that sprang up around the Fleet Prison and near the ports. This "underground marital industry," as Lord Hardwicke would later call it, thrived in the later seventeenth and early eighteenth centuries, despite the increasingly stern prohibitions of Parliament against it.[38]

The 1753 Parliamentary Act for the Better Preventing of Clandestine Marriage – "Lord Hardwicke's Act," as it came to be called – sought to put a forceful end to this practice of clandestine marriage in England as well as to the recognition of its colonial American cousin, "common law marriage." The Act returned the licensing exception to its traditional narrow limits under strict control of the Anglican clergy. And for valid marriages it required parental consent, two witnesses, formal banns, civil registration, and church consecration. Only marriages formed in strict compliance with all these rules were lawful, and children born to couples who had violated these rules were now illegitimate. Parish registrars and record-keepers were ordered to keep close tabs on these requirements and report breaches of the rules. The old canon law rules of marital formation – crystallized by the Fourth Lateran Council of 1215, and again by the Council of Trent in 1563 – were now back as firm new common law requirements.[39]

Lord Hardwicke's Act of 1753 had the inevitable, if ironic, effect of increasing the numbers of recorded illegitimate children in early modern England. Studies of English and Scottish parish records from 1750–1850 show marked increases in the percentage of illegitimates born and registered after 1753 – from averages of 2–3 percent in the five decades before the Act, to averages of 5–7 percent in the five decades afterward.[40] Rates well over 10 percent could be

---

[38] See George Elliott Howard, *A History of Matrimonial Institutions,* 3 vols. (Chicago: University of Chicago Press, 1904), II:435–60.

[39] 26 Geo II, c. 33. See above p. 79 for the Fourth Lateran Council rules.

[40] Peter Laslett and Karla Oosterveen, "Long Term Trends in Bastardy in England: A Study of the Illegitimacy Figures in the Parish Registers and in the Reports of the Registrar General, 1561–1960," *Population Studies* 27 (1973): 255–86; Peter Laslett, "Introduction," to

found in some English cities and in some rural regions of Scotland by the turn of the nineteenth century.[41] These same records also show a sharp spike in the number of cases of abortion, abandonment, and infanticide, often involving illegitimates.[42] Many factors, of course, contributed to these increased rates of illegitimacy. Local studies have pointed variously to the effect of growing urbanization and industrialization, increased use of live-in seasonal laborers and apprentices, a housing shortage in the cities that forced more contact if not cohabitation, increased numbers of single women apprentices and workers who were open both to sexual experimentation of their own or sexual exploitation because they were on their own, shifting courtship practices with increased premarital sex and longer engagements, economic downturns that discouraged marriages or broke consummated engagements, among other factors.[43] Peter Laslett has also pointed to "bastard-bearing subcultures" in England, in which a few local women produced a good number of the illegitimates in their community, and their daughters and granddaughters continued their loose habits[44] – a theory borne

Peter Laslett, Karla Oosterveen, and Richard M. Smith, eds., *Bastardy and Its Comparative History* (London: Edward Arnold, 1980); Peter Laslett, *Family Life and Illicit Love in Earlier Generations: Essays in Historical Sociology* (Cambridge: Cambridge University Press, 1977).

[41] Leah Leneman and Rosalind Mitchison, "Scottish Illegitimacy Ratios in the Early Modern Period," *Economic History Review*, 2nd ser., 40(1) (1987): 41–63; Leah Leneman and Rosalind Mitchinson, *Sin in the City: Sexuality and Social Control in Urban Scotland, 1660–1780* (Edinburgh: Scottish Cultural Press, 1998); Andrew Blaikie, "A Kind of Loving: Illegitimacy, Grandparents, and the Rural Economy of North East Scotland, 1750–1900," *Scottish Economic and Social History* 14 (1994): 41–57; Andrew Blaikie, *Illegitimacy, Sex, and Society: Northeast Scotland, 1750–1900* (Oxford: Clarendon Press, 1993); George Sexton, *The Causes of Illegitimacy Particularly in Scotland* (Edinburgh: Edmonston and Douglas, 1860). Though Lord Hardwicke's Act did not formally apply in Scotland, local judges and consistories did begin insisting on comparable rules of marital formation soon after its promulgation.

[42] See, e.g., Lawrence Stone, *The Family, Sex, and Marriage in England, 1500–1800* (San Francisco: Harper & Row, 1979), 296–7.

[43] Ibid.; Alyssa Levine, Thomas Nutt, and Samantha Williams, eds., *Illegitimacy in Britain, 1700–1920* (Basingstoke/New York: Palgrave Macmillan, 2005); Nicholas Rogers, "Carnal Knowledge: Illegitimacy in Eighteenth-Century Westminster," *Journal of Social History* 23 (1989): 355–75; Susan Scott and C.J. Duncan, "Interacting Factors Affecting Illegitimacy in Preindustrial Northern England," *Journal of Biosociological Science* 29 (1997): 151–69; Cissie Fairchilds, "Female Sexual Attitudes and the Rise of Illegitimacy: A Case Study," *Journal of Interdisciplinary History* 8 (1978): 627–67.

[44] Peter Laslett, "The Bastard Prone Sub-Society," in Laslett *et al.*, eds., *Bastardy*, 217ff.

out in other local studies.[45] Edward Shorter and Lawrence Stone have even pointed to a growing "sexual libertinism" – if not a "sexual revolution" – that erupted in the century wedged between the puritan disciplinary programs of the seventeenth century and the evangelical revival and morals reforms of the nineteenth.[46] Whatever the relative weight of these factors might be in individual communities, "no single-cause analysis" can explain the sharp increases in illegitimacy rates in the later eighteenth century.[47]

What also drove up the numbers sharply after 1753 was a combination of the simple clarity of the old law of illegitimacy with the stern rigor of the new law of valid marriage. More bastards were no doubt being produced after the passage of Lord Hardwicke's Act of 1753, but more children were also being counted as bastards. Newly included on the bastard rolls were children of secret and common law marriages and of informally married couples whose families had never bothered with all the legal and sacerdotal niceties of proper marital union. In the old days, these children were treated as legitimate. Now they were branded as bastards, and, lacking any legal means of legitimation, their parents could do nothing about it.[48]

THE LIMITS AND SUPPORTS OF BASTARDS

At medieval and early modern common law, a bastard was regarded at once as a "child of no one" (*filius nullius*) and as "a child of everyone" (*filius populi*). As a child of no one, a bastard had no name or reputation, no voice or representation, no kin or family home. This was not necessarily all bad. Bastards were sometimes assigned guardians or sent to institutions that could be better

---

[45] See, e.g., Barry Reay, "Sexuality in Nineteenth-Century England: The Social Context of Illegitimacy in Rural Kent," *Rural History* 1(2) (1990): 219–47.

[46] Stone, *The Family*, 330–1, 390–404; Edward Shorter, "Illegitimacy, Sexual Revolution, and Social Change in Modern Europe," *Journal of Interdisciplinary History* 2(2) (1971): 237–72; Edward Shorter, *The Making of the Modern Family* (New York: Basic Books, 1977), chaps. 3–4.

[47] Laslett and Oosterveeen, "Long Term Trends," 256.

[48] See Belinda Meteyard, "Illegitimacy and Marriage in Eighteenth-Century England," *Journal of Interdisciplinary History* 10 (1980): 479–89; but with the caveats of Joan Schellekens, "Courtship, the Clandestine Marriage Act, and Illegitimate Fertility in England," *Journal of Interdisciplinary History* 25 (1995): 433–44.

caretakers than their parents. Bastards could choose their own names and professions without family pressure. If they made it to adulthood, they were exempt from the obligations that fell on legitimate children: They had no duty of care to their parents, no obligation to seek parental consent to marry, no responsibility for their family's torts, debts, or taxes – even if their parents and siblings had taken them in and supported them.[49] But, despite the occasional braggadocios to freedom uttered by famous bastards in history and in literature,[50] few children in medieval and early modern England would have freely chosen the status of bastardy over legitimacy.

From infancy to adulthood, an English bastard was "liable to reproach," John Brydall wrote in 1703. "For he was begotten and born out of matrimony, which is the first step to honor, and therefore the apostle calls marriage honorable (Heb. 13.4). Upon which it necessarily follows that the opposite or contrary thereof is shame and disgrace; for though it be of no fault to the bastard to be such a one, yet it is a dishonor derived from the parents of the child, and a thing easily subject to contumely and reproach." "The condition of bastards was heretofore among the people of God very contemptible," Brydall continued, quoting the condemnations of bastardy in Deuteronomy 23:2; Sirach 23:24–6; and Wisdom 3:16–17. "Children born of unlawful unions are witnesses of evil against their parents" both historically and today.[51]

The laws and customs of the Christian nation of England have long maintained these godly standards concerning bastardy, Brydall went on to demonstrate. Lacking the honor of legitimate birth,

---

[49] Stephen, *New Commentaries*, II:329–30.

[50] See literature in Lisa Zunshine, *Bastards and Foundlings: Illegitimacy in Eighteenth-Century England* (Columbus, OH: Ohio State University Press, 2005); Glenn Arbery, "'Why Bastard? Wherefore Base?' Legitimacy, Nature, and the Family in Post-Renaissance Literature," *Liberty, Life, and the Family* 2(1) (2005): 99–119. In addition to Shakespeare's plays discussed in ibid., see also Cosmo Manuche, *The Bastard: A Tragedy* (London: M.M. T. Collins and Gabrielle Bedell, 1652).

[51] Brydall, *Lex Spuriorum*, 15–34. This was only a sampling of the many biblical texts brought forward more forcefully by Sir George Meriton against the "depravity" and "debauchery" of "bastard-getting." George Meriton, *Immorality, Debauchery, and Profaneness, Exposed to the Reproof of Scripture and the Censure of the Law: Containing a Compendium of the Laws Now in Force Against . . . Debauched Incontinency and Bastard-Getting* (London: John Harris and Andrew Bell, 1698), 103–19.

bastards were formally precluded or informally shunned from various honorable positions, particularly high political, military, admiralty, and judicial offices, as well as service as coroners, jurors, prison wardens, church wardens, parish vestryman, or comparable positions of social visibility and responsibility. However well-propertied they became, bastards were also often denied access to local polls, clubs, schools, learned societies, and licensed professions. However well qualified they might be, they were also, for a time, precluded from ordination in the established Church of England. These "great disadavantages children born out of holy matrimony do lie under" should "very much deter men and women from ever pursuing unlawful and exorbitant embraces, of which this nation, as well as foreign countries, have been deeply guilty."[52]

While most of these social disabilities fell away in the course of the eighteenth century, various property and testamentary disabilities persisted, some of them dating from the early Middle Ages.[53] As a child of no one, Blackstone wrote in 1765, a bastard has "no ancestor from whom any inheritable blood can be derived."[54] Bastards could thus inherit nothing from fathers, siblings, or from anyone else, whether name, property, title, honor, business, license, charter, or other devisable private or public claim or good. This was true even in cases where the child's father or mother, who had supported him in his lifetime, died intestate and there were no other heirs to take on their property. Moreover, the common law included bastards on a roll with "apostates, traitors, felons, outlaws, famous libellers, manifest usurers, sodomites, uncertain persons, and recusants" who could not serve as executors of the estates of their parents.[55]

Illegitimate children, in turn, were limited in their capacities to alienate or devise their own property. Contrary to some of the firmer medieval canonists, the common law did allow illegitimates to marry as adults, and to support their wives and children during and after their lifetimes. But the estates of childless bastards, or of

[52] Brydall, *Lex Spuriorum*, A3, 15–34; Godolphin, *Repertorium Canonicum*, 86–7, 279–80.
[53] Coke, *Institutes*, I:3b.   [54] Blackstone, *Commentaries*, bk. I, ch. 16.2.3.
[55] John Godolphin, *The Orphans Legacy*, 2nd. enlarged edn. (London: Chr. Wilkinson, 1677), 86–7, 279–80. See also Nelson, *Lex Testamentarium*, 98–9, 331.

those who died intestate or with defective wills, were seized by officials upon their deaths. Even those illegitimates who donated or devised their property to surviving spouses or children by proper instruments were sometimes subject to special gift and inheritance taxes.[56]

While as "children of no one" bastards were liable to reproach and restrictions, as "children of everyone" they deserved support and protection, particularly in their tender years. The common lawyers decried the classical Roman law rules that barred parents from giving spurious children any support during or after their lifetimes. Such callous and calculated cruelty to "innocent offspring of his parents' crimes" is "odious and unjust . . . to the last degree," Blackstone wrote. How could a legal tradition "so boasted for its equitable decisions make bastards in some cases incapable even of a gift from their parents"?[57] "However profligate and wicked the parents" were in committing their sexual debauchery, Henry John Stephen added, to deny them the right and duty to maintain their children "was neither consonant to nature nor reason."[58]

Henry Swinburne said he understood that the law of the Christian emperors had a higher moral aim: "to restrain the unbridled lusts of some and to preserve the charity of others." But it makes no sense, said Swinburne, for any law to defy the law of nature and equity in an effort to stamp out unnatural acts: "[N]ature has taught all creatures to provide for their young so that the very brute beasts have a natural care to bring up whatever they bring forth." "[I]n equity the poor infants ought not to be punished, at least not to perish for want of food, by occasion of the father's fault, whereof they are altogether faultless." It is thus "more agreeable to nature, equity, and humanity," Swinburne continued, for the common law to follow the medieval canon law "in providing as well for the convenient relief and keeping of poor and miserable children, begotten and born out of lawful matrimony at the charges [so far as possible] of the reputed father or mother – without distinction

---

[56] Stephen, *New Commentaries*, II:329. But see the sensational sixteenth-century case testing these rules, as described in Charles M. Gray and Maija Jansson Cole, "*Bowdler's* Case: The Intestate Bastard," *University of Toronto Law Journal* 30 (1980): 46–74.

[57] Blackstone, *Commentaries*, bk. I, ch. 16.3.   [58] Stephen, *New Commentaries*, II:327.

whether such infants were begotten in incest and adultery, or fornication."[59]

This is precisely what the English common law did after the dust of the Protestant Reformation had settled. In the Poor Law of 1576 (which, amply amended, remained in place until the Poor Law Reforms of 1834[60]), Parliament enacted a comprehensive new program to support and protect illegitimate children.[61] This replaced the centuries-old church-based system of care for illegitimates that had dissolved with the dissolution of the monasteries in the 1530s and 1540s. Now, two justices of the peace in each parish, working with church wardens and overseers of the poor, were charged with the care, nurture, and education of any illegitimate child born in that parish. This care could be given directly through church offices or through wet nurses, foster homes, or foundling houses, especially when the children were young. As the children grew older, and the poor law programs developed, the parishes, separately and together, established all manner of poorhouses, workhouses, orphanages, hospitals, bonded apprenticeships, and service and trade training programs for various poor and needy children, a good number of them illegitimate. As Charles Dickens' novels would later famously depict, these programs could be hard and cruel on children, and several studies have shown that children put out to nurse or lease as infants, or put into bonded apprenticeships and trades as youths, died at alarmingly high rates.[62] But these parish-based programs provided many illegitimate children with a better life than they could have managed on their own.

The 1576 Poor Law also empowered the justices of the peace to mete out "punishment of the mother and the reputed father" for their sexual offenses that had caused such "great Dishonor" to "the laws of man and of Almighty God."[63] A 1610 poor law became

---

[59] Swinburne, *Testaments and Last Willes*, 200a–b.

[60] On these see Lisa Forman Cody, "The Politics of Illegitimacy in an Age of Reform: Women, Reproduction, and Political Economy in England's New Poor Law of 1834," *Journal of Women's Studies* 11(4) (2000): 131–56.

[61] 18 Eliz. I, c. 3, 1576.

[62] For a good distillation and systematization of these programs, and the problems they encountered in application, see Poor Relief Act, 1782, 22 Geo. III, c. 83. See further James, "The Illegitimate and Deprived Child," 39–55.

[63] 18 Eliz. I, c. 2.

sterner, calling for the justices of the peace to imprison for a year and set to hard labor "every lewd woman which shall have any bastard which shall be chargeable to the parish." Repeat offenders could be imprisoned again and released only upon "sureties for good behavior."[64] In application, proven fathers, too, could be convicted under these laws as accessories to the woman's "lewd behavior" and put to work or into prison.

The proper care of bastards proved to be a costly burden on the parishes, particularly in cities, where the numbers of bastards continued to rise. A whole tangle of special rules emerged in the seventeenth and eighteenth centuries to deal with cases of fraud – say, where mothers moved to more generous parishes just before birth to ensure better treatment, or where an aggressive parish overseer sought to move mothers and their children along to avoid the costs of their further care. Other rules emerged to exclude dissenters, known felons, and other "undeserving poor" from all parish care, and to condition anyone's continued care on their good standing in the Anglican communion – a form of "redemptive charity."[65] Parliament and local governments eventually developed an elaborate system of bonding, indemnification, and affiliation of parishes to protect them against fraud and to ensure them of sufficient funding.[66]

One important source of funding for the care of bastards was the mother and the putative father of the illegitimate child – and their respective families. Already the 1576 Poor Law empowered the justices of the peace to charge the mother and the reputed father with weekly support payments of their bastard child, until the child reached the age of majority, or was bonded out as a servant or apprentice, or engaged to be married. Later laws made it easier for a mother to identify the father of her bastard child, and for the justices of the peace to investigate closely his reputed paternity. If he

---

[64] 7 Jac. I, c. 4.

[65] The phrase is from Brian S. Pullan, "Support and Redeem: Charity and Poor Relief in Italian Cities from the Fourteenth to the Seventeenth Century," *Continuity and Change* 3 (1988): 177, 188. See also Brian S. Pullan, *Rich and Poor in Renaissance Florence: The Social Institutions of a Catholic State to 1620* (Oxford: Oxford University Press, 1971).

[66] See a good sampling in Richard Burn, *The Justice of the Peace, and Parish Officer*, 16th edn. by John Burn (London: A. Strahan and W. Woodfall, 1788), 181–226.

proved to be the father – by his own confession or by strong evidence to corroborate the mother's claim – the justices could punish the man for his fornication and irresponsibility, and lay claim on him and his family for the costs of support, maintenance, and education of the child. A 1662 law dealt harshly with "putative fathers and lewd mothers of bastard children" who "run away out of the parish, and sometimes out of the county, and leave the said bastard children upon the charge of the parish where they are born." The law authorized the justices of the peace "to take and seize so much of the goods and chattels, and to receive so much of the annual rents and profits of the lands of such putative father or lewd mother" as needed "for the bringing up and providing for such bastard child."[67] In application, this law allowed the courts to reach even across the Atlantic to the American colonies to recoup from parents the maintenance costs of the child they had abandoned in England.[68]

As criminal sanctions and support orders escalated in the seventeenth and eighteenth centuries, some desperate mothers (and occasionally fathers) found it easier to abandon their bastard children in churches, hospitals, or public places. A few mothers chose to smother the children during or after birth or to leave them with reputed "killer nurses who were willing to quietly starve bastard infants left in their custody."[69] Tomas Coram in 1727 complained of "the daily sight of infant corpses thrown on the dust heaps of London," many of them discarded illegitimates.[70] The authorities came down hard on such offenses in the later seventeenth and eighteenth centuries. Parents who intentionally abandoned their infant children faced a public whipping, a spell in the stocks, and various other types of shame punishments. Repeat offenders were put in prison and could have their properties seized. If their

---

[67] 13 & 14 Car. II, c. 12; see also 7 Jac. I, c. 4 with discussion in Burn, *Ecclesiastical Law*, I:246–50; R.H. Helmholz, "Support Orders, the Church Courts, and the Rule of *Filius Nullius:* A Reassessment of the Common Law," *Virginia Law Review* 63 (1977): 431–48.

[68] Stephen, *New Commentaries,* II:327–8.

[69] Zunshine, *Bastards and Foundings,* 4; Richard Adair, *Courtship, Illegitimacy, and Marriage in Early Modern England* (Manchester: Manchester University Press, 1996), 44.

[70] Quoted in Zunshine, *Bastards and Foundlings,* 4. See also Laslett *et al.,* eds., *Bastardy,* 52, showing that illegitimate infants died at "often twice" the rate as legitimate infants in early modern England.

abandoned infant died from exposure, they faced murder charges, and not a few of these convicts were executed.

To deal with the growing problem of intentional infanticide, Parliament had already passed "An Act to Prevent the Destroying and Murthering of Bastard Children" in 1623, which remained in force until 1803.

Whereas many lewd women that have been delivered of bastard children, to avoid their shame, and to escape punishment, do secretly bury or conceal the death of their children, and after, if the child be found dead, the said women do allege, that the said child was born dead, whereas it falleth out sometimes (although hardly it is to be proved) that the said child or children were murdered by the said women, their lewd mothers, or by their assent or procurement:

For the preventing therefore of this great mischief, be it enacted by the authority of the present Parliament, That if any woman . . . be delivered of any issue of her body, male or female, which being born alive, should by the laws of this realm be a bastard, and that she endeavour privately, either by drowning, or secret burying thereof, or any other way, either by herself, or the procuring of others, so to conceal the death thereof, as that it may not come to light, whether it were born alive or not, but be concealed: In every such case, the said mother so offending shall suffer death as in case of murder, except such mother can make proof by one witness at the least, that the child (whose death was by her so intended to be concealed) was born dead.[71]

This law did not hold a woman guilty until proven innocent. But it did shift the burden of persuasion to the woman to demonstrate what had become of her child, and it greatly strengthened the hand of the prosecutor if there was evidence of wrongdoing and coverup. A recent study of prosecutions of women under this statute in the eighteenth century shows that well over 90 percent of the defendants were poor and desperate single women who had simply run out of options.[72] The prosecution and execution of mothers

---

[71] 21 Jac. I, c. 27 (1623); see later detailed discussion in William Cummin, M.D., *The Proofs of Infanticide Considered, Including Dr. Hunter's Tract on Child Murder* (London: Green and Longman, 1836).

[72] See Mark Jackson, *New-Born Child Murder: Women, Illegitimacy, and the Courts in Eighteenth-Century England* (Manchester: Manchester University Press, 1996); with analysis of later developments in Ann R. Higginbotham, "'Sin of the Age,': Infanticide and Illegitimacy in Victorian London," *Victorian Studies* 32 (Spring, 1999): 319–37.

convicted under this statute sparked a small English cottage industry of sermons and pamphlets decrying the "debauched incontinency" of "bastard-getting."[73] Colonial and early American legislators maintained comparable laws against the infanticide of bastards, and their preachers launched a fusillade of fire-and-brimstone sermons against the sins of the fathers and mothers.[74]

SUMMARY AND CONCLUSIONS

England was a vital part of the Western legal tradition, and its jurists and theologians made formidable contributions to the development of many familiar Western ideas and institutions of law, politics, and society. On many legal topics, the English common law was in accord with the civil law and canon law, and the common lawyers freely adapted the norms and practices of the Continent to local conditions, and vice versa.

On the topic of illegitimacy, however, the English common law introduced a number of striking changes to the Western legal tradition. Most notably, the common law rejected legitimation by adoption, by putative or subsequent marriage, or by any other means. They rejected illegitimation by sacrilege, interreligious marriage, or by various sexual crimes committed by engaged or married women. And they rejected the imposition of restrictions on

---

[73] The quotation is from the subtitle of Meriton, *Immorality, Debauchery, and Profaneness*. For sermons and pamphlets, see, e.g., John Scott, *The Fatal Consequences of Licentiousness: A Sermon, Occasioned by the Trial of a Young Woman for the Alleged Murder of Her Illegitimate Child*, 6th edn. (London: L.B. Seeley & Sons, 1828); *The Trial of Mary Gibbs for the Murder of Her Female Bastard Child* (London, 1814); J. Penrose, *The Rev. Mr. Penrose's Account of the Behavior, Confession, and Last Dying Words of . . . J. Williams for the Murder of Her Bastard Child* (Bristol, 1741); Lydia Neeve, *The True Account of the Confession and Behaviour of Lydia Neeve for That Barbarous . . . Murder, by the Cutting off the Head of Her Bastard Child* (Norwich?, 1702); *A Full, True and Particular Account of the Trial, Sentence, and Execution of John Webb . . . for the Murder of a Male Bastard Child . . . to Which Is Added His Extraordinary Case, and the Substance of an Excellent Sermon Preached on This Most Solemn Occasion* (London: J. Pitts, 1911).

[74] See, e.g., Thomas Foxcroft, *Lessons of Caution to Young Sinners: A Sermon Preached . . . upon the Affecting Occasion of an Unhappy Young Woman Present in the Assembly under Sentence of Death* (Boston: S. Kneeland and T. Green, 1733); *The Trial of Alice Clifton, for the Murder of Her Bastard-Child* (Philadelphia, 1787). See further Ronald A. Bosco, "Lectures at the Pillory: The Early American Execution Sermon," *American Quarterly* 30 (3) (1978): 156–76; Howard, *A History of Matrimonial Institutions*, III:191, n. 3.

illegitimates proportionate to the gravity of the sins of their parents.[75] Taken together, these legal changes narrowed the category of illegitimacy, but hardened the boundaries between legitimates and illegitimates.

The common law of illegitimacy was considerably simpler than that of the canon law and civil law. Children born in marriage were legitimate; children born outside of marriage were not. It did not matter where, how, or by whom the children were conceived. Even children conceived in sacrilege, adultery, incest, concubinage, prostitution, or other infamous unions were legitimate so long as their mother was validly married by the time of the birth. The parents might be punished severely for their sexual sins, but their marriage kept the sins from being visited on their children. There was no small irony in this. The common lawyers insisted that "the holiness of the matrimonial state is left entirely to the ecclesiastical law," while "our law considers marriage in no other light than as a civil contract."[76] But it was the civil contract, not the holy sacrament, of marriage, that proved more effective in protecting the children from their parents' sin, and sanctifying them from their illicit conception.

The simplicity of the common law of illegitimacy, however, came at the cost of flexibility. At common law, illegitimacy was tantamount to an immutable condition, like gender or race. Once born illegitimate, a person could not be legitimated. A bastard remained a child of no one for life, with no opportunity for adoption or legitimation. This status was sealed in parish birth, marriage, and death certificates. There was a strong flavor of predestinarianism at work in this. Perhaps that explains why it was the early modern Calvinists, notably Oliver Cromwell in the 1650s, who most strongly resisted making changes to the common law of illegitimacy, even though the Calvinists eagerly reformed so many other laws.[77]

---

[75] Two other changes are less significant: the common law accepted as valid the marriages of the mentally handicapped, and their children were viewed as legitimate. Moreover, the common law courts were loath to accept challenges to a person's legitimacy after his or her death.

[76] Blackstone, *Commentaries*, bk. I, ch. 15.1.

[77] See sources and discussion in John Witte, Jr., *The Reformation of Rights: Law, Religion, and Human Rights in Early Modern Calvinism* (Cambridge: Cambridge University Press, 2007), chaps. 4–5.

The Continental canon law and civil law, by contrast, were considerably more flexible in their treatment of illegitimates. Though they had a more expansive category of illegitimacy, the canonists and civilians also held out more avenues of partial or complete escape from the consequences of illegitimate birth. Some of these were based on the sacraments of baptism, penance, or marriage; others were based on the laws of adoption, legitimation, and dispensation. Some of these avenues could be pursued by the children themselves, others only through the actions of their fathers, parents, state officials, or church officers. Only the most infamous bastards – those born of adultery, incest, and sacrilege – found themselves with few options at canon and civil law. The civil law, in fact, prohibited the parents from giving these spurious children any support, whether by gift or by testament. These children were regarded as the most "rightless" citizens of Christendom.

It was precisely these latter spurious children – born of adultery, incest, and sacrilege – who most deserved the support of their parents and society, the common lawyers insisted. Just because these were the most infamous, they deserved the most support. "[N]ature has taught all creatures to provide for their young . . . whatever they bring forth," Henry Swinburne reminded his fellow common lawyers. And Scripture has taught that "as much as you do it to the least of those in society, you do it to" Christ himself (Matt. 25:31–46).[78] And thus, after the Reformation, the common lawyers thought it "more agreeable to nature, equity, and humanity" to reject the civil law and to follow the traditional canon law rules of supporting these spurious children, even if they could not be legitimated. Ironically, it was because the canon law did not allow these spurious children to be legitimated that the common lawyers found its rules of support for these children so agreeable. Even proud English nationalists like Sir Edward Coke, who often decried the civil and canon law as "contrary to the law and custom of England," saw the wisdom and justice of the medieval canon law on this point.[79]

Indeed, after the Reformation, the common law transplanted a good deal of the medieval church's pastoral care for all illegitimates into the state's new poor laws. Under the poor laws, mothers and

---

[78] Swinburne, *Testaments and Last Willes*, 200a.   [79] Coke, *Institutes*, II:96.

fathers alike had to support these illegitimate children, and faced severe sanctions if they proved delinquent – and execution if they killed their illegitimate children. Some desperate mothers of illegitimate children went to the gallows for the crime of infanticide; a few such felons who tried to escape to colonial America met their end at the end of a rope as well. But each parish was also obligated to give whatever supplemental support was needed to feed, nurture, and educate illegitimate children who were born there. Guardians could also be assigned to give further care, and special tithes and taxes were collected if parish funds ran short.

Commenting on the relative leniency of the English common law toward illegitimates compared to the canon law and civil law of the Continent, the great English historians Pollock and Maitland wrote: "it may well be that the divergence of English from continental law is due to no deeper cause than the subjection of England to kings who proudly traced their descent from a mighty bastard" – William the Conqueror. The Norman laws of illegitimacy that William brought with him to England in 1066 were certainly more generous to bastards than the classical Roman laws.[80] And, perhaps in emulation of their great king, the royalty and aristocracy of England, at least in medieval times, seemed less preoccupied with wallowing in the shame of extramarital sex or visiting the sins of the fathers upon their children.[81]

But "descent from a mighty bastard" also had a more subtle influence on the common law. From the Middle Ages forward, the common law of illegitimacy shifted its focus from a logic of morality to a logic of pedigree. Not mortal sin, but heritable blood, not the wrongs of conception, but the rights of inheritance, not just royal succession after King William, but property succession for each and every family became the new driving logic of the common law of illegitimacy. As Blackstone put it, the "main inducement for marriage is usually not only the desire of having *children,* but procreating lawful *heirs.*" The main point of legitimacy law is to

[80] Pollock and Maitland, *History of English Law,* II:397. See further Hooper, *Illegitimacy,* 5–7; Selden, *Opera Omnia,* III:1335ff., 1768ff., 1962ff.; Aileen Quigley, *King Bastard: The Story of William the Conqueror* (London: Hale, 1973).
[81] Chris Given-Wilson and Alice Curteis, *The Royal Bastards of Medieval England* (London/ Boston: Routledge & Kegan Paul, 1984).

settle upon those heirs who are truly lawful. It is a telling anecdote that the first full treatise on the common law of bastardy, written by William Clerke in 1594, devotes its whole first chapter to the topic, "of possessions and nativities, their cognizance and trial."[82]

This gave a decidedly different orientation to Western illegitimacy law than the rigid morality and retributive measures codified by the Christian Roman emperors or the elegant hierarchies of sexual sin and sacramental grace offered by the medieval canon lawyers. The common law of illegitimacy at once softened the moralism of the Roman law and flattened the hierarchies of the canon law. The common law did express ample outrage at sexual sin. But it visited more of the sins upon the guilty parents than upon their innocent children.

[82] Clerke, *The Triall of Bastardie,* fol. 1.

CHAPTER 5

The rights of all children: The new law of non-marital childhood in America and beyond

If succession from William the Conqueror helps to explain the English law of bastardy, then secession from England helps to explain the corresponding American law. Before the Revolution, the American colonies shared England's focus on inheritance, property, and devisable blood in crafting their laws on bastardy. After the 1776 Revolution, the American states gradually shifted their focus to the rights and liberties of children, including illegitimates. This was part and product of the natural rights ideas championed in the American Declaration of Independence and in the new state and federal constitutions. Beginning with Thomas Jefferson's new Virginia laws on legitimation and inheritance in 1785 and ending with the Supreme Court's equal protection jurisprudence two centuries later, American law slowly drew the sting and stigma from the traditional common law of illegitimacy. Illegitimacy laws still remain on the books today, but they have been reduced to dead or dying letters in most American states. The rights and best interests of the child, regardless of its birth status, are now the dominant legal logic respecting all children.[1] Virtually all formal restrictions on illegitimates have fallen or been thrown aside, though cultural barriers and opportunity costs to illegitimates still remain high.

This chapter analyzes this American development as an illustration of the broader Western story of the modern law of

---

[1] Albert E. Wilkerson, ed., *The Rights of Children: Emergent Concepts in Law and Society* (Philadelphia: Temple University Press, 1973).

Figure 7 Léon Augustin Lhermitte (1844–1925), *Taking in Foundlings.*

illegitimacy. Parallel accounts can be given of the gradual eclipse of the common law of bastardy in England and other commonwealth countries, though their developments usually came later and sometimes featured other logics besides children's rights.[2] And parallel stories can be told of the amelioration of the plight of illegitimate children in the modern constitutional law of many Continental nations,[3] and in the new protection of "nonmarital children" under the European Convention of Human Rights.[4] Furthermore, some scholars are showing that the concept of children's rights has ancient and medieval Western roots, and they have used that historical insight to press for further reforms of the law and theology of illegitimacy today.[5]

---

[2] J.M. Eekelaar, "Reforming the English Law Concerning Illegitimate Persons," *Family Law Quarterly* 14 (1980): 41–58.

[3] See the careful comparative law study of Norway, France, and Germany in Harry D. Krause, *Illegitimacy: Law and Social Policy* (Indianapolis: Bobbs-Merrill, 1971), 175–229; Ernst Freund, *Illegitimacy Laws of the United States and Certain Foreign Countries* (Washington, DC: Government Printing Office, 1919), 243–60. See further Mark Abrahamson, *Out of Wedlock Birth: The United States in Comparative Perspective* (Westport, CT: Praeger, 1998).

[4] See, e.g., A.G. Chloros, ed., *The Reform of Family Law in Europe (The Equality of the Spouses – Divorce – Illegitimate Children)* (Deventer: Kluwer, 1978); Hugh Cunningham, *Children and Childhood in Western Society since 1500*, 2nd edn. (New York: Pearson Longman, 2005), 161ff.; Wolfgang P. Hirczy De Mino, "From Bastardy to Equality: The Rights of Nonmarital Children and Their Families in Comparative Perspective," *Journal of Comparative Family Studies* 31 (2000): 231–62. See also the series of recent judgments by the European Convention of Human Rights, striking down discrimination against illegitimates as violations of the European Convention of Human Rights (1950), arts. 6, 8, and 14. See below note 71 and cases listed at www.echr.coe.int/echr, and careful analysis of the first main case, *Marckx v. Belgium* (1979), in Marc Salzberg, "The *Marckx* Case: The Impact of European Jurisprudence of the European Court of Human Rights' 1979 *Marckx* Decision Declaring Belgian Illegitimacy Statutes Violative of the European Convention on Human Rights," *Denver Journal of International Law and Policy* 13 (1984): 283–99; J.S. Davidson, "The European Convention on Human Rights and the 'Illegitimate' Child," in *Children and the Law: Essays in Honour of Professor H. K. Bevan*, ed. D. Freestone (Hull: Hull University Press, 1990), 75–106.

[5] See, e.g., Patrick M. Brennan, ed., *The Vocation of the Child* (Grand Rapids, MI: Wm. B. Eerdmans, 2008); Symposium, "What's Wrong with Rights for Children?" *Emory International Law Review* 20 (2006): 1–239; Charles J. Reid, Jr., *Power over the Body, Equality in the Family: Rights and Domestic Relations in Medieval Canon Law* (Grand Rapids, MI: Wm. B. Eerdmans, 2004); Marcia J. Bunge, ed., *The Child in Christian Thought* (Grand Rapids, MI: Wm. B. Eerdmans, 2001).

FROM FATHER'S PROPERTY TO CHILDREN'S RIGHTS[6]

Before 1776, the American colonies largely replicated the English common law of illegitimacy.[7] Children born within marriage were legitimate and heritable. Those born out of marriage were illegitimate and not heritable – products of fornication, concubinage, prostitution, adultery, incest, or bigamy. Like the English motherland, the American colonies maintained the very strong presumption that a child born to a married couple was their legitimate heir, regardless of the suspicious circumstances of its conception. The colonies, too, dropped the canon law category of sacrilegious illegitimates born of breached vows of chastity or celibacy. They also dropped

---

[6] This is the title of Mary Ann Mason, *From Father's Property to Children's Rights: The History of Child Custody in the United States* (New York: Columbia University Press, 1994). Among numerous studies of colonial family law, see Edmund S. Morgan, *The Puritan Family: Religion and Domestic Relations in Seventeenth-Century New England,* rev. edn. (New York: Harper & Row, 1966); Daniel Blake Smith, *Inside the Great House: Planter Family Life in Eighteenth-Century Chesapeake Society* (Ithaca, NY: Cornell University Press, 1980); John Ruston Pagan, *Anne Orthwood's Bastard: Sex and Law in Early Virginia* (Oxford: Oxford University Press, 2003); Else L. Hambleton, *Daughters of Eve: Pregnant Brides and Unwed Mothers in Seventeenth-Century Massachusetts* (New York: Routledge, 2004). On the American law of illegitimacy before and after the Revolution, see Mason, *From Father's Property,* 24–30, 68–75; Michael Grossberg, *Governing the Hearth: Law and the Family in Nineteenth-Century America* (Chapel Hill, NC: University of North Carolina Press, 1985), 196–233; Elizabeth Urban Alexander, *Notorious Woman: The Celebrated Case of Myra Clark Gaines* (Baton Rouge: Louisiana State University Press, 2001); Robert Wells, "Illegitimacy and Bridal Pregnancy in Colonial America," in *Bastardy and Its Comparative History,* ed. Peter Laslett, Karla Osterveen, and Richard M. Smith (London: Edward Arnold, 1980), 349–61; Daniel Scott Smith, "The Long Cycle in American Illegitimacy and Premarital Pregnancy," in Laslett *et al.,* eds., *Bastardy,* 362–78; Stephen B. Presser, "The Historical Background of the American Law of Adoption," *Journal of Family Law* 11 (1972): 443–516; Jamil S. Zainaldin, "The Emergence of an American Family Law: Child Custody, Adoption, and the Courts, 1796–1851," *Northwestern University Law Review* 73 (1979): 1038–89; and the various historical legal treatises cited in the notes below. See also the comprehensive collection and analysis of state statutes on illegitimacy and related topics in Freund, *Illegitimacy Laws of the United States;* Chester G. Vernier, *American Family Laws: A Comparative Study of the Family Law of the Forty-Eight American States . . . (to Jan. 1, 1935),* 5 vols. (Stanford: Stanford University Press, 1936), IV:148–270.

[7] On the distinctive civil law of family and illegitimacy in colonial Louisiana and other parts of Spanish North America, which remained closer to Continental developments, see Ann Twinam, *Public Lives, Private Secrets: Gender, Honor, Sexuality, and Illegitimacy in Colonial Spanish America* (Stanford: Stanford University Press, 1999), esp. 126–83; Hans W. Baade, "The Form of Marriage in Spanish North America," *Cornell Law Review* 61 (1975): 1–89. See also the influence of civil law in California as described in Herma Hill Kay, "The Family and Kinship System of Illegitimate Children in California Law," *American Anthropologist* 67(6) (1965): 57–81.

the concept of putative marriage that the canon law used to legitimate children born of incestuous or polygamous unions innocently entered. Several colonies added a category of illegitimates born of unions between whites and African-Americans, and between whites and native American Indians. Most American colonies accepted secret or common law marriages, and usually regarded the children of such unions as legitimate. The stern rules of valid marital formation set by Lord Hardwicke's Act in 1753 had only a modest impact on colonial life before the American Revolution.[8] The American colonies had no formal church courts as in England, and most legal questions affecting legitimates were resolved by colonial courts and legislatures. Day-to-day legal issues regarding bastards were left to the justices of the peace, who sometimes worked with local churchwardens, sextons, and deacons.

As in England, so in colonial America, the parents of illegitimate children were punished for their sexual sins by fines, imprisonment, time in the stocks, a public whipping, or other shame punishments – the mothers generally more often and more severely than the fathers. Custody of illegitimates was usually left with the mothers, especially in the child's tender years, though the child could be "put out" in the care of relatives or other caretakers. If they could be found, the fathers (and occasionally their families, too) were charged with their child's support until the child reached the age of seven, or was engaged or bonded out as an apprentice or servant. Counties and townships gave illegitimates further support as needed, usually through an informal nursing, fostering, and apprentice system, often working in cooperation with the local established churches. Justices of the peace sought to recoup their public costs for support of the illegitimate child from their mothers and fathers. If the parents were too poor to pay, they could be put under indentures. These were contracts that required them to deliver future services to the holder of the indenture, whether the town itself or private parties to whom the town could sell the indenture. If the indentured parties compounded their problems with further sexual crimes, their indentures could be lengthened by months or years. Those found guilty of repeating serious sexual crimes faced

----

[8] See above p. 120.

banishment or execution. Masters whose live-in servants gave birth to illegitimate children could sometimes be saddled with the costs of child support as well – especially if they had been delinquent in their supervision and housing of these servants, or if the masters or their sons were suspected of siring the illegitimate children. Abandonment of one's bastard child, and even worse infanticide, was punished severely, sometimes by execution.[9]

Like English common law, colonial American law had no formal methods of legitimation, save by a rare act of the colonial legislature. Colonial law rejected legitimation by a father's declaration or testament, by subsequent marriage of the parents, by adoption into a new family, or by any formal method of legitimation by church or state. Once born illegitimate, colonial Americans remained so all their lives, as signified on their birth, marriage, death, tax, and property certificates and registrations. Also like English law, colonial laws did little to differentiate the status or treatment of bastards based on the severity of their parents' sin, as had been the custom of the canon and civil law. All common law bastards faced the same legal disabilities: most notably they lacked the right to inherit property from anyone and the right to devise their own property, save to their own wives and children.

Reform of this law of illegitimacy began already on the eve of the American Revolution, and it continued with alacrity in the nineteenth and early twentieth centuries. A number of these reforms were self-conscious importations of canon law and civil law provisions that England had rejected but that American lawyers found more consonant with their revolutionary ideology of rights and liberties. The civil law of Louisiana proved to be a convenient local source of such provisions, though many jurists cited to European law codes and legal treaties, too. The general legal picture that emerged in America at the turn of the twentieth century was a collage of all the traditional canon, civil, and common law rules that were the most favorable to illegitimates. The American states also introduced several striking legal innovations that granted illegitimates further rights and protections.

---

[9] James Ewing, *A Treatise on the Office and Duty of a Justice of the Peace* (Trenton, NJ: James Oram, 1805), 146–59.

First, the American states legitimated bastards upon the subsequent marriage of their parents. This reversed the ancient common law rule that the English barons had so fiercely defended at the Council of Merton in 1234.[10] Thomas Jefferson was the first to push for this reform in Virginia in 1779, and it became the new state law in 1785.[11] Jefferson later described this law as part of his effort to make concrete the natural rights ideals of the American Declaration of Independence and the Virginia Bill of Rights. He bundled this law on legitimation with a series of other acts designed to foster religious freedom, to end slavery, to "establish the natural right of man to expatriate himself at will," to reform criminal law, procedure and punishment, and to give rights of "inheritance to all children, etc. equally." Buoyed by the success of the American Revolution and the ideas of the Declaration of Independence, Jefferson believed that "the public mind was ripe" for this kind of reform of the common law of illegitimacy.[12]

The public mind of many other states proved to be ripe for this reform, too. By 1870, more than half the states had adopted the rule that subsequent marriage of the parents automatically legitimated their child. By 1930, all but three states had fallen in line – though many states still required the husband to acknowledge that the child was his own. Both courts and commentators welcomed this reform as a way of protecting children from the sins of the parents. Timothy Walker, for example, wrote in his commentary of 1833: "The justice and humanity of these provisions cannot fail to strike every mind. How cruel and unreasonable the law, which would visit the sins of the parents upon the unoffending offspring of their unlawful intercourse. And, on the other hand, how wise and humane the law that gives to such parents the strongest motives to repair, by subsequent marriage, the wrongs they would otherwise have done."[13]

---

[10] See above pp. 105–6.

[11] W.W. Hening, *The Statutes at Large, Being a Collection of All the Laws of Virginia*, 12 vols. (Richmond: George Cochran, 1823), XII:139–40.

[12] Thomas Jefferson, *The Writings of Thomas Jefferson*, ed. P.L. Ford, 10 vols. (New York: G.P. Putnam's Sons, 1892–9), VII:476–7.

[13] Timothy Walker, *Introduction to American Law; Designed As a First Book for Students* (Philadelphia: P.H. Nicklin and T. Johnson, 1837), 233. See also Grossberg, *Governing the Hearth*, 204–5.

A few states extended this rule to allow for the legitimation of children by the subsequent marriage of adulterous paramours – something that the Western legal tradition had always rejected. The whole point of legitimation by subsequent marriage, a Maryland court put it in 1875, "was to remove the taint and disabilities of bastardy from the unoffending children, whenever their parents did marry, without regard to the deepness of guilt on the part of the parents, in which they were conceived and born."[14] This new rule, a Maine court added, is more "consistent with equity and justice," and with "the tender promptings of humanity toward innocent and unoffending children." It allows all children, regardless of the manner of their conception and their status at birth to benefit equally from "the honorable relation of lawful matrimony." If marriage can redeem children from the sins of intentional fornication, why not from the sins of intentional adultery as well, which is a sin of "the same sort"?[15] Such reasoning proved strong enough to convince a few states to accept this extension of the subsequent marriage rule to adulterous paramours. But the traditional argument, which went back to biblical times, still dominated the states well into the twentieth century: to allow adulterous paramours to marry each other and to have their adulterine children legitimated would only reward the couple for their serious sin and encourage others to divorce their current spouses, or even worse to kill them.

Second, the same Virginia law of 1785 adopted the old canon law rule of putative marriage. The canon law regarded as legitimate those children who were born of putative marriages that were later annulled on discovery of an absolute impediment of incest or polygamy (or precontract). So long as the husband and/or wife had been ignorant of the impediment, and so long as they had married in good faith in the face of the church, their children remained legitimate and heritable – even if their parents were permanently separated thereafter, and indeed were married to others. England had rejected this canon law rule as a fiction that confused inheritance rights and clouded property titles. It also betrayed the ancient

---

[14] *Hawbecker v. Hawbecker*, 43 Md. 516, 520 (1875). See further examples in Grossberg, *Governing the Hearth*, 222–3, 376–7.
[15] *Brewer v. Hamor*, 83 Me. 251 (1891).

common law rule that ignorance of the law and mistake of the facts are no excuse for punishment from wrongdoing.

Virginia and many later American states thought the common law position to be "extremely harsh and unsatisfying."[16] It was also inconsistent with their new rule of legitimation by subsequent marriage. If the intentional crime of premarital fornication or even adultery could be forgiven by the subsequent marriage of the parents, American jurists reasoned, then surely the innocently committed crime of incest or bigamy should be forgivable as well, at least with respect to the children of such putative marriages. The jurists pushed even harder on the rights of children. A Texas court put it this way in 1852:

> The rights of the children do not depend on the legality or illegality of the marriage of the parents. If there be crime, if there be offense against the laws in such marriage, they are considered as unconscious of the guilt, and not the proper subject for the infliction of its retributive consequences . . . The issue of marriages deemed null in law, without regard to the grounds of nullity, are legitimated, and are, consequently, endowed with all the rights of the legitimate issue.[17]

This is a "very just and humane provision," a Wisconsin court elaborated. It "serves to mitigate somewhat the severity of the old law which visited upon the children the sins of the parents" – even "the unintended sins."[18]

By 1860, about half the states had adopted this rule that putative marriages later annulled on discovery of an impediment of incest or polygamy still yielded legitimate children. By 1930, all but seven states had this rule in place, though the matters remained controversial. One authority explained the lingering ambivalence neatly: "The idea of incestuous or of bigamous marriage is abhorrent to common instincts and a widespread and deep-seated prejudice exists against [it]; . . . it is therefore not surprising that there should be a tendency to carry the invalidity of such unions to every logical consequence. Where, moreover, a formal celebration of marriage is made mandatory and an informal or so-called common-law

---

[16] Vernier, *American Family Laws*, IV:186.   [17] *Hartwell* v. *Jackson*, 7 Tex. 576 (1852).
[18] *Watts* v. *Owens*, 62 Wis. 512 (1885); see further Walter C. Tiffany, *Handbook on the Law of Persons and Domestic Relations* (St. Paul, MN: West Publishing, 1896), 215–16.

marriage is made illegal and null, it will be asked, What is the sanction of such a rule if the issue of the union is not made illegitimate?"[19]

While such arguments proved strong enough to convince a minority of states to reject putative marriage rules well into the twentieth century, a majority of states accepted these rules. Some states went further and waived the traditional requirements that the married couple enter their putative marriage innocently, and celebrate their wedding in church. The new presumption was that if the law had recognized the couple as validly married at the time of their child's birth, the child should remain legitimate, regardless of what happened to the marriage afterwards. It should not make a difference whether the parents entered the union in innocent or knowing violation of an impediment, or whether they had formally celebrated their wedding in a church or had informally married or eloped. To declare their child illegitimate after the fact was akin to imposing on that child a form of *ex post facto* law, in violation of the spirit if not the letter of the constitution.[20] This was a markedly different logic of putative marriage rules than the concerns for sacramental purity and individual piety that had informed the medieval canon law provisions.

The emerging American rule of putative marriage faced its sternest test with the rise of Mormon polygamy in the second half of the nineteenth century.[21] The Mormon Church's founder, Joseph Smith, had developed a new Scripture to supplement the Bible – the *Book of Mormon* (1830) – together with a separate *Book of Commandments* (1833) for the Mormon faithful. These sacred texts offered a number of novel teachings, such as the efficacy of proxy baptism for the dead, the pre-existence of man, and a metaphysical materialism that stood in tension with the traditional biblical story

---

[19] Freund, *Illegitimacy Laws,* 15.

[20] See US Constitution, Art. 1.9 prohibiting *ex post facto* laws, those which hold a person liable for a previously innocent act that was later declared illegal. Example: in 2005, drinking alcohol is legal, and defendant has a drink. In 2006, the legislature bans drinking alcohol. In 2007, defendant is arrested for having a drink in 2005. This is an unconstitutional *ex post facto* law.

[21] See analysis and sources in Sarah Barringer Gordon, *The Mormon Question: Polygamy and Constitutional Conflict in Nineteenth-Century America* (Chapel Hill, NC: University of North Carolina Press, 2002).

of the creation *ex nihilo*. Such novel teachings, and the ardent advocacy of them by Mormon missionaries, soon led to severe repression of the Mormon Church. The church was driven first from New York to Ohio, then to Missouri and Illinois. After severe rioting and the murder of Joseph Smith and his brother in 1844, the Mormon members escaped to the frontier, establishing themselves in what became in 1850 the Territory of Utah.

Far on the frontier, the Mormon Church may well have been left to itself, like many other new religious communities born of the Second Great Awakening in nineteenth-century America. But in 1852, the church leadership issued a manifesto commending polygamy to the faithful. For one man to have several wives, the church taught, was an appropriate and scriptural form of communal living. It also increased the opportunities for women to enjoy the spiritually salutary steps of marriage and motherhood. To set an example for the reticent, the church's leaders took several wives. They further reported that Joseph Smith and other church leaders had done the same in the 1830s and 1840s.

When word of this practice and policy of polygamy reached Congress, it prompted instant denunciation and a mounting political crusade against the Mormon Church. An 1862 law made polygamy a federal crime. An 1882 law disqualified polygamists from holding political office, voting in elections, and sitting on juries, among other rights. Related statutes required parties to swear oaths denying any practice or advocacy of polygamy and subjected them to close scrutiny for suspected participation or even belief in the same. An 1887 law called for the forfeiture of the Mormon Church's property altogether if it persisted in its preaching and practice of polygamy.

The Mormons mounted dozens of cases in the territorial courts challenging these laws as violations of their First Amendment rights to the free exercise of religion. The lower courts and the United States Supreme Court upheld federal law in each instance.[22] But the Supreme Court accepted the Mormons' claim that children born of polygamy should not be rendered illegitimate, even if the unions of

---

[22] See analysis of these statutes and cases in my *Religion and the American Constitutional Experiment*, 2nd. edn. (Boulder, CO: Westview Press, 2005), chap. 6.

their parents were later annulled. The court noted that Congress, like most states, had accepted the rules of putative marriage, and had even permitted legitimation of adulterine children by subsequent marriage. It made no sense, in that context, to penalize the children of polygamy by illegitimating them:

Legislation for the protection of children born in polygamy is not necessarily legislation favorable to polygamy. There is no inconsistency in shielding the one, and in denouncing the other as a crime. It has never been supposed that the acts of the several states legitimating natural children, whose parents intermarry after their birth, had the slightest tendency to shield or countenance illicit cohabitation, but they were rather designed to protect the unfortunate children of those who were willing to do all in their power towards righting a great wrong. So, if the act in question had been passed in any other jurisdiction, it would have been considered as a perfectly harmless, though possibly indiscrete, exercise of the legislative power, and would not be seriously claimed as a step towards the establishment of a polygamous system.[23]

It followed naturally from this law of putative marriage, that children of divorce should remain legitimate as well. Unlike England, the young American states recognized the private right to sue one's spouse for divorce on grounds of adultery, desertion, cruelty, and crime, among other faults. A divorce decree left the innocent spouse free to remarry another and often saddled the guilty party with child support and alimony payments. After some hesitation, every state mandated that children born to a couple while they were married remained legitimate after that couple divorced. This was true even if the cause for the divorce was the wife's adultery, which had brought an unwelcome child into the married couple's home. So long as the child was born within the marriage, or within forty weeks of the divorce, the child was viewed as the legitimate heir of both the father and the mother.

Third, American states partly rejected the English common law doctrine of *filius nullius,* that bastards have no "heritable blood" at least from their mothers. Jefferson's 1785 statute was again the first to introduce this reform. The Virginia law provided that bastards "shall be capable of inheriting or transmitting inheritance on the

---

[23] *Cope* v. *Cope,* 137 U.S. 682, 687 (1891). See also Grossberg, *Governing the Hearth,* 223–4.

part of their mother, in like manner as if they had been lawfully begotten of such mother."[24] Jefferson combined this reform with the eradication of the old common laws of primogeniture (which gave the eldest son the lion's share of the father's estate) and entail (which restricted how and to whom the heirs could later dispose of their inherited property). Taken together, Jefferson said, these reforms would remove the "aristocratic," "feudal and unnatural distinctions" between families and among family members, and lay the "foundation" "for a government truly republican." These reforms would further ensure, a Delaware law added, "equality amongst its citizens, by maintaining the balance of property as far as it is consistent with the rights of the individual."[25]

This Virginia reform of inheritance law – which allowed bastards to inherit the properties of their mothers and to transmit their own property to their mothers and maternal kin – caught on quickly among other states. It was part of a broader set of reforms that shifted to mothers principal parental responsibility for their children, whether legitimate or illegitimate, and left fathers with enhanced responsibilities for child support.[26] These reforms were premised, in James Kent's words, on "a very reasonable principle that the relation of mother and child ... in all its native and binding force" ought to be preserved and promoted so far as possible.[27] By 1830, thirteen states had granted mothers and their illegitimate children the right to inherit property from each other. By 1860, more than half the states had joined in. By 1930, this was the clear rule in all but one state. A handful of states in 1930 still limited the illegitimate child's right to inherit when their mothers had other legitimate siblings or had later married a man who was not the child's father. But many other states allowed illegitimate and legitimate children alike to inherit equally from their mothers regardless of the mother's later marriage.[28] Some states even allowed

[24] Hening, *Statutes at Large,* XII:688.
[25] Quoted and discussed in Grossberg, *Governing the Hearth,* 211–12.
[26] See Mason, *From Father's Property,* 68–73.
[27] James Kent, *Commentaries on American Law,* 2 vols. (New York: O. Halsted, 1827), II:176.
[28] These laws became more common in the later nineteenth century as women for the first time gained rights to marital property. See Mary Lynn Salmon, *Women and the Law of Property in Early America* (Chapel Hill, NC: University of North Carolina Press, 1986).

illegitimates to inherit from siblings and relatives on their mother's side as well.

Though these new laws of maternal succession to and from illegitimates remained controversial in application, both federal and state courts upheld these laws against direct challenges. Already in an 1840 case, the United States Supreme Court upheld one such law in Maryland. The case was brought against illegitimate children who were born of a longstanding incestuous marriage of a father and his daughter. Surely, the law could not countenance such "animalistic barbarism," counsel argued in seeking to block these children from inheriting from their mother. The court disagreed. While acknowledging that the parents had engaged in a "shocking crime" of incest, the court held that "it is unjust to punish the offspring for the crime of the parents. The right of the children, therefore, is not made to depend upon the degree of guilt of which they were the offspring. All illegitimate children are the fruits of crime; differing indeed, greatly, in its degree of enormity." But a legislature may properly assign rights to inheritance based on "the unoffending character of the children, rather than on the criminal conduct of the parents, of whom they were the offspring."[29] A Connecticut court put it similarly in 1875: "The fundamental maxim of the common law, that a bastard is *nullius filius*, is entirely rejected here, and such a child is here recognized by law as the child of its mother, with all the rights and duties of a child ... The feudal, repulsive doctrine of the common law, that a bastard child has no parent, no protector, not even a mother, has never found favor in this state."[30]

While illegitimates gained the right of succession from and to their mothers (and sometimes their maternal relatives), succession from and to their fathers remained rare until later in the twentieth century. Fathers could give gifts to their illegitimate children, and they were compelled to give them child support in their tender years. But few fathers had either the right or the duty to provide their illegitimate children with an inheritance. In 1930, only four states allowed for paternal inheritance by illegitimates. California

---

[29] *Brewer's Lessee* v. *Blougher*, 39 U.S. 178, 199 (1840).
[30] Appeal of *Dickinson*, 42 Conn. 491, 498 (1875) (internal quotations and citations omitted).

was one of the first such states, and the state supreme court defended its reform on both principle and pragmatics. The old common law "visited the sins of the fathers upon the children," the court wrote in a 1945 case. The theory was that such cruelty would "discourage bastardy if illegitimate children are denied any right to inheritance or support or recognition from the father." But the reality is that these old common law rules have not worked, given the rising numbers of illegitimates. So, in California, the court continued,

the common law has given way in large measure to the concept that the onus for the act of the parents cannot be visited justly upon the child and that placing responsibility for the support of the child upon the father equally with the mother, permitting it to become legitimated and to have a right to his name and to inheritance from him, will tend as well or better to deter the potential father than did the common-law doctrine of irresponsibility, and at the same time conform more closely to our present ideas of justice. Indeed, aside from considerations of justice, it may be suggested that the complete freedom from legal responsibility for illegitimate children, which the common law afforded the father, may have been a doctrine which to the male in licentious moments was more encouraging than deterrent, and were better abandoned.[31]

Such arguments proved prescient of arguments that would become commonplace in the second half of the twentieth century. But before 1950, most American states retained the ancient rule, which went back to Justinian, that bastards could not inherit from their fathers. When pressed to reform this rule, in fact, several states embroidered their law to prohibit bastards from claiming wrongful death damages in tort, residual life or disability insurance proceeds, and other proceeds that were generically earmarked for the children of a deceased father. Fathers who wished to leave property to their illegitimate children would have to legitimate them first. Many states did make that step considerably easier.

Fourth, the American states eventually imported other methods of legitimation of illegitimate children besides subsequent marriage of their parents. The English practice of legitimation by private legislation continued in some states, but this method proved just as

---

[31] In re *Lund's Estate*, 26 Cal. 2d 472, 480–1 (1945).

cumbersome, expensive, and rare as it had been in England. In place of this, a handful of states passed laws that allowed fathers simply to apply to a court for a declaration that their child was legitimate and heritable. But the more popular method, adopted by more than half the states by 1930, was the civil law rule that allowed a father simply to declare on his own – by letter, formal declaration, or by last will and testament – that his child was legitimate and heritable.

Fifth, American states adopted another civil law institution that helped illegitimate children and others, namely the ancient Roman practice of adoption. English common law had roundly rejected this institution. "Only God can make an heir," the medieval common lawyer Glanvill once put it, and adoption was thus always dismissed as "mere artifice."[32] Only a child born within marriage was a true heir. This left illegitimates without legacies, and it left childless couples without much hope for perpetuating their family name, home, or business. The new law of adoption served to remedy that.

Already earlier in the nineteenth century, courts recognized informal private adoptions, particularly when a father assumed responsibility for the support, care, and nurture of his illegitimate child, and left his property in trust on death as a form of further child support.[33] Massachusetts was the first state to enact a formal law of adoption, which involved close state regulation and court supervision of the adoption of non-relatives. An 1851 statute allowed for the permanent transfer of parental power and rights of a child to a third-party adopting adult, who was usually biologically unrelated to the child. Adopting parents had to meet basic qualification requirements, and the biological mothers (and in some states the fathers, too) had to consent to the adoption. Older children had to consent to the adoption, too. Courts or agencies would oversee this process. Once the adoption process was completed, and a judicial decree of adoption was issued, the adopted child became the adopting parent's own child, received the adopting family's name, and acquired all the rights and privileges of a natural-born child.

---

[32] Quoted and discussed in Stephen B. Presser, "Law, Christianity, and Adoption," in *The Morality of Adoption: Social-Psychological, Theological, and Legal Perspectives,* ed. Timothy P. Jackson (Grand Rapids, MI: Wm. B. Eerdmans, 2005), 219–45, at 220–2.

[33] Yasuhide Kawashima, "Adoption in Early America," *Journal of Family Law* 20 (1982): 677–96; Kent, *Commentaries,* 178.

Adoption "cannot, and does not purport to do, the work of nature, and create one a child who by nature is a stranger," one jurist put it. "But it can and does fix the status of the adoptive child and the adoptive parent as substantially the same as the status of a natural child . . . with all the legal consequences."[34] Adoption became the norm in all American states by 1900, and England eventually instituted its own adoption law in 1926.

Advocates for adoption presented this legal reform as both necessary and just. Adoption was needed to provide homes and relief to the rapidly escalating numbers of illegitimates, orphans, and poor children that appeared in America in the nineteenth century. These were legitimate and illegitimate children brought with the massive immigration to America after the 1830s. They were children who lost their parents to industrialization, or who were born illegitimate in the crowded new cities with their more permissive and exploitative sexual practices. They were illegitimate children produced through rape and fornication during the Civil War, or orphans left by the hundreds of thousands of soldiers and civilians who died in that war. They were African-American children suddenly released onto the world by the Emancipation Proclamation, many long bereft of natural family ties. These were joined by the thousands of "mulatto children" who were born in violation of miscegenation laws, and often products of rape or forced concubinage of African-American slaves or servants with their masters.[35]

Stephen Presser has shown that it was evangelical Christians, many associated with the Social Gospel movement, who helped lead a nationwide campaign for the states to adopt laws of adoption to help these numerous needy children. Reverend Charles Loring Brace, the evangelical head of New York Children's Aid Society, was a particularly visible leader. Brace argued from Scripture that it is our divine duty to help children, "the least of our brethren," and that adoption is a biblically sanctioned means of helping those without parents. All children, even those born of the most awful poverty and sinfulness, Brace insisted, will be transformed into

[34] Tiffany, *Handbook,* 222–5.
[35] Amanda C. Pustilnik, "Private Ordering, Legal Ordering, and the Getting of Children: A Counterhistory of Adoption Law," *Yale Law and Policy Review* 20 (2002): 263–96.

"upstanding Christian citizens" if placed in the right environment and family. We must "put these poor creatures – the vagrant, the houseless, the needy and criminal, and the uncared for children of the great cities, where they could be most easily reached by Christian influences." We must help "inculcate" in them "refinement, purity, self-sacrifice and Christian obligation." "[W]e assert boldly, that a poor child taken in thus by the hand of Christian charity, and placed in a new world of love and of religion, is *more likely to be tempted to good*, than to tempt others to evil." "The family is God's Reformatory; and every child of bad habits who can secure a place in a Christian home, is in the best possible place for his improvement."[36]

Such sentiments led Brace and others to institute the famous orphan trains at the turn of the twentieth century that brought needy children from New York and other east coast cities to the nation's heartland, where they were put into fostering or adoptive homes. Inevitably, some children and their families were exploited and abused in this campaign, and there were also some streaks of anti-urbanism, anti-Catholicism, and white racism at work. Catholic city boys and girls were placed in unusually large numbers in rural Protestant homes. And white children were by far the greatest number placed. That said, this was a remarkable campaign to protect innocent children, many of whom thrived. From 1890 to 1929, this campaign placed more than a quarter million children in new homes.[37]

The reforms of legitimation, inheritance, and adoption laws were only part of the growing campaign in early twentieth-century America to ameliorate the plight of illegitimate and other needy children.[38] Especially during and after the New Deal in the 1930s, many American states reformed their criminal and private laws to give new protection to illegitimate (and legitimate) children. Firm new laws against assault and abuse of children offered substantive and procedural protection, particularly for those who suffered under intemperate parents and guardians. New criminal laws punished

---

[36] Presser, "The Historical Background of the American Law of Adoption," 480–8.
[37] Ibid. See further Presser, "Law, Christianity, and Adoption," 219–45.
[38] Gail Reekie, *Measuring Immorality: Social Inquiry and the Problem of Legitimacy* (Cambridge: Cambridge University Press, 1998).

more firmly abortion and infanticide. Ample new federal and state tax appropriations were made available to support orphanages and other children's charities, and to establish new children's aid and social welfare societies. Child labor, particularly the cruel industrial exploitation of illegitimate children in factories and workhouses, was firmly outlawed by both federal and state laws. Educational opportunities for children were substantially enhanced through the rapid expansion of public schools, and the introduction of mandatory school attendance laws in every state. The modern welfare state came increasingly to stand *in loco parentis* for needy children, offering them care, protection, and nurture, regardless of the legitimacy of their birth.[39]

Even where children were not or could not be legitimated, American states after 1950 gradually removed a good number of the common law disabilities against them. A number of states allowed legitimization upon marriage of a child's mother to any man, not necessarily the father of the child. Illegitimate children themselves gained firmer standing in courts and surer footing through agencies to file paternity suits and claim support from their parents beyond their tender years. All states left mothers and maternal relatives free to give their illegitimate children property by gift or testament. Illegitimate children, in turn, were equally entitled with their legitimate siblings to receive property from mothers who had died intestate. Between 1940 and 1970, the majority of states revised their inheritance laws to allow fathers to leave bequests to their illegitimate children, though many restrictions remained.

FROM THE SEXUAL SINS OF THE PARENTS TO THE EQUAL RIGHTS OF CHILDREN

None of these reforms of the traditional American laws of illegitimacy and legitimation came without controversy. Strong arguments in favor of the old rules sounded throughout the nineteenth and early twentieth centuries. The biblical story of Ishmael's banishment from Abraham's home, and the biblical adage that "the sins of the fathers are visited upon their children" came up repeatedly.

[39] Krause, *Illegitimacy,* 21–104.

In 1845, for example, the Virginia jurist Tapping Reeve defended the old common law of bastardy as "partly founded in that anxiety which the law every where exhibits, to secure domestic tranquility, and partly in policy, to discourage illicit commerce betwixt the sexes. If a bastard might inherit either to his father or his mother, where they had married, and had a family of children, it might be a great source of domestic uneasiness. Sarah was not willing that Ishmael should inherit with Isaac."[40]

The Massachusetts jurist James Schouler wrote matter-of-factly in 1870 of the stigma that bastards bear because of their parents' sins:

The rights of a bastard are very few at common law; children born out of a lawful marriage having been from the earliest times stigmatized with shame, and made to suffer through life with reproach which was rightfully visited upon those who brought them into being. The dramatist depicts the bastard as a social Ishmaelite, ever bent upon schemes for the ruin of others, fully determined to prove a villain; thus fitly indicating the public estimates of such characters centuries ago in England. The law-writers, too, pronounce the bastard to be one whose only rights are such as he can acquire; going so far as to demonstrate, by cruelly irresistible logic, that an illegitimate cannot possibly inherit, because he is the son of nobody.[41]

William C. Rodgers echoed this view a couple of decades later: "A bastard is an unhappy species of being, deprived of many of the rights and privileges of society. Aside from the unfortunate disgrace which he must receive as a humiliating heritage because of the sins of his parents, he is regarded by the common law as a kin of no one."[42]

Other legal writers echoed the old images of bastards as unsavory villains who were a menace to society. George H. Napheys, for example, an authority on medical jurisprudence, drew together what he called the "prevailing sentiments of numerous clergymen and university presidents" in his testimony of 1870: "It is a vicious and vulgar error which pretends that the unnatural ardor, the

---

[40] Tapping Reeve, *The Law of Baron and Femme,* 2nd edn. (New York: Banks, Gould and Company, 1845), 274.

[41] James Schouler, *A Treatise on the Law of Domestic Relations* (Boston: Little, Brown, and Company, 1870), 379.

[42] William C. Rodgers, *A Treatise on the Law of Domestic Relations* (Chicago: T.H. Flood and Company, 1899), 538.

anxiety, and the sweetness of the stolen fruit, which are associated with illicit love, tend to produce a more felicitously constituted being. Illegitimate children are notorious for their mortality" and their immorality. "Some celebrated bastards there have been, it is true, but they are the exceptions, and generally they have a taint of viciousness or of monomania running in their blood, which spoils their lives."[43] In 1939, another writer defended the formal legal disabilities on illegitimates with these words: "The bastard, like the prostitute, thief, and beggar, belongs to that motley crowd of disreputable social types which society has generally resented, always endured. He is a living symbol of social irregularity, and undeniable evidence of contramoral forces."[44] As late as 1961, an Ohio family court ordered the removal of two illegitimate children from their mother on the grounds that she was utterly "devoid of morals and intelligence" and "incapable of ordering her own life in accordance with the prevailing legal and moral codes." Rebutting arguments that this solution would harm her children, the court said: "It might perhaps be mentioned that the Decalog, which is the basis of our moral code, specifically states that the sins of the father may be visited upon the children unto the third and fourth generation."[45]

But these traditional refrains about visiting the sins of the parents upon the children were gradually drowned out by the robust new judicial orchestrations on the equal rights of children, regardless of their birth status. A number of federal and state courts went out of their way to reject the ancient biblical adage about the sins of the fathers as a rule of American law. An 1846 federal district court, for example, characterized a more favorable property arrangement for an illegitimate child as a decision "not to visit the iniquities of the father upon the children, but to adopt a more benevolent principle of doing to others as they would wish that others should do unto

[43] George H. Naphey, *The Transmission of Life: Counsels on the Nature and Hygiene of the Masculine Function*, new edn. (Philadelphia: David McKay, 1887), 188. I am grateful to Amy Laura Hall for bringing this passage to my attention, and for her excellent book, *Conceiving Parenthood: American Protestantism and the Spirit of Reproduction* (Grand Rapids, MI: Wm. B. Eerdmans, 2008).

[44] Kingsley Davis, "Illegitimacy and the Social Structure," *American Journal of Sociology* 45 (1939): 215–33.

[45] *In re Dakle*, 180 N.E. 2d 646, 87 Ohio Law Abs. 493 (1961). See further Krause, *Illegitimacy*, 9.

them."[46] A 1901 federal appellate court proclaimed: "The visitation of the sins of the fathers upon the children may be the inexorable decree of physical law, and, possibly, an essential tenet of orthodox faith, but is not the policy of the state."[47]

Several later cases argued that visiting the sins of the fathers on the children was not an "inexorable decree" of the Bible, either. A 1950 New York court, for example, pointed out that the notion of "visiting the sins of the fathers upon the children" concerned the sins of idolatry, not adultery, and that it was thus both "harsh and unreasonable" for the state's illegitimacy laws to apply the adage "to an extent not contemplated by the Decalogue."[48] A 1959 New York court argued that the Decalogue makes clear that "[t]he sins of the father may not be visited on the children *by mortal man*," only by God. "'His [God's] thoughts are not our thoughts'," the court went on, quoting Isaiah 55:8. Thus "any visitation" of sin can only be done "with that infinite compassion as well as depthless wisdom which belong to Providence alone."[49]

This reading followed early rabbinic and patristic interpretations.[50] A later Texas court, in fact, quoted directly from the Talmud to show that the Bible did not countenance vicarious liability within the family, or even testimony against family members: "What is the implication of the text, 'The fathers shall not be put to death for the sins of the children?' If it implies the fathers shall be put to death for the *iniquity* of the fathers, that has already been stated (Deut. 24:16): 'every man shall be put to death for his own sin.' But the text implies that the fathers shall not be put to death *on the testimony* of the children and the children *on the testimony* of their fathers."[51] In a 1958 case, a federal district court emulated the Church Fathers in balancing "the sins of the fathers"

---

[46] *Hunter v. Marlboro*, 2 Woodb. & M. 168, 12 F.Cas. 957 (C.C.Mass.) (1846).

[47] In re *Mayer*, 108 F. 599, 615 (Ct. App. 7th Cir., 1901). See also *Flanagan v. O'Dwyer*, 197 Misc. 5, 11 (1950) (internal citations omitted): "Illegitimate children are quite as much dependents, legally as well as morally, as legitimate children [and] in any event it is alien to the competent province of this Court, to visit the sins of the father upon any of his children."

[48] *Novak v. State*, 199 Misc. 588, 591 (1950) (citations omitted).

[49] *Larkin v. Larkin*, 219 Misc. 172, 175 (1959).   [50] See above pp. 21–4, 38–40.

[51] *Diehl v. State*, 698 S.W.2d 712 (Tex. App. 1 Dist., 1985), quoting in part Sanhedrin 27b (emphasis in original). See above pp. 21–4 for further Talmudic texts.

passages with several more favorable biblical texts. In place of "the stern admonition of a familiar Old Testament passage [of] 'visiting the iniquity of the fathers upon the children'," the court argued, it is "more appropriate to recall the more charitable language of other Biblical contexts: ... 'But every one shall die for his own iniquity: every man that eateth the sour grape, his teeth shall be set on edge' (Jeremiah 31:30) ... 'The son shall not bear the iniquity of the father, neither shall the father bear the iniquity of the son: the righteousness of the righteous shall be upon him, and the wickedness of the wicked shall be upon him' (Ezekiel 18:19–20)."[52]

"[A]n intuition that sons and daughters must sometimes be punished for the sins of the father may be deeply rooted in our consciousness," Justice Brennan of the US Supreme Court wrote in 1987.[53] But "modern society shrinks from the application of the Old Testament (Exodus 20:5) commandment 'visiting the iniquity of the fathers upon the children ...' as we progress to the more humanitarian view that there are no illegitimate children, only illegitimate parents."[54]

Whatever doubts may have still lingered about the propriety of reforming traditional illegitimacy laws were met by a series of strong Supreme Court cases supporting the equal protection and treatment of illegitimate children. In ten major cases from 1968 to 1986, the court used the Fourteenth Amendment Equal Protection Clause (and the equal protection reading of the Fifth Amendment Due Process Clause) to draw much of the remaining sting from the traditional laws of illegitimacy. The court held that illegitimate children are equally entitled with legitimate children to recover tort damages or workman's compensation benefits for the wrongful death of their

---

[52] *Robbins* v. *Prudential Ins. Co. of America*, 168 F.Supp. 668, 670–71 (D.C.Fla. 1958). See similar arguments in *Snediker Developers Ltd. Partnership* v. *Evans*, 773 F.Supp. 984 (E.D. Mich., 1991); *Warren* v. *U.S.*, 932 F.2d 582, 583 (Ct. App. 6th Cir. 1991).

[53] *Tison* v. *Arizona*, 481 U.S. 137, 184 (1987) (Brennan, J. dissenting). His footnote reads: "The prophets warned Israel that theirs was 'a jealous God, visiting the iniquity of the fathers upon the children unto the third and fourth generation of them that hate [Him].' Exodus, 20:5 (King James version). See, *e.g.*, Horace, Odes III, 6:1 (trans C. Bennett, 1939) ('Thy fathers' sins, O Roman, thou, though guiltless, shall expiate'); W. Shakespeare, The Merchant of Venice, Act III, scene 5, line 1 ('Yes, truly, for look you, the sins of the father are to be laid upon the children'); H. Ibsen, Ghosts (1881)."

[54] *In Interest of Miller*, 605 S.W.2d 332 (Tex. Civ. App., 1980).

parents. A mother, in turn, has the right to collect tort damages for the wrongful death of her illegitimate and legitimate children alike. An illegitimate child is equally entitled with legitimate children to make claims on the property and estate of his father, regardless of whether his father ever acknowledged him, or whether his parents were ever married. Moreover, in making these claims, the illegitimate child cannot be subject to special procedural requirements or shortened statutes of limitation not imposed on legitimate children. An illegitimate child is equally entitled to draw residual social security benefits, disability benefits, and life insurance proceeds from either of its deceased parents.[55]

The court has not rejected altogether the category of illegitimacy. It has allowed federal agencies to impose extra procedural burdens on illegitimate children born abroad who have sought to claim American citizenship or federal benefits through their citizen parents. And it has upheld, as a necessary protection against fraud, modest procedural requirements that states still impose on illegitimate children to prove their relationship to their parents.[56] But blatant discrimination between legitimate and illegitimate children in virtually all areas of life and law is now unconstitutional.

These cases produced a number of famous statements on the equal rights of the illegitimate child that have echoed loudly in the lower federal and state courts. In the first major case in this series, *Levy v. Louisiana* (1968), the Supreme Court struck down a state statute that denied illegitimate children any claim to the tort damages paid to compensate for the wrongful death of their mother. Justice Douglas wrote for the court:

Why should the illegitimate child be denied rights merely because of his birth out of wedlock? He certainly is subject to all the responsibilities of a citizen, including the payment of taxes and conscription under the Selective Service Act. How under our constitutional regime can he be

---

[55] *Reed* v. *Campbell*, 476 U.S. 852 (1986); *Pickett* v. *Brown*, 461 U.S. 1 (1983); *Mills* v. *Habluetzel*, 456 U.S. 91 (1982); *Trimble* v. *Gordon*, 430 U.S. 762 (1977); *Jiminez* v. *Weinberger*, 417 U.S. 628 (1974); *New Jersey Welfare Rights Organization* v. *Cahill*, 411 U.S. 619 (1973); *Gomez* v. *Perez*, 409 U.S. 535 (1973); *Weber* v. *Aetna Casualty & Surety Co.*, 406 U.S. 164 (1972); *Glona* v. *American Guarantee Company*, 391 U.S. 73 (1968); *Levy* v. *Louisiana*, 319 U.S. 68 (1968).

[56] *Tuan Anh Nguyen* v. *I.N.S.*, 533 U.S. 53 (2001); *Miller* v. *Albright*, 523 U.S. 420 (1998); *Fiallo* v. *Bell*, 430 U.S. 787 (1977).

denied correlative rights which other citizens enjoy? Legitimacy or illegitimacy of birth has no relation to the nature of the wrong allegedly inflicted on the mother. These children, though illegitimate, were dependent on her; she cared for them and nurtured them; they were indeed hers in the biological and the spiritual sense; in her death they suffered wrong in any sense that a dependent would. We conclude that it is invidious to discriminate against them when no action, conduct, or demeanor of theirs is possibly relevant to the harm that was done to the mother.[57]

Four years later, the court struck down a state statute that denied a man's unacknowledged illegitimate children from an equal claim to his residual workmen's compensation benefits. Justice Powell wrote for the court:

The status of illegitimacy has expressed through the ages society's condemnation of irresponsible liaisons beyond the bonds of marriage. But visiting this condemnation on the head of an infant is illogical and unjust. Moreover, imposing disabilities on the illegitimate child is contrary to the basic concept of our system that legal burdens should bear some relationship to individual responsibility or wrongdoing. Obviously, no child is responsible for his birth and penalizing the illegitimate child is an ineffectual – as well as an unjust – way of deterring the parent. Courts are powerless to prevent the social opprobrium suffered by these hapless children, but the Equal Protection Clause does enable us to strike down discriminatory laws relating to status of birth.[58]

In a 1973 case, the court struck down a state statute that allowed illegitimate children to claim support from their father only if he had married their mother. In a *per curiam* opinion, the court wrote: "A state may not invidiously discriminate against illegitimate children by denying them substantial benefits accorded children generally ... [O]nce a State posits a judicially enforceable right on behalf of children to needed support from their natural fathers there is no constitutionally sufficient justification for denying such an essential right to a child simply because its natural father has not married its mother. For a State to do so is 'illogical and unjust'."[59]

There is ample irony in the protection afforded by the Fourteenth Amendment, however. The Fourteenth Amendment Equal Protection Clause does remove much of the legal stigma from

[57] *Levy*, 391 U.S. at 71–2. [58] *Weber*, 406 U.S. at 175. [59] *Gomez*, 409 U.S. at 538.

illegitimate birth. But the Fourteenth Amendment Due Process Clause removes most of the legal sanction from extramarital sex. In a series of Due Process cases from 1965 onward the court has outlawed various traditional prohibitions on contraception, fornication, promiscuity, and sodomy as violations of the emerging constitutional right of privacy, liberty, and sexual autonomy.[60] In the first case of this series, *Griswold v. Connecticut* (1965), the court struck down a state law banning the use of contraceptives by a married couple as a violation of their freedom to choose whether to have or to forgo children.[61] The court then extended this ruling to protect access of unmarried couples and minors to contraceptives.[62] In a 1972 case, the court stated its rationale clearly: "The marital couple is not an independent entity with a mind and heart of its own, but an association of two individuals, each with a separate emotional and intellectual makeup. If the right of privacy means anything, it is the right of the *individual*, married or single, to be free from unwanted governmental intrusion into matters so fundamentally affecting the person as the decision whether to bear or beget a child."[63]

With the illegal consequences of both illegitimacy and promiscuity largely removed, the number of illegitimates has exploded. In the 1980s and 1990s, more than one third of all American children were born illegitimate. In 2007, 38 percent of all American children were born out of wedlock: 25 percent of all white children, 46 percent of all Hispanic children, and 69 percent of all African-American children.[64] While many of these illegitimate children

---

[60] E.R. Rubin, *The Supreme Court and the American Family* (Westport, CT: Greenwood Press, 1986); David J. Garrow, *Sexuality and Liberty: The Right to Privacy and the Making of Roe v. Wade*, rev. edn. (Berkeley/Los Angeles: University of California Press, 1998).

[61] 381 U.S. 479 (1965).

[62] *Eisenstadt* v. *Baird*, 405 U.S. 438 (1972); *Carey* v. *Population Services International*, 431 U.S. 678 (1977).

[63] *Eistenstadt*, 405 U.S. at 453.

[64] See www.census.gov. For earlier numbers, see Robert M. Franklin, *Crisis in the Village: Restoring Hope in African-American Communities* (Minneapolis: Fortress Press, 2007); Steven M. Tipton and John Witte, Jr., eds. *Family Transformed: Religion, Values, and Society in American Life* (Washington, DC: Georgetown University Press, 2005); David Popenoe and Barbara DaFoe Whitehead, *The State of Our Unions* (Rutgers, NJ: National Marriage Project, 1998–2000); David Blankenhorn, *Fatherless America: Confronting Our Most Urgent Social Problem* (New York: Basic Books, 1995).

thrive in single, blended, and adoptive households, many more do not. Illegitimate children today suffer roughly three times the rates of poverty and penury, poor education and health care, juvenile delinquency and truancy, criminal conduct and conviction when compared to their legitimate peers. Illegitimate children and their mothers also draw considerably more heavily upon federal and state welfare programs, with all the stigmatizing by self and others that such dependency often induces. While the legal and moral stigma of illegitimacy may no longer sting much, the social and psychological burdens of illegitimacy remain rather heavy, and the taxation and regulation burdens are enormous.[65]

There is an even greater irony to the protection afforded by the Fourteenth Amendment. In *Roe v. Wade* (1973), the court held that the Due Process right of privacy also includes the right of an married or unmarried woman to abort her fetus during the first trimester of pregnancy – without interference by the state, her husband, parent, or other third party.[66] While the formal *Roe* holding has been qualified somewhat through subsequent statutes and cases, in *Planned Parenthood v. Casey* (1992), the court upheld the basic right to abortion framework adopted by *Roe*, and in *Stenberg v. Carhart* (2003), the court extended this right to include partial-birth abortion.[67]

This extension of the Due Process guarantee to include the right of abortion has sanctioned a whole new class of "illegitimates" in the past three decades. These new illegitimates are not innocent children who are born out of wedlock, but unwanted innocents who are aborted before their birth. These unwanted innocents pay not with a sort of a civil death as in the past, but with an actual physical death without hope of a future.

---

[65] See Reekie, *Measuring Immorality*; Llewellyn Hendrix, *Illegitimacy and Social Structures* (Westport, CT: Bergin & Garvey, 1996); Martin T. Zingo and Kevin E. Early, *Nameless Persons: Legal Discrimination against Non-Marital Children in the United States* (Westport, CT: Praeger, 1994). A new study estimates that single parentage – brought on by divorce and out-of-wedlock birth – "costs U.S. taxpayers $112 billion each year, or $1 trillion per decade." Benjamin Scafidi, *The Taxpayer Costs of Divorce and Unwed Childbearing: First-Ever Estimates for the Nation and All Fifty States* (New York: Institute for American Values, 2008), 18.

[66] 410 U.S. 113 (1973).

[67] 505 U.S. 833 (1992); 530 U.S. 914 (2003); but cf. *Gonzales v. Carhart*, 127 S.Ct. 1610 (2007) (upholding a federal statute limiting one form of partial birth abortion).

I know this is an exceedingly tender topic. I am not saying that children conceived out of wedlock are the only or even the majority of those being aborted. Nor am I saying that we must return to a system of criminalizing abortion and thus exposing unwanted innocents and their mothers to more desperate and dangerous measures. But I dare say that it is worth pondering the analogies between the current plight of the innocent being *in utero* and the historical plight of the innocent youngster in limbo. Indeed, if the historical doctrine of illegitimacy was a Christian theology of original sin gone wrong, this new form of illegitimacy is a constitutional theory of sexual liberty gone wild. What to do in response to all this will be the topic of the "Concluding reflections" that follow.

SUMMARY AND CONCLUSIONS

"Transplantation has been the major mode of legal development in virtually all Western states," Alan Watson writes in his classic title, *Legal Transplants*.[68] Historically, legal transplantation often occurred through colonization and conquest. In those instances, both the colonizer and the colonized, the conqueror and the conquered, inevitably absorbed some of the legal rules, procedures, structures, and customs of the other. Historically and today, legal transplantation also occurs when a community's law becomes outmoded, ossified, arbitrary, or abusive and in need of reform, or when a community comes upon a new problem or subject matter which local law does not address properly. In those instances, communities will look to other laws for edification – sometimes to ancient and authoritative sources such as Hebrew law or Roman law or to the laws of a people with whom the community shares "an inner spiritual or psychic relationship."[69]

---

[68] Alan Watson, *Legal Transplants: An Approach to Comparative Law* (Charlottesville, VA: University of Virginia Press, 1974), 7. See further Alan Watson, *The Evolution of Law* (Baltimore, MD: Johns Hopkins University Press, 1985); Alan Watson, *Sources of Law, Legal Change, and Ambiguity* (Philadelphia: University of Pennsylvania Press, 1984); Alan Watson, *The Making of the Civil Law* (Cambridge, MA: Harvard University Press, 1981).

[69] Watson, *Legal Transplants,* 8, quoting Fritz Pringsheim, "The Inner Relationship between English and Roman Law," in Fritz Pringsheim, *Gesammelte Abhandlungen,* 2 vols. (Heidelberg: C. Winter, 1961), I:76, 78.

The history of American illegitimacy law certainly bears out Professor Watson's provocative metaphor. In the colonial era, England transplanted its law of illegitimacy into the new world, and cultivated this law both through the learning of the common lawyers and the supervision of the royal courts. While the common law of illegitimacy continued to grow after the Revolution, Americans began to reform this law in favor of the rights of the child. They transplanted several bastard-friendly rules of legitimation, adoption, putative marriage, and inheritance which they had plucked selectively from the civil law and canon law. Once set in American legal soil, some of these transplanted rules, notably those on putative marriage and legitimation by subsequent marriage, grew well beyond the moral confines which the Western tradition had long maintained. Americans went even further beyond tradition when they transplanted the constitutional law of equal protection into their laws of illegitimacy, and used this instrument to weed out many remaining federal and state laws that still discriminated against illegitimates.

American laws of illegitimacy and legitimation, in turn, were transplanted back to England and the Continent. A generation or two after the American states had made their piecemeal reforms to the laws of legitimation, adoption, and inheritance, England and other common law countries reformed their laws along the same lines, sometimes citing American prototypes.[70] A decade after the United States Supreme Court began to strike down discriminatory laws against illegitimates as violations of the Equal Protection Clause, the European Court of Human Rights issued its first opinion protecting "non-marital children" against discrimination in inheritance. The court has, since 1979, issued several cases in favor of these children, interpreting the privacy provisions of the European Convention on Human Rights (1950).[71] Here, too, American

---

[70] T.E. James, "The Illegitimate and Deprived Child," in *A Century of Family Law*, ed. R.H. Graveson and F.R. Crane (London: Sweet & Mawell, Ltd., 1957), 39–55.

[71] See, e.g., *Mazurek* v. *France* (34406/97), 1 February 2000 [Section III]; *Elsholz* v. *Germany* (25735/94), 13 July 2000 [Grand Chamber]; *Glaser* v. *United Kingdom* (32346/96) 19 September 2000 [Section III]; *Sahin* v. *Germany* (30943/96), 11 October 2001 [Section IV]; *Sahin* v. *Germany* (30943/96) 8 July 2003 [Grand Chamber]; *Hoffmann* v. *Germany* (34045/96) 11 October 2001 [Section IV]; *Yousef* v. *Netherlands* (33711/96), 5 November 2002 [Section II]; *Sommerfeld* v. *Germany* (31871/96), 8 July 2003 [Grand Chamber]; *Haas* v.

cases have sometimes proved to be valuable prototypes, if not precedents. The Charter of Fundamental Rights of the European Union (2000) now specifically protects children's rights and prohibits any discrimination based on a child's birth status – provisions which a number of European nation-states also maintain in their own laws.[72]

Comparable guarantees of the equal rights of legitimate and illegitimate children can be found in other recent international human rights instruments. Already the 1948 Universal Declaration of Human Rights called for equal treatment of all children "whether born in or out of wedlock."[73] The 1966 Covenant on Civil and Political Rights prohibits discrimination based on one's "birth"; the parallel Covenant on Social, Cultural and Economic Rights prohibits discrimination against children "for reasons of parentage."[74] The 1969 American Convention on Human Rights provides more concretely that "the law shall recognize equal rights for children born out of wedlock and those born in wedlock."[75] The 1989 United Nations Convention on the Rights of the Child sets out an elaborate panoply of private, public, and procedural rights for all children which must be applied "without discrimination of any kind, irrespective of the child's or his or her parent's ... birth or other status." The Child Convention further calls on States Parties to "take all appropriate measures to ensure that the child is protected against all forms of discrimination or punishment on the basis of the status, activities, expressed opinions, or beliefs of the child's parents, legal guardians, or family members."[76] And in specific rejection of the classic common law doctrine of *filius nullius*,

---

Netherlands (36983/97), 13 January 2004 [Section II]; *Görgülü* v. *Germany* (74969/01), 26 February 2004 [Section III]; *Lebbink* v. *Netherlands* (45582/99), 1 June 2004 [Section II]; *Pla and Puncernau* v. *Andorra* (69498/01), 13 July 2004 [Section IV]; *Merger and Cros* v. *France* (68864/01), 22 December 2004 [Section I]; *Bove* v. *Italy* (30595/02), 30 June 2005 [Section III].

[72] Arts. 21.1, 24.1–3 at www.europarl.europa.eu/charter/ (visited June 24, 2008).
[73] GA Resolution 217A (III), GAOR, 3rd Session, Part I, Resolutions, p. 71.
[74] 9 ILM 673 (1970).
[75] UKTS 6 (1977); (1967) ILM 360, 368. See further provisions in Davidson, "The European Convention," 76–8.
[76] Art. 2.1, 2.2, U.N. Doc. A/44/25.

the Child Convention requires that every "child shall be registered immediately after birth and shall have the right from birth to a name, the right to acquire a nationality and, as far as possible, the right to know and be cared for by his or her parents."[77]

It would be a gross exaggeration, of course, to say that current international human rights protection for all children, whether legitimate or illegitimate, is simply American law writ large. Many other nations, within and beyond the West, contributed to the development of these modern formulations of children's rights, some calling upon early formulations of children's rights that go back to classical Roman law and medieval canon law. Moreover, when it comes to children's rights, America today is notorious for being the only nation on earth, besides Somalia, to refuse to ratify the United Nations Convention on the Rights of the Child.[78]

What America did contribute, however, was an early example of a law of illegitimacy, legitimation, and adoption that gradually sought to make natural rights real for all children. This was Thomas Jefferson's early insight. Three years after writing into the Declaration of Independence that "all men are created equal and endowed with certain inalienable rights," Jefferson sought to translate that ideal into concrete terms in his reforms of the Virginia law of legitimation and inheritance. It would take two more centuries for American law to realize fully that legitimate and illegitimate children alike are "created equal." But it was Jefferson who put the nation on the right(s) path.

---

[77] Ibid., art. 7.
[78] For analysis of American contributions to the Child Convention, and continued reservations about ratification, see Symposium, "What's Wrong with Rights for Children?"

Figure 8 Étienne Jeaurat (1699–1769), *The Broken Contract.*

Concluding reflections

Bastards, like the poor, will doubtless always be with us – subjects of pity and scorn, romance and ribaldry at once. Bastards may now have passed largely beyond the daily concerns and calculations of Western law. But they live on in our language and literature, with all the ambivalence surrounding the first biblical story of Ishmael. Contrast the sound still today of the pitying phrase, "Oh, you poor bastard," with the angry rebuke, "You Damned Bastard!!" Read still today of the checkered career of the illegitimate love-child in Hawthorne's *Scarlet Letter,* Dickens' *Bleak House,* or Shakespeare's plays.[1]

Shakespeare's *King Lear* puts this perennial ambivalence about illegitimacy best in the character of Edmund, the scheming bastard son of the Duke of Gloucester whose life nonetheless evokes sympathy. Edmund was born to the duke and a prostitute: "[T]here was good sport at this making," the duke admitted, but now "the whoreson must be acknowledged" (I.i.23–4). His father thus paid for Edmund's care and education, albeit from afar: "He hath been out nine years, and away he shall again," the duke remarked (I.i.32–3). But Edmund had no claim to his father's land and title. Illegitimate children could not inherit from anyone, per the common law of Shakespeare's day. Moreover, Edmund had an older brother, Edgar, who had the superior claim of primogeniture. Edmund, therefore, true to the caricature of a scheming bastard, forged a letter, falsely signed by his brother Edgar, that called for the death of their father, the duke. If this letter fell into the hands of his father, Edmund

---

[1] See Glenn Arbery, "'Why Bastard? Wherefore Base?' Legitimacy, Nature, and the Family in Post-Renaissance Literature," *Liberty, Life, and the Family* 2(1) (2005): 99–119.

calculated, the duke would become so enraged by the treachery that he would disown Edgar and embrace Edmund as his true son and heir. His father would see the natural injustice of Edmund's status as a bastard despite the formality of the law. He would see that an illegitimate son conceived in loving passion deserves at least as much as a lawful heir born of dutiful conjugality. Shakespeare puts in the mouth of Edmund the bastard his own "most nakedly modern thought" that legitimate and illegitimate children deserve equal treatment and protection.[2]

> Thou, Nature, art my goddess; to thy law
> My services are bound. Wherefore should I
> Stand in the plague of custom, and permit
> The curiosity of nations to deprive me,
> For that I am some twelve or fourteen moonshines
> Lag of a brother? Why bastard? Wherefore base,
> When my dimensions are as well compact,
> My mind as generous, my shape as true,
> As honest madam's issue? Why brand they us
> With base? with baseness? Bastardy base? Base?
> Who, in the lusty stealth of nature, take
> More composition and fierce quality
> Than doth within a dull, stale, tired bed,
> Go to th'creating a whole tribe of fops
> Got 'tween sleep and wake? Well then
> Legitimate Edgar, I must have your land.
> Our father's love is to the bastard Edmund
> As to the legitimate. Fine word "legitimate."
> Well, my legitimate, if this letter speed,
> And my invention thrive, Edmund the base
> Shall top the legitimate. I grow. I prosper.
> Now, gods, stand up for bastards (I.ii).

The dialectics at work in Edmund's speech – between nature and custom, charity and justice, rights and wrongs – reflect many of the dialectics at work in the history of Western illegitimacy law. For nearly two millennia, Western theologians and jurists vacillated between an ethic of charity that counseled tenderness for illegitimate children and an ethic of morality that thundered anathema on

---

[2] Ibid., 104.

illicit sex. They vacillated between a policy of inclusion that welcomed every child regardless of its pedigree, and a politics of exclusion that graded each child on the purity of its conception. They vacillated between a theory of natural rights and a theology of family wrongs.

The early rabbis and Church Fathers chose charity over morality, inclusion over exclusion, rights over wrongs as their starting point for dealing with illegitimate children. Perhaps as minorities themselves in a hostile world, these early religious leaders understood what it meant to be an outsider. ("We are all bastards" in the eyes of the law, Augustine once put it.)[3] The early rabbis and Fathers thus worked hard to incorporate innocent children into the community and commanded everyone to take them in and care for them with the help of local synagogues and churches. By contrast, later Christian emperors, Catholic popes, and Protestant princes reversed their starting presumption from inclusion to exclusion of bastards. Perhaps as leaders of vast communities of faithful, they could afford to be selective in their assignations of citizenship and dispensations of grace. They worked hard in their laws to place illegitimate children at various removes from their communities, allowing only some of them to enter and only through legally sanctioned means of adoption or legitimation. Anglo-American common lawyers eventually abandoned these historical dialectics in favor of more secular criteria. Initially, their preoccupation with heritable blood led the early common lawyers to policies of exclusion and reproach that were even more arbitrary than the calculus of sin and grace at work in medieval civil law and canon law. This was the common law policy that Shakespeare, through Edmund, so bitterly denounced. Eventually, however, the common lawyers declared that all children are equally vested with natural rights, and equally entitled to the care and protection of their parents and their communities. By the end of the twentieth century, common lawyers concluded, and the international human rights community with them, that "there are no illegitimate children, only illegitimate parents."[4]

Some of the historical dialectics reflected in Edmund's speech have long been based on a selective reading of the Bible, the anchor

---

[3] See above p. 39.   [4] *In Interest of Miller*, 605 S.W.2d 332 (Tex. Civ. App., 1980).

text for much of the West's speculation on and regulation of bastardy. Several biblical texts seem to condemn bastards – not least the fourfold admonition of the Torah that "the sins of the fathers shall be visited on their children." But other texts command the protection of all children – particularly the fourfold rejoinder of Moses and the prophets that "the son shall not suffer for the iniquity of the father." The Bible recounts several stories of bastards who are banished from their homes, communities, and assemblies of the Lord – notably Ishmael, the illegitimate son of Abraham and Hagar, who was cast out of his home and disinherited. But several other stories place bastards at the center of the drama of redemption – most poignantly, Christ himself, the seemingly illegitimate son of Mary and Joseph, who was forsaken even by his divine father in order that all could inherit eternally.[5]

Read comprehensively and in context, the Bible does not countenance a doctrine of illegitimacy. The ancient Talmudic rabbis and Church Fathers already said this, and modern biblical scholars have again made this clear. The biblical story of Abraham and Ishmael, which Western jurists and theologians through the ages repeatedly cited as a proof text for illegitimacy, is just that – a story, which must be read as part of the full biblical *nomos* and narrative. It is a powerful, troubling, and sobering tale. Modern biblical scholars view it as an injunction to human faithfulness and patience in light of God's promises, a warning against concubinage and adultery, which can only lead to domestic strife, and a testimony to God's mercy for all despite repeated acts of human frailty. All of these moral lessons are underscored many times later in the Bible. Modern commentators variously blame Sarah for her injustice to Hagar or Abraham for his "fainthearted faith."[6] Others blame Ishmael for his abuse of Isaac, or Abraham for his abuse of Hagar. Modern commentators also dispute whether Ishmael received more than his due in receiving Abraham's gifts and provisions, or less than his due in being deprived of his rights to primogeniture. But all agree that the name "Ishmael" means literally that "God hears"

---

[5] See Jane Shaberg, *The Illegitimacy of Jesus: A Feminist Theological Interpretation of the Infancy Narratives* (New York: Crossroad, 1990).
[6] Gerhard von Rad, *Genesis* (Philadelphia: The Westminster Press, 1961), 191.

the cries of all children, however ill-conceived or abused they might be by their fathers and mothers. And all agree that Abraham's banishment of Ishmael is no more to be emulated and implemented today than the later story of Abraham carrying his legitimate son Isaac to the top of a mountain in order to sacrifice him on an altar.[7]

The ancient Talmudic rabbis and modern biblical scholars also agree that the injunction of Deuteronomy 23:2 ("No bastard shall enter the assembly of the Lord") is no warrant for banishing illegitimate children from the religious community altogether. For the rabbis, this passage meant only that bastards could not marry in the synagogue, but they were free to do anything else. Modern Christian writers have echoed this narrow reading. They have further emphasized that this passage is a transient ceremonial law of temple purity and not an enduring moral law of domestic relations. This is like other ceremonial laws in the Torah, concerning diet, sacrifice, and worship, that have been fulfilled and replaced with the coming of Christ. The Torah's moral laws (such as "thou shalt not commit adultery") and even some of its juridical laws (such as the laws on tithing or sanctuary) hold enduring teachings for the Christian community. But not so the ceremonial laws: Christians cannot base their laws upon them.[8]

Ancient and modern biblical scholars have also rejected the four "sins of the fathers" passages in the Torah as warrants for punishing illegitimate children (Ex. 20:5; 34:7; Num. 14:18; Deut. 5:9): "You shall not make for yourself a graven image . . . for I the Lord your God am a jealous God, visiting the iniquity of the fathers upon the children of the third and the fourth generation of those who hate

---

[7] Hans Urs von Balthasar, *The Glory of the Lord: A Theological Aesthetics, vol. VI, Theology: The Old Covenant* (San Francisco: Ignatius Press, 1991), 196ff.; F.F. Bruce, "'Abraham Had Two Sons': A Study in Pauline Hermeneutics," in *New Testament Studies: Essays in Honor of Ray Summers*, ed. Huber L. Drumwright, Jr. and Curtis Vaughan (Waco, TX: Baylor University Press, 1975), 71–84; Walter Brueggemann, *Genesis* (Atlanta: John Knox Press, 1982), 111ff., 184ff.; Bruce Vawter, *On Genesis: A New Reading* (Garden City, NY: Doubleday & Company, Inc., 1977), 216ff; Claus Westermann, *Genesis 12–36: A Commentary* (Minneapolis: Augsburg Publishing House, 1985), 249ff.

[8] Walter Brueggemann, *Deuteronomy* (Nashville: Abingdon Press, 2001), 227ff.; Walter Brueggemann, *Theology of the Old Testament: Testimony, Dispute, Advocacy* (Minneapolis: Fortress Press, 1997), 367ff.; Gerhard von Rad, *Deuteronomy* (Philadelphia: The Westminster Press, 1966), 146ff.; Gerhard von Rad, *Old Testament Theology*, 2 vols. (New York: Harper & Brothers Publishers, 1962), I:190ff.

me, but showing steadfast love to thousands of those who love me
and keep my commandments" (Ex. 20:4–6). As even our modern
federal judges have noted, the sin prohibited in these passages is
idolatry, not adultery. God jealously retains the power to punish
idolaters; he does not share it with human tribunals. God mercifully
postpones any punishment for three or four generations rather than
exacting immediate retribution, in hopes that the children will
come back to him. And God draws no distinction between legitimate or illegitimate children of the next generations. He threatens
to punish any subsequent generations of children who continue to
"hate God" or perpetuate their parents' sin. But he offers "steadfast
love" to those who love God and keep the commandments. These
passages do not teach a doctrine of double original sin for illegitimates. They preach the need for all to repent and be righteous,
knowing that God is both just and merciful. As Psalm 103 puts it:

The Lord works vindication and justice for all who are oppressed. He
made known his ways to Moses, his acts to the people of Israel. The Lord
is merciful and gracious, slow to anger and abounding in steadfast love. He
will not always chide, nor will he keep his anger for ever. He does not deal
with us according to our sin, nor requite us according to our iniquities. For
as the heavens are high above the earth, so great is his steadfast love toward
those who fear him; as far as the east is from the west, so far does he move
his transgressions from us. As a father pities his children, so the Lord pities
those who fear him . . . The steadfast love of the Lord is from everlasting to
everlasting upon those who fear him, and his righteousness to children's
children, to those who keep his covenant and remember to do his commandment (Ps. 103: 6–13, 17).

Later passages in the Torah and in the prophets repeat this
instruction, ancient and modern biblical scholars point out. In
Deuteronomy 24, for example, Moses lays out various laws of crime
and tort, and then explicitly rejects the law of vicarious liability
within the family: "The fathers shall not be put to death for the
children, nor shall the children be put to death for the fathers; every
man shall be put to death for his own sin" (Deut. 24:16). This
passage not only prohibits imposing vicarious liability on a son for
his father's crime, biblical scholars point out. It even prohibits
adverse testimony by a father against his son. The prophet Ezekiel
repeats this admonition, for any community that has dedicated

itself to "Godly justice." "You say, 'Why should not the son suffer
for the iniquity of the father?' [I say:] When the son has done what
is lawful and right, and has been careful to observe all my statutes,
he shall surely live. The soul that sins shall die. The son shall not
suffer for the iniquity of the father, nor the father suffer for the
iniquity of the son; the righteousness of the righteous shall be upon
himself, and the wickedness of the wicked shall be upon himself"
(Ezek. 18:19–20). Jeremiah 31:30 and Isaiah 3:10–11 teach the same.

This Hebrew Bible teaching of individual accountability and
liability is further underscored by New Testament teaching. If
Christ's atonement for sin means anything for Christians, it means
that no one, not least unborn or newborn children, need be
scapegoats for the sins of their parents. In Christian theology, one
Scapegoat for others' sins was enough. The New Testament says
repeatedly that each individual soul will stand directly before the
judgment seat of God to answer for what he or she has done in this
life, and to receive final divine judgment and mercy (see esp. Matt.
25:31–46). Before the judgment seat of God, there will be no class
actions, and no joint or vicarious liability for which the individual
soul must answer.

To be sure, some of the ancient prophets included some jarring
statements and threats against children of adultery. Hosea, for
example, declares: "Upon her children also I will have no pity
because they are the children of harlotry. For their mother has
played the harlot; she that conceived them has acted shamefully"
(Hosea 2:4–5). The Wisdom of Solomon threatens that the
"children of adulterers will not come to maturity, and the offspring
of an unlawful union will perish. Even if they live long they will
be held of no account, and finally their old age will be without
honor . . . For children born of unlawful unions are witnesses of evil
against their parents when God examines them" (Wisd. 3:16–17;
4:6). Similar threats recur in Jeremiah 31:20; Lamentations 5:7; and
Sirach 3:11, 23:24–26.

These prophetic passages, however, are part of a grand ongoing
metaphor used by the ancient prophets to decry the idolatry of the
Jews and to drive them to repentance. In this metaphor, Yahweh's
special covenantal relationship with Israel is analogized to the
special covenant relationship between husband and wife. Israel's

disobedience to Yahweh, particularly its proclivity to worship false gods, is described as a form of adultery, of "playing the harlot." Idolatry, like adultery, can lead to divorce, and Yahweh threatens this and other punishments many times on the idolaters and their children. But God also, in his mercy, withholds this punishment. He chooses instead to revisit the question in the third and fourth generation, calling his elect people to reconciliation in the interim. This metaphor plays out repeatedly in the writings of the prophets: Hosea (2:2–23); Isaiah (1:21–22; 54:5–8; 57:3–10; 61:10–11; 62:4–5); Jeremiah (2:2–3; 3:1–5, 6–25; 13:27; 23:10; 31:32); and Ezekiel (16:1–63; 23:1–49). The denunciations of illegitimates that appear in these passages, several modern commentators insist, have to be read as part and product of this ongoing metaphor, not as new commandments against illegitimacy.[9]

Modern biblical scholars have used this same argument about metaphors to explain Christ and Paul's denunciation of those in the New Testament who continue to rely upon the Mosaic law as an avenue to salvation. Playing the rules of "rhetorical hardball,"[10] in the New Testament world, Christ and Paul describe those who insist on following the law as the new Ishmaels of the world, who will be cast out. Those who follow the Gospel are like the new Isaacs, who will receive their full inheritance (John 8:31–59; Gal. 4:21–31). Here, again, modern scholars argue, the point of these passages is not to license the doctrine of illegitimacy. Rather, Christ and Paul have seized on a story very familiar to the Pharisees and teachers of the day and twisted it to make their point about the new dispensation in Christ. Paul, in particular, "inverts the conventional exegesis" of the story of Ishmael by putting the Jews, not the Ishmaelites, in the place of exclusion. To his Jewish interlocutors,

---

[9] See detailed study in Gordon P. Hugenberger, *Marriage as Covenant: A Study of Biblical Law and Ethics Governing Marriage Developed from the Perspective of Malachi* (Leiden: E.J. Brill, 1994); Edward Schillebeeckx, *Marriage* (New York: Sheed and Ward, 1965), esp. 59ff; Michael Kolarcik, *The Book of Wisdom* (Nashville: Abingdon Press, 1997), esp. 473ff.; James M. Reese, *The Book of Wisdom, Song of Songs* (Wilmington, DE: Michael Glazier, Inc., 1983).

[10] Luke Timothy Johnson, "Religious Rights and Christian Texts," in *Religious Human Rights in Global Perspective: Religious Perspectives*, ed. John Witte, Jr. and Johan D. van der Vyver (The Hague: Martinus Nijhoff Publishers, 1996), 65–95, at 76.

this exegesis "must have appeared preposterous."[11] That was the whole point: to show that God "chooses the barren and the deserted rather than the privileged and favoured woman. Thus the physical descendants of Sarah become the spiritual descendants of Hagar, and the physical descendants of Hagar (generalized into the Gentiles) become the spiritual descendants of Sarah, who inherit the divine promise."[12] There is nothing in all this word play and inverted exegesis that commands or even commends the theological and legal doctrine of illegitimacy.

To castigate the traditional doctrine of illegitimacy, however, does nothing to ameliorate the current plight of outcast children. If biblical theology no longer should support illegitimacy, and the law no longer should stigmatize illegitimates, what can be done about the current problem of so many children born out of wedlock, with all the predictions of social pathos and problems, dependency and delinquency that await them? The ancient angel's description of Ishmael's bane still seems altogether too apt a prediction of the plight of the modern illegitimate child: "He will be a wild ass of a man, his hand will be against every man and every man's hand against him; and he shall dwell over against all his kinsmen" (Gen. 16:11–12). With 38.5 percent of all American children now born out of wedlock – and even higher numbers in other parts of the West – what can we do to help them? With $112 billion being spent in America each year to care for our non-marital children, what new laws and policies should we begin to consider?

One obvious measure is to assign further responsibility where it is due: on both the mother and the father of the unwanted child – as well as on the families and guardians who are responsible for these new parents. Historically, adulterers, fornicators, and other sexual criminals paid dearly for their crimes – by fine, prison, or banishment, by execution in extreme cases. But this remedy often only exacerbated the plight of their illegitimate child, who in extreme cases was now often left with no or little natural network of family

---

[11] Bruce, "Abraham Had Two Sons," 75–6. See the probing analysis of Galatians 4, in Hans Dieter Betz, *Galatians* (Philadelphia: Fortress Press, 1979).

[12] Charles Kingsley Barrett, "The Allegory of Abraham, Sarah, and Hagar in the Argument of Galatians," *Rechtfertigung: Festschrift für Ernst Käsemann zum 70. Geburtstag,* ed. Johannes Friedrich, Johannes Pöhlman, and Peter Stuhlmacher (Tübingen: J.C.B. Mohr, 1976), 16.

resources and support. Today, adulterers and fornicators pay little if anything for their sexual behavior – protected in part by new cultural mores and constitutional laws of sexual privacy. Even if one wanted to pursue a neo-puritan path – I, for one do not! – it is highly unlikely that a new criminalization of adultery or fornication could pass constitutional or cultural muster.

But the elimination of criminal punishment for non-marital sex should, to my mind, be coupled with a much firmer imposition of ongoing civil responsibility for the care and support of an innocent child born of such conduct. After all, the same constitutional text that exonerates promiscuity also licenses contraception, which is widely and cheaply available now; indeed it is free in many quarters. Those who choose to have children out of wedlock notwithstanding these options need to pay dearly for their children's support. I am no fan of shotgun marriages or forced cohabitation for a couple suddenly confronted with the prospect of a new child but not really compatible: too often a forced marriage compounds the misery for everyone. But I support aggressive paternity and maternity suits, now amply aided by the growing availability of cheap genetic technology. I support firm laws that compel stiff payments of child support for non-custodial parents, and that garnish the wages, put liens on the properties, and seek reformation of insurance contracts and testamentary instruments of those parents, particularly fathers, who choose to ignore their dependent minor children. I also support tort suits by illegitimate children who seek compensatory and punitive damages from their parents or their parents' estates in instances where these children have been cavalierly abandoned or notoriously abused. These and a good number of comparable provisions are happily emerging in American states today, with several federal laws providing interstate support and enforcement, and both federal and state criminal laws standing ready with sanctions when civil orders are chronically breached.

These are, in fact, modern applications of insights that go back to the medieval canon law and early modern common law: that both fathers and mothers, and sometimes their families as well, must pay for the support of children born out of marriage. Fathers, in fact, should pay more dearly in material goods given the heavier biological burdens borne by mothers who carry the children to term.

This is not neo-conservative dogmatism, but elementary political liberalism. Every right has a corresponding duty, and the misuse of a right can trigger ongoing responsibilities. There may be a right to bear arms in the United States, but there is a duty not to kill another except in proper self-defense. A single impulsive act of unjustly killing another may trigger a lifetime of responsibilities of paying back the victim's family and society. So it is with the right to have sex. Government has no business policing the consensual sex of able adults. But a single impulsive act of conceiving a child should trigger a lifetime of responsibilities to care for that child. As with the taking of life, so with the making of life, there are no statutes of limitation on these responsibilities. Sex may be free, but children are not.

The state imposes child support obligations automatically if the child is born to a married couple; the father or mother will pay dearly if they ignore, abuse, or desert their child, especially in its tender years. It should be no different for a child born out of wedlock. Ongoing support for that child should not just depend upon the voluntary good will of the father, or a successful paternity suit by the mother. Absent adoption by another, that child is the moral and fiscal responsibility of its father and mother until it reaches the age of majority. And the state needs to impose these costs automatically and hold parents of illegitimate children accountable if they fail to pay.

This points to another lesson that can be drawn from medieval and early modern poor laws. Particularly in its English and early American forms, the poor law imposed the costs of care for illegitimate children locally – on local parishes and townships, in addition to the parents and grandparents of the illegitimate children. Under this regime, the exact costs of an illegitimate child to each local person were immediately calculable and visible to all. The more illegitimate children that were produced, the more incentive the local community had to deter the illicit sex that produced them. And the more readily these local communities taught responsible sexual practice by all and demanded repayment from those who proved irresponsible. They imposed indentures on the parents of these illegitimate children, filed liens on their family's homes, and stood in line at the probate courts to recoup their remaining costs from their estates.

The immense bureaucracy of the modern welfare state has now tended to abstract the true costs of illegitimacy. America paid roughly $112 billion to care for its non-marital children last year, but it's hard to see and feel how those costs affect each of us at the local level.[13] If the costs of illegitimacy are just passed along generically to all tax payers, the incentives for self-restraint and responsibility and for local control and local caretaking go down.

We cannot go back to a system of indentured servitude for delinquent parents administered by local justices or courts. Indentured servitude has long been outlawed as a species of slavery, and leaving enforcement of child support to local justices does not work, given our modern means and rights to travel. But we need to find creative new ways of re-engaging our families and neighborhoods, our worship centers and schools, our charities and voluntary associations in the great task of responsible sex and childrearing.[14] Moreover, we need to use modern technology to hold irresponsible parents accountable to support their children, regardless of where they go. Birth certificates should carry more specific information about both the child's parents – not just their names and addresses as now, but their social security numbers, blood types, and genetic data as well. And a national registry of these birth certificates should be developed to ensure that parents can be found regardless of where they move. Having those more refined parental data available will enable an unsupported child, an abandoned parent, or, if necessary, a government official to track down a delinquent parent and hold that party to account in the case of delinquency. This might sound Orwellian at first blush. But is it really any more intrusive on our liberty than government reaching into all taxpayers' pockets to collect the extra $112 billion a year needed to pay for our non-marital children?

The government must, of course, develop procedures and safeguards to ensure the privacy and proper use of these parental personal data. The government must also provide back-up support

[13] See Benjamin Scafidi, *The Taxpayer Costs of Divorce and Unwed Childbearing: First-Ever Estimates for the Nation and All Fifty States* (New York: Institute for American Values, 2008).

[14] See the excellent manifesto for one community by Robert M. Franklin, *Crisis in the Village: Restoring Hope in African-American Communities* (Minneapolis: Fortress Press, 2007).

when parents cannot be found or cannot afford support for their children, despite their best efforts. No child in a nation with our wealth and values should be left uninsured, undernourished, or poorly educated. But we need a much better organized and advertised state and federal system of holding parents financially accountable for the children they bring into the world. That will do much to deter irresponsible sex and to promote responsible child-bearing within marriage.

A second obvious response to the modern explosion of illegitimacy is a more robust engagement of the doctrine of adoption. For all the pro- and anti-abortion lobbying and litigation that has emerged in the post-*Roe v. Wade* era, relatively little attention has been paid to the alternative of adoption. Historically, adoption legitimated illegitimate children, removing the cultural stigma and civil shadow that attended their birth. Today, adoption provides not only this protection, but also one of the best hopes and remedies to the new illegitimates who are condemned *in utero*. Adoption should, to my mind, be much more aggressively advocated and actively facilitated – and amply celebrated and rewarded when a natural mother chooses to make this heroic sacrifice for the sake of her child.

Adoption still remains a theologically tender topic today. Until a few generations ago, it was still severely frowned on if not barred in a number of conservative Christian quarters, particularly among those who thought blood ties were essential to faithful and stable family life and love. Kin altruism, of course, is an ancient classical insight, which came most famously into Christian theology via Thomas Aquinas' appropriation of Aristotle.[15] There is something fundamentally sound and sensible in the notion that a parent, particularly a father, will be naturally inclined to invest in the care of a child who carries his blood and name, who looks and acts like him, and who needs him in those tender years to survive.

But it is easy to press this naturalist argument for kin altruism too far, and to make blood ties a dangerous and discriminating idol.[16]

---

[15] See Don S. Browning *et al.*, *From Culture Wars to Common Ground: Religion and the American Family Debate,* 2nd edn. (Louisville, KY: Westminster John Knox Press, 2000).

[16] This preoccupation with blood can cut two ways. The common law's preoccupation with the purity of heritable blood made it insist on procreation within marriage. See above pp. 109, 124–5. By contrast, the Nazis' preoccupation with the purity of Aryan blood in the

After all, the same Christian theology that insists on blood ties between parent and child insists on no blood ties between husband and wife. Indeed, to marry within the prohibited degrees of consanguinity is to commit the crime of incest, a serious offense if it is done intentionally. But why should the legitimacy of parental love turn essentially on the presence of blood ties, but the legitimacy of marital love turn essentially on the absence of blood ties? The sacrificial love and charity demanded of a parent and a spouse are not the same, but they are certainly comparable, and they must be discharged concurrently. Why is a blood tie so essential to one and not to the other loving relationship? This strikes me as a peculiar form of transubstantiation doctrine gone badly awry.

This is not to argue, as some do today, that the crime of incest must be dropped and that siblings and blood relatives must be left free to marry each other. It is instead to argue that natural blood ties between parent and child are not essential to stable families. Parental love, like marital love, is in its essence not only an instinct but also a virtue, not only a bodily inclination but also a spiritual intuition.[17] Blood ties between parents and children should not be easily severed. But parental ties to children should not be predicated on blood ties alone. Real family kinship goes beyond "birth, biology, and blood," in Stephen Post's apt words.[18]

Moreover, adoption is one of the deepest forms and examples of Christian charity. A Christian need only look so far as the example of the first Christian family. Joseph, after all, adopted Jesus, the purportedly illegitimate child of Mary, and raised him in a stable family despite the absence of a blood tie to him. A Christian might further look at how the New Testament describes God's mechanism

---

notorious *Lebensborn* program led to a policy of promiscuity for the purest. See, e.g., Catrine Clay and Michael Leapman, *Master Race: The Lebensborn Experiment in Nazi Germany* (London: Hodder & Stoughton, 1995), esp. 53–77; Hans Peter Bleuel, ed., *Sex and Society in Nazi Germany,* trans. J. Maxwell Brownjohn (Philadelphia: J.B. Lippincott Company, 1973), 54–74, 148–79; Paul Weindling, *Health, Race and German Politics between National Unification and Nazism, 1870–1945* (Cambridge: Cambridge University Press, 1989). I am grateful to Timothy P. Jackson for alerting me to this striking contrast.

[17] See Timothy P. Jackson, *The Priority of Love: Christian Charity and Social Justice* (Princeton: Princeton University Press, 2003).

[18] Stephen G. Post, *More Lasting Unions: Christianity, the Family, and Society* (Grand Rapids, MI: Wm. B. Eerdmans, 2000), 124.

for dispensing grace: Christians are adopted as heirs of salvation, despite the sins that they inherit (Rom. 8:15, 23; 9:4; Gal. 4:5; Eph. 1:5).[19] Adoption by grace is the theological means by which God removes the stigma of original sin and the eternal punishment it carries, and vests each person with a new name, a new home, and new liberties to be enjoyed eternally. As the Westminster Confession of Faith (1647) puts it:

All those that are justified God vouchsafeth, in and for his only Son Jesus Christ, to make partakers of the grace of adoption; by which they are taken into the number, and enjoy the liberties and privileges of the children of God; have his name put upon them; receive the Spirit of adoption; have access to the throne of grace with boldness; are enabled to cry, Abba, Father; are pitied, protected, provided for, and chastened by him as by a father; yet never cast off; but sealed to the day of redemption, and inherit the promises as heirs of everlasting salvation.[20]

Modern scholars are now beginning to mine these biblical and confessional texts in earnest, and these efforts hold great promise for both the theology and the law of adoption.[21]

Adoption is not only a theologically tender topic today, but also a legally stunted doctrine. The law of adoption has improved somewhat in recent years in the United States, and both state and federal

---

[19] See the immense literature gathered in James M. Scott, *Adoption As Sons of God* (Tübingen: J.C.B. Mohr (Paul Siebeck), 1992).

[20] The Westminster Confession of Faith (1647), ch. XII, in Philip Schaff, ed., *The Creeds of Christendom, with a History and Critical Notes*, reprint of 6th edn. by David S. Schaff, 3 vols. (Grand Rapids, MI: Baker Books, 2007), III:628. For discussion of this and the half dozen other Protestant confessions in which the doctrine of adoption appears, see Tim Trumper, "The Metaphorical Import of Adoption: A Plea for Realization," *Scottish Bulletin of Evangelical Theology* 14 (1996): 129–45; Tim Trumper, "The Theological History of Adoption," *Scottish Bulletin of Evangelical Theology* 20 (2002): 4–28, 177–202; Douglas F. Kelly, "Adoption: An Underdeveloped Heritage of the Westminster Standards," *The Reformed Theological Review* 52 (1993): 110–20; Joel R. Beeke, "Transforming Power and Comfort: The Puritans on Adoption," *The Faith Once Delivered: Essays in Honor of Dr. Wayne R. Spear*, ed. Anthony T. Selvaggio (Phillipsburg, NJ: P & R Publishing, 2007), 63–106.

[21] See, e.g., Timothy P. Jackson, *The Morality of Adoption: Social-Psychological, Theological, and Legal Perspectives* (Grand Rapids, MI: Wm. B. Eerdmans, 2005); Jeanne Stevenson-Moessner, *The Spirit of Adoption: At Home in God's Family* (Louisville, KY: Westminster John Knox Press, 2003); Trevor Burke, "Pauline Adoption: A Sociological Approach," *The Evangelical Quarterly* 73 (2001): 119–34.

regulations and appropriations have made it easier and cheaper than in past decades. International conventions and bilateral treaties on adoption and cross-border migration of children have made further advances. But adoption is still a clumsy and expensive procedure to pursue in the United States and abroad and still remains reserved primarily for the substantially well-to-do. It is made worse by the continued insistence of many states that natural fathers and mothers have an effective veto over adoptions – however irresponsible they may have been in conceiving the child and however notorious they may have been in neglecting or abusing it *in utero* or upon birth. It is too easy to say that blood ties should mean nothing and that children should be placed only with the fittest parents. That is a dangerous step along the way to the bleak anonymous regime of parenting contemplated coldly in Plato's *Republic* and B.F. Skinner's *Walden Two*. But a much more generously funded, administered, and applied law of adoption would do much to alleviate the plight of the modern illegitimates.

The most important response to the mounting problem of illegitimacy is a more robust legal and cultural embrace of marriage as the best institution for having and raising children. Other forms of civil union and intimate association might work for consenting adults, but marriage is the best institution for children. This has been the perennial teaching of the Western tradition – before, during, and after the days of Christian legal establishment. It is now confirmed by mounting social science evidence as well. A long series of studies over the past two decades report that children born and raised within intact marital homes fare far better on many counts than children raised in single-parent, foster-parent, or institutional homes. Infant children from intact marital homes have physical survival rates that are more than 50 percent higher. As these children grow up, they generally have a larger pool of economic resources to sustain them and correspondingly higher standards of nutrition, living, education, recreation, and health care. They have a larger network of caretakers who support, socialize, and help them in their tender years, and a larger kin network that sustains them as they move from adolescence to adulthood. They have nearly triple the educational and vocational achievement records, and less than half the rates of drop-out, truancy, delinquency, tobacco, drug

Figure 9 George Bernard O'Neill (1828–1917), *Not Forgotten.*

and alcohol abuse, teenage pregnancy, criminality, and eventually incarceration.[22]

---

[22] See, e.g., Timothy P. Jackson, *The Best Love of the Child* (forthcoming); Linda J. Waite and Maggie Gallagher, *The Case for Marriage: Why Married People Are Happier, Healthier and Better Off Financially* (New York: Broadway Books, 2001); Kristian Anderson More, "Marriage from a Child's Perspective: How Does Family Structure Affect Children, and

These new social science data on the benefits of marriage for children do not pretend to describe every particular case. There are plenty of heroic single parents and foster families, plenty of extraordinary youth homes and community programs, plenty of remarkable and resilient children who defy every prediction of failure and rise to greatness in life. We all know these stories, and they bring tears of joy. But the new social science data suggest strongly that these exceptions, though ample and diverse in number, do not overcome the basic presumption that children do much better when born and raised in intact marital homes. Perhaps it takes a village to raise a child, but it takes a marriage to make one.

What Can We Do about It?" (Washington, DC: Child Trends Research Brief, June 2002); "Marriage Promotion in Low-Income Families, Fact Sheet" (Minneapolis: National Council of Family Relations, April 2003). See also the sources in chapter 5, note 64.

Bibliography

Adair, Richard, *Courtship, Illegitimacy, and Marriage in Early Modern England* (Manchester: Manchester University Press, 1996)

Alexander, Elizabeth Urban, *Notorious Woman: The Celebrated Case of Myra Clark Gaines* (Baton Rouge: Louisiana State University Press, 2001)

Althusius, Johannes, *Dicaeologicae libri tres, totum et universum jus, quo utimur, methodice complectentes* (Frankfurt am Main: Christophe Corvin, 1618)

Andreae, Johannes, *Novella in Sextum* [Venice, 1499], repr. edn. (Graz: Scientia Verlag, 1963)

The Ante-Nicene Fathers: The Writings of the Fathers Down to A.D. 325, repr. edn., trans. and ed. Alexander Roberts, 10 vols. (Peabody, Mass: Hendrickson Publishers, 1995)

Arbery, Glenn, "'Why Bastard? Wherefore Base?' Legitimacy, Nature, and the Family in Post-Renaissance Literature," *Liberty, Life, and the Family* 2(1) (2005): 99–119

Augustine, *The Works of Saint Augustine*, trans. and ed. John E. Rotelle (Charlottesville, VA: Intelex Corporation, 2001)

Ayer, John C., "Legitimacy and Marriage," *Harvard Law Review* 16 (1902): 22–42

Baade, Hans W., "The Form of Marriage in Spanish North America," *Cornell Law Review* 61 (1975): 1–89

Bacon, Matthew, *A New Abridgement of the Law* (London: A. Strathan, 1798)

Balch, David and Carolyn Osiek, *The Family in Early Christianity* (Louisville: Westminster John Knox Press, 1997)

eds., *Early Christian Families in Context: An Interdisciplinary Dialogue* (Grand Rapids, MI: Wm. B. Eerdmans, 2005)

Barrett, Charles Kingsley, "The Allegory of Abraham, Sarah, and Hagar in the Argument of Galatians," in *Rechtfertigung: Festschrift für Ernst Käsemann zum 70. Geburtstag*, ed. Johannes Friedrich, Johannes Pöhlman, and Peter Stuhlmacher (Tübingen: J.C.B. Mohr, 1976), 16–31

Bartolus de Sassoferrato, *In primam ff. veteris commentaria* (Venice, 1585)

Barzis, Benedecti de, *De filiis non legitimè natis*, in *Tractatus universi iuris*, vol. VIII/2, 24a–29b

Bassett, W. J., ed., *The Bond of Marriage: An Ecumenical and Interdisciplinary Study* (Notre Dame/London: University of Notre Dame Press, 1968)

"Bastard," in *The Universal Jewish Encyclopedia*, ed. Isaac Landman, 10 vols. (New York: The Universal Jewish Encyclopedia, Inc., 1942), VII:587–92

Beeke, Joel R., "Transforming Power and Comfort: The Puritans on Adoption," *The Faith Once Delivered: Essays in Honor of Dr. Wayne R. Spear,* ed. Anthony T. Selvaggio (Phillipsburg, NJ: P & R Publishing, 2007), 63–106

Betz, Hans Dieter, *Galatians* (Philadelphia: Fortress Press, 1979)

Bischof, L., *Die Rechtsstellung der ausserehelichen Kinder nach den zürcherischen Rechtsquellen* (Diss. Zurich, 1931)

Blackstone, William, *Commentaries on the Laws of England*, 4 vols. (Oxford: Clarendon Press, 1765)

Blaikie, Andrew, "A Kind of Loving: Illegitimacy, Grandparents, and the Rural Economy of North East Scotland, 1750–1900," *Scottish Economic and Social History* 14 (1994): 41–57

Illegitimacy, Sex, and Society: Northeast Scotland, 1750–1900 (Oxford: Clarendon Press, 1993)

Blankenhorn, David, *Fatherless America: Confronting Our Most Urgent Social Problem* (New York: Basic Books, 1995)

Bleuel, Hans Peter, ed., *Sex and Society in Nazi Germany*, trans. J. Maxwell Brownjohn (Philadelphia: J.B. Lippincott Company, 1973)

Blume, Fred H., "Legitimation under the Roman Law," *Tulane Law Review* 5 (1931): 256–66

Bosco, Ronald A., "Lectures at the Pillory: The Early American Execution Sermon," *American Quarterly* 30(3) (1978): 156–76

Boswell, John, *The Kindness of Strangers: The Abandonment of Children in Western Europe from Late Antiquity to the Renaissance* (New York: Pantheon Books, 1988)

Bracton on the Laws and Customs of England, trans. Samuel E. Thorne, 4 vols. (Cambridge, MA: Harvard University Press, 1968)

Brennan, Patrick M., ed., *The Vocation of the Child* (Grand Rapids, MI: Wm. B. Eerdmans, 2008)

Brinton, Crane, *The French Revolutionary Legislation on Illegitimacy* (Cambridge, MA: Harvard University Press, 1936)

Brissaud, Jean, *A History of French Private Law*, 2nd edn., trans. R. Howell (Boston: Little, Brown, and Company, 1912)

Brown, Peter, *Poverty and Leadership in the Later Roman Empire* (Hanover, NH/London: University Press of New England, 2000)

Browning, Don S., "Family Law and Christian Jurisprudence," in *Christianity and Law: An Introduction*, ed. John Witte, Jr. and Frank S. Alexander (Cambridge: Cambridge University Press, 2008), 163–84

Browning, Don S., Bonnie J. Miller-McLemore, Pamela D. Couture, K. Brynolf Lyon, and Robert M. Franklin, *From Culture Wars to Common Ground: Religion and the American Family Debate*, 2nd edn. (Louisville, KY: Westminster John Knox Press, 2000)

Broyde, Michael J., "Adoption, Personal Status, and Jewish Law," in *The Morality of Adoption: Social-Psychological, Theological, and Legal Perspectives*, ed. Timothy P. Jackson (Grand Rapids, MI: Wm. B. Eerdmans, 2005), 128–47

Marriage, Divorce, and the Abandoned Wife in Jewish Law (Hoboken, NJ: Ktav Publishing House, 2001)

"Proselytism and Jewish Law: Inreach, Outreach, and the Jewish Tradition," in *Sharing the Book: Religious Perspectives on the Rights and Wrongs of Proselytism*, ed. John Witte, Jr. and Richard C. Martin (Maryknoll, NY: Orbis Books, 1999), 45–60

Broyde, Michael J., and Michael Ausubel, eds., *Marriage, Sex, and Family in Judaism* (Lanham, MD: Rowman & Littlefield, 2005)

Bruce, F. F., "'Abraham Had Two Sons': A Study in Pauline Hermeneutics," in *New Testament Studies: Essays in Honor of Ray Summers*, ed. Huber L. Drumwright, Jr. and Curtis Vaughan (Waco, TX: Baylor University Press, 1975), 71–84

Brueggemann, Walter, *Deuteronomy* (Nashville: Abingdon Press, 2001)

Genesis (Atlanta: John Knox Press, 1982)

Theology of the Old Testament: Testimony, Dispute, Advocacy (Minneapolis: Fortress Press, 1997)

Brundage, James A., *Law, Sex, and Christian Society in Medieval Europe* (Chicago: University of Chicago Press, 1987)

Sex, Law, and Marriage in the Middle Ages (Aldershot: Variorum, 1993)

Brydall, John, *Lex Spuriorum, or the Law Relating to Bastardy Collected from the Common, Civil, and Ecclesiastical Laws* (London: Assigns of Richard and Edwards Atkins, 1703)

Bückling, G., *Die Rechtstellung der unehelichen Kinder im Mittelalter und in der heutigen Reformbewegung* (Breslau: M. and H. Marcus, 1920)

Bullough, Vern L. and James A. Brundage, *Sexual Practices and the Medieval Church* (Buffalo, NY: Prometheus Books, 1982)

Bunge, Marcia J., ed., *The Child in Christian Thought* (Grand Rapids, MI: Wm. B. Eerdmans, 2001)

Burke, Trevor, "Pauline Adoption: A Sociological Approach," *The Evangelical Quarterly* 73 (2001): 119–34

Burn, Richard, *Ecclesiastical Law*, 6th edn., 4 vols. (Philadelphia: 1787)

The Justice of the Peace, and Parish Officer, 16th edn. by John Burn (London: A. Strahan and W. Woodfall, 1788)

Cardwell, Edward, ed., *Synodalia: A Collection of Articles of Religion, Canons, and Proceedings of Convocations in the Province of Canterbury* (Oxford: University Press, 1842)

Carlson, Eric Josef, *Marriage and the English Reformation* (Oxford: Blackwell, 1994)

Carpzov, Christian, *De legitima, quae vocantur ab Hotomano quarta legitima* (Wittenberg: Johannis Gormanni, 1631)

Chloros, A. G., ed., *The Reform of Family Law in Europe (The Equality of the Spouses – Divorce – Illegitimate Children)* (Deventer: Kluwer, 1978)

Clay, Catrine and Michael Leapman, *Master Race: The Lebensborn Experiment in Nazi Germany* (London: Hodder & Stoughton, 1995)

Clerke, William, *The Triall of Bastardie* (London: Adam Islip, 1594)

Code Napoleon, or The French Civil Code, trans. George Spence (London: William Benning, 1827)

Cody, Lisa Forman, "The Politics of Illegitimacy in an Age of Reform: Women, Reproduction, and Political Economy in England's New Poor Law of 1834," *Journal of Women's Studies* 11(4) (2000): 131–56

Coing, Helmut, ed., *Handbuch der Quellen und Literatur der neueren europäischen Privatrechtsgeschichte,* 3 vols. (Munich: Beck, 1973–88)

Coke, Sir Edward, *The Second Part of the Institutes of the Laws of England,* repr. of the 1797 edn., 4 vols. (Buffalo, NY: William S. Hein, 1986)

Corbett, P. E., *The Roman Law of Marriage* (Oxford: Oxford University Press, 1930)

Couvreur, Gilles, *Les pauvres on-ils des droits?* (Rome: Libraria editrice dell' Universita Gregoriana, 1961)

Cummin, William, M.D., *The Proofs of Infanticide Considered, Including Dr. Hunter's Tract on Child Murder* (London: Green and Longman, 1836)

Cunningham, Hugh, *Children and Childhood in Western Society since 1500,* 2nd edn. (New York: Pearson Longman, 2005)

Davidson, J. S., "The European Convention on Human Rights and the 'Illegitimate' Child," in *Children and the Law: Essays in Honour of Professor H. K. Bevan,* ed. D. Freestone (Hull: Hull University Press, 1990), 75–106

Davis, Kingsley, "Illegitimacy and the Social Structure," *American Journal of Sociology* (1939): 215–33

De Mino, Wolfgang P. Hirczy, "From Bastardy to Equality: The Rights of Nonmarital Children and Their Families in Comparative Perspective," *Journal of Comparative Family Studies* 31 (2000): 231–62

Deferrari, R. J., ed., *St. Augustine: Treatises on Marriage and Other Subjects* (New York: Fathers of the Church, Inc., 1955)

Desan, Suzanne, *The Family on Trial in Revolutionary France* (Berkeley: University of California Press, 2004)

Didascalia Apostolorum, trans. R. Hugh Connolly (Oxford: Clarendon Press, 1929)

The Digest of Justinian, ed. Theodor Mommsen and Paul Krueger, trans. Alan Watson, 4 vols. (Philadelphia: University of Pennsylvania Press, 1985)

Dixon, Suzanne, *The Roman Family* (Baltimore: The Johns Hopkins University Press, 1992)

Donahue, Charles, *Law, Marriage, and Society in the Later Middle Ages: Arguments about Marriage in Five Courts* (Cambridge: Cambridge University Press, 2008)

Early Church Fathers: Nicene and Post-Nicene Fathers, First Series, trans. and ed. Philip Schaff [1886–9], repr. edn., 14 vols. (Peabody, MA: Hendrickson Publishers, 1994)

Early Church Fathers: Nicene and Post-Nicene Fathers, Second Series, trans. and ed. Philip Schaff and Henry Wace [1886–9], repr. edn., 14 vols. (Peabody, MA: Hendrickson Publishers, 1994)

Eekelaar, John M., *Family Life and Personal Life* (Oxford: Oxford University Press, 2006)

"Reforming the English Law Concerning Illegitimate Persons," *Family Law Quarterly* 14 (1980): 41–58

Elon, Menachem, *Jewish Law: History, Sources, Principles,* trans. Bernard Auerbach and Melvin J. Sykes, 4 vols. (Philadelphia: The Jewish Publication Society, 1994)

ed., *The Principles of Jewish Law* (Jerusalem: Keter Publishing House, 1975)

Epstein, Louis M., *Marriage Laws in the Bible and the Talmud* (Cambridge, MA: Harvard University Press, 1942)

Sex Laws and Customs in Judaism (New York: Ktav Publishing House, 1967)

Etzensperger, C., *Die Rechtsstellung des ausserehelichen Kinder nach den schaffhauserischen Rechtsquellen* (Diss. Zurich, 1931)

Ewing, James, *A Treatise on the Office and Duty of a Justice of the Peace* (Trenton, NJ: James Oram, 1805)

Fairchilds, Cissie, "Female Sexual Attitudes and the Rise of Illegitimacy: A Case Study," *Journal of Interdisciplinary History* 8 (1978): 627–67

Finch, Sir Henry, *Law or a Discourse Thereof* (London: Henry Lintot, 1759)

Fliscus, Sinibaldus [Innocent IV], *Commentaria Apparatus in V Libros Decretalium* [1570], repr. edn. (Frankfurt am Main: Minerva, 1968)

Foxcroft, Thomas, *Lessons of Caution to Young Sinners: A Sermon Preached ... upon the Affecting Occasion of an Unhappy Young Woman Present in the Assembly under Sentence of Death* (Boston: S. Kneeland and T. Green, 1733)

Franklin, Robert M., *Crisis in the Village: Restoring Hope in African-American Communities* (Minneapolis: Fortress Press, 2007)

The Frederician Code, 2 vols. (Edinburgh: A. Donaldson and J. Reid, 1791)

Freund, Ernst, *Illegitimacy Laws of the United States and Certain Foreign Countries* (Washington, DC: Government Printing Office, 1919)

Friedberg, Emil, *Corpus Iuris Canonici,* 2 vols. (Leipzig: Bernard Tauchnitz, 1879–81)

Frier, Bruce W. and Thomas A. J. McGinn, *A Casebook on Roman Family Law* (Oxford: Oxford University Press, 2004)

A Full, True and Particular Account of the Trial, Sentence, and Execution of John Webb . . . for the Murder of a Male Bastard Child . . . to Which Is Added His Extraordinary Case, and the Substance of an Excellent Sermon Preached on This Most Solemn Occasion (London: J. Pitts, 1911)

Gaius, *Institutiones,* ed. Paul Krüger and William Studemund (Berlin: Weidemann, 1877)

Gardner, Jane F., *Family and* Familia *in Roman Law and Life* (Oxford: Clarendon Press, 1998)

Garnsey, Peter, *Social Status and Legal Privilege in the Roman Empire* (Oxford: Clarendon Press, 1970)

Garrow, David J., *Sexuality and Liberty: The Right to Privacy and the Making of Roe v. Wade,* rev. edn. (Berkeley/Los Angeles: University of California Press, 1998)

Gaudemet, Jean, "Les transformations de la vie familiale au bas empire et l'influence du christianisme," *Romanitas* 4 (1962): 58–85

"Tendances nouvelles de la legislation familiale aux ivme siècle," *Antiquitas* 1 (1978): 187–207

Génestal, R., *Histoire de la légitimation des enfants naturels en droit canonique* (Paris: Ernst Leroux, 1905)

Germain, Christopher Saint, *Doctor and Student,* rev. edn. by William Muchall (Cincinnati, OH: Robert Clarke & Co., 1874)

Ginzberg, Louis, *The Legends of the Jews,* trans. Henrietta Szold and Paul Radin (Philadelphia: The Jewish Publication Society, 2003)

Given-Wilson, Chris, and Alice Curetis, *The Royal Bastards of Medieval England* (London/Boston: Routledge & Kegan Paul, 1984)

Glanvill, Ranulf de, *A Translation of Glanville,* trans. John Beames, repr. edn. (Littleton, CO: Fred B. Rothman & Co., 1980)

Goldin, Judah, *Studies in Midrash and Related Literature* (Philadelphia: The Jewish Publication Society, 1988)

Godolphin, John, *The Orphans Legacy,* 2nd. enlarged edn. (London: Chr. Wilkinson, 1677)

Repertorium Canonicum, 3rd edn. (London: Assigns of R. & E. Atkins, 1687)

Goody, Jack, *The Development of the Family and Marriage in Europe* (Cambridge: Cambridge University Press, 1983)

Gordon, Sarah Barringer, *The Mormon Question: Polygamy and Constitutional Conflict in Nineteenth-Century America* (Chapel Hill, NC: University of North Carolina Press, 2002)

Gottlieb, Beatrice, "The Meaning of Clandestine Marriage," in Robert Wheaton and Tamara K. Hareven, eds., *Family and Sexuality in French History* (Philadelphia: University of Pennsylvania Press, 1980), 49–83

Graveson, Ronald H., and F. R. Crane, eds., *A Century of Family Law: 1857–1957* (London: Sweet & Maxwell, 1957)

Gray, Charles M. and Maija Jansson Cole, *"Bowdler's* Case: The Intestate Bastard," *University of Toronto Law Journal* 30 (1980): 46–74

Grayzel, Solomon, *The Church and the Jews in the XIIIth Century* (Philadelphia: Dropsie College, 1933)

Grossberg, Michael, *Governing the Hearth: Law and the Family in Nineteenth-Century America* (Chapel Hill, NC: University of North Carolina Press, 1985)

Grubbs, Judith Evans, *Law and Family in Late Antiquity: The Emperor Constantine's Marriage Legislation* (Oxford: Clarendon Press, 1995)

  "Marrying and Its Documentation in Later Roman Law," in *To Have and to Hold: Marrying and Its Documentation in Western Christendom, 400–1600,* ed. Philip L. Reynolds and John Witte, Jr. (Cambridge: Cambridge University Press, 2007), 43–94

  Women and the Law in the Roman Empire: A Sourcebook on Marriage, Divorce, and Widowhood (London/New York: Routledge, 2002)

Guttmann, Alexander, *Rabbinic Judaism in the Making* (Detroit: Wayne State University Press, 1970)

Hagn, Hans, *Illegitimität und Thronfolge: zur Thronfolgeproblematik illegitimiter Merowinger, Karolinger, und Ottonen* (Neureid: Ars Una, 2006)

Halivni, David Weiss, *Midrash, Mishnah, and Gemara: The Jewish Predilection for Justified Law* (Cambridge, MA: Harvard University Press, 1986)

Hall, Amy Laura, *Conceiving Parenthood: American Protestantism and the Spirit of Reproduction* (Grand Rapids, MI: Wm. B. Eerdmans, 2008)

Hambleton, Else L., *Daughters of Eve: Pregnant Brides and Unwed Mothers in Seventeenth-Century Massachusetts* (New York: Routledge, 2004)

Harms-Ziegler, Beate, *Illegitimität und Ehe: Illegitimität als Reflex des Ehediskurses in Preussen im 18. und 19. Jahrhundert* (Berlin: Duncker & Humblot, 1991)

Hartley, Shirley, *Illegitimacy* (Berkeley: University of California Press, 1975)

Hayes, Christine E., *Gentile Impurities and Jewish Identities: Intermarriage and Conversion from the Bible to the Talmud* (Oxford: Oxford University Press, 2002)

The Hebrew–English Edition of the Babylonian Talmud, trans. Israel W. Slotki, ed. I. Epstein (London: Soncino Press, 1984)

Helmholz, R. H., "Bastardy Litigation in Medieval England," *American Journal of Legal History* 13 (1969): 361–83

    The Oxford History of the Laws of England, vol. I, The Canon Law and Ecclesiastical Jurisdiction, 597 to the 1640s (Oxford: Oxford University Press, 2004)

    Roman Canon Law in Reformation England (Cambridge: Cambridge University Press, 1990)

    "Support Orders, the Church Courts, and the Rule of *Filius Nullius*: A Reassessment of the Common Law," *Virginia Law Review* 63 (1977): 431–48

Hendrix, Llewellyn, *Illegitimacy and Social Structures* (Westport, CT: Bergin & Garvey, 1996)

Hening, W. W., *The Statutes at Large, Being a Collection of All the Laws of Virginia*, 12 vols. (Richmond: George Cochran, 1823)

Herrmann, H., *Die Stellung der unehelichen Kinder nach kanonischen Recht* (Amsterdam: Grüner, 1971)

Hess, Hamilton, *Sexuality and Power: The Emergence of Canon Law at the Synod of Elvira* (Philadelphia: University of Pennsylvania Press, 1972)

Higginbotham, Ann R., "'Sin of the Age': Infanticide and Illegitimacy in Victorian London," *Victorian Studies* 32 (Spring, 1989): 319–37

Hooper, Wilfrid, *The Law of Illegitimacy* (London: Sweet & Maxwell, Ltd., 1911)

Hotman, François, *De spuriis et legitimatione*, appended to Barnabé Brisson, *De verteri ritu nuptiarum et jure connubiorum* (Amsterdam: Petrus le Grand, 1662)

Howard, George Elliott, *A History of Matrimonial Institutions,* 3 vols. (Chicago: University of Chicago Press, 1904)

Hugenberger, Gordon P., *Marriage As Covenant: A Study of Biblical Law and Ethics Governing Marriage Developed from the Perspective of Malachi* (Leiden: E.J. Brill, 1994)

Hunter, David G., *Marriage, Celibacy, and Heresy in Ancient Christianity: The Jovinianist Controversy* (Oxford: Oxford University Press, 2007)

Ingram, Martin, *Church Courts, Sex and Marriage in England, 1570–1640* (Cambridge: Cambridge University Press, 1987)

Isidore of Seville, *The* Etymologies *of Isidore of Seville*, trans. and ed. Stephen A. Barney, W.J. Lewis, J.A. Beach, and Oliver Berghof (Cambridge: Cambridge University Press, 2006)

Jackson, Mark, *New-Born Child Murder: Women, Illegitimacy, and the Courts in Eighteenth-Century England* (Manchester: Manchester University Press, 1996)

Jackson, Timothy P., ed., *The Morality of Adoption: Social-Psychological, Theological, and Legal Perspectives* (Grand Rapids, MI: Wm. B. Eerdmans, 2005)

The Priority of Love: Christian Charity and Social Justice (Princeton: Princeton University Press, 2003)

ed., *The Best Love of the Child* (forthcoming)

James, T. E., "The Illegitimate and Deprived Child: Legitimation and Adoption," in *A Century of Family Law*, ed. R. H. Graveson and F. R. Crane (London: Sweet & Mawell, Ltd., 1957), 39–55

Jefferson, Thomas, *The Writings of Thomas Jefferson,* ed. P. L. Ford, 10 vols. (New York: G.P. Putnam's Sons, 1892–9)

Johnson, Luke Timothy, "Religious Rights and Christian Texts," in *Religious Human Rights in Global Perspective: Religious Perspectives,* ed. John Witte, Jr. and Johan D. van der Vyver (The Hague: Martinus Nijhoff Publishers, 1996), 65–95

Jonkers, Engbert J. J., *Invloed van het Christendom op de romeinsche wetgeving betreffende het concubinaat en de echtscheiding* (Wageningen: H. Veenman, 1938)

Joyce, George Hayward, *Christian Marriage: An Historical and Doctrinal Study,* 2nd. rev. edn. (London: Sheed and Ward, 1948)

Kawashima, Yasuhide, "Adoption in Early America," *Journal of Family Law* 20 (1982): 677–96

Kay, Herma Hill, "The Family and Kinship System of Illegitimate Children in California Law," *American Anthropologist* 67(6) (1965): 57–81

Kelly, Douglas F., "Adoption: An Underdeveloped Heritage of the Westminster Standards," *The Reformed Theological Review* 52 (1993): 110–20

Kelly, Henry Ansgar, *The Matrimonial Trials of Henry VIII* (Stanford: Stanford University Press, 1976)

Kent, James, *Commentaries on American Law,* 2 vols. (New York: O. Halsted, 1827)

Kertzer, David I. and Marzio Barbagli, eds., *Family Life in Early Modern Times, 1500–1789* (New Haven, CT: Yale University Press, 2001)

Kolarcik, Michael, *The Book of Wisdom* (Nashville: Abingdon Press, 1997)

Krause, Harry D., *Illegitimacy: Law and Social Policy* (Indianapolis: Bobbs-Merrill, 1971)

Krüger, Paul, ed., *Codex Theodosianus* (Berlin: Weidmann, 1923–6), translated as *The Theodosian Code and Novels and the Sirmonidian Constitutions,* trans. C. Pharr (Princeton: Princeton University Press, 1952)

ed., *Corpus Iuris Civilis,* 3 vols. (Berlin: Weidmann, 1928–9)

ed., *Justinian's Institutes,* trans. Peter Birks and Grant McLeod (Ithaca, NY: Cornell University Press, 1987)

Kuehn, Thomas, *Illegitimacy in Renaissance Florence* (Ann Arbor, MI: University of Michigan Press, 2002)

"A Medieval Conflict of Laws: Illegitimacy and Legitimation in *Ius Commune* and *Ius Proprium,*" *Law and History Review* 15 (1997): 243–73

Landau, Peter, "Sakramentalität und Jurisdiktion," in *Das Recht der Kirche,* ed. Gerhard Rau, Hans-Richard Reuter, and Klaus Schlaich, 4 vols. (Gütersloh: Chr. Kaiser, 1994–7), II:58–95

Laslett, Peter, *Family Life and Illicit Love in Earlier Generations: Essays in Historical Sociology* (Cambridge: Cambridge University Press, 1977)

and Karla Oosterveen, "Long Term Trends in Bastardy in England: A Study of the Illegitimacy Figures in the Parish Registers and in the Reports of the Registrar General, 1561–1960," *Population Studies* 27 (1973): 255–86

Karla Oosterveen, and Richard M. Smith, eds., *Bastardy and Its Comparative History: Studies in the History of Illegitimacy and Marital Non-Conformism in Britain, France, Germany, Sweden, North America, Jamaica, and Japan* (Cambridge, MA: Harvard University Press, 1980)

Laudensis, Martinus, *De Legitimatione,* in *Tractatus universi iuris,* vol. VIII/2, 90b–98a

Leclercq, Jean, *Monks on Marriage: A Twelfth Century View* (New York: Seabury Press, 1982)

Leineweber, Anke, *Die rechtliche Beziehung des nichtehelichen Kindes zu seinem Erzeuger in der Geschichte des Privatrechts* (Königstein: Peter Hanstein Verlag, 1978)

Leneman, Leah and Rosalind Mitchison, "Scottish Illegitimacy Ratios in the Early Modern Period," *Economic History Review,* 2nd ser., 40(1) (1987): 41–63

Sin in the City: Sexuality and Social Control in Urban Scotland, 1660–1780 (Edinburgh: Scottish Cultural Press, 1998)

Lettmann, Reinhard, *Die Diskussion über die klandestinen Ehen und die Einführung einer zur Gültigkeit verpflichtenden Eheschliessung auf dem Konzil von Trent* (Münster: Aschendorff, 1967)

Levine, Alyssa, Thomas Nutt, and Samantha Williams, eds., *Illegitimacy in Britain, 1700–1920* (Basingstoke/New York: Palgrave Macmillan, 2005)

Linder, Amnon, ed., *The Jews in the Legal Sources of the Early Middle Ages* (Detroit: Wayne State University Press, 1997)

The Jews in Roman Imperial Legislation (Detroit: Wayne State University Press, 1987)

Locke, John, *Two Treatises on Government,* ed. Peter Laslett (Cambridge: Cambridge University Press, 1960)

Maimonides, Moses, *The Code of Maimonides (Mishneh Torah)*, Book 5, The Book of Holiness, ed. Leon Nemoy, trans. Louis I. Rabinowitz and Philip Grossman (New Haven, CT: Yale University Press, 1965)

Maitland, F. W., *Roman Canon Law in the Church of England: Six Essays* (London: Methuen, 1898)

Manuche, Cosmo, *The Bastard: A Tragedy* (London: M.M.T. Collins and Gabrielle Bedell, 1652)

"Marriage Promotion in Low-Income Families, Fact Sheet" (Minneapolis: National Council of Family Relations, April 2003)

Mason, Mary Ann, *From Father's Property to Children's Rights: The History of Child Custody in the United States* (New York: Columbia University Press, 1994)

Mayali, Laurent, "Note on the Legitimization by Subsequent Marriage from Alexander III to Innocent III," in *The Two Laws: Studies in Medieval Legal History Dedicated to Stephan Kuttner*, ed. Laurent Mayali and Stephanie A. J. Tibbets (Washington, DC: Catholic University of America Press, 1990), 55–75

McDevitt, Gilbert J., *Legitimacy and Legitimation: An Historical Synopsis and Commentary* (Washington, DC: Catholic University of America Press, 1941)

Menochius, Jacobus [Giacomo Menochio], *De arbitrariis iudicium quaestionibus et causis libri II* (Venice, 1624)

Meriton, George, *Immorality, Debauchery, and Profaneness, Exposed to the Reproof of Scripture and the Censure of the Law: Containing a Compendium of the Laws Now in Force Against . . . Debauched Incontinency and Bastard-Getting* (London: John Harris and Andrew Bell, 1698)

Merlinus, Mercurialus, *De legitima tractatus* (Venice, 1651)

Meteyard, Belinda, "Illegitimacy and Marriage in Eighteenth-Century England," *Journal of Interdisciplinary History* 10 (1980): 479–89

Meyer, Paul, *Der römischen Konkubinat nach den Rechtsquellen und den Inschriften* (Leipzig: G.B. Teubner, 1895)

The Minor Tractates of the Talmud, 2nd edn., trans. and ed. A. Cohen, 2 vols. (London: Soncino Press, 1971)

The Mishnah, trans. Herbert Danby (Oxford: Oxford University Press, 1987)

More, Kristian Anderson, "Marriage from a Child's Perspective: How Does Family Structure Affect Children, and What Can We Do about It?" (Washington, DC: Child Trends Research Brief, June 2002)

Morgan, Edmund S., *The Puritan Family: Religion and Domestic Relations in Seventeenth-Century New England*, rev. edn. (New York: Harper & Row, 1966)

Naphey, George H., *The Transmission of Life: Counsels on the Nature and Hygiene of the Masculine Function*, new edn. (Philadelphia: David McKay, 1887)

Neeve, Lydia, *The True Account of the Confession and Behaviour of Lydia Neeve for That Barbarous ... Murder, by the Cutting off the Head of Her Bastard Child* (Norwich?, 1702)

Nelson, William, *Lex Testamentaria* (London: J. Nutt, 1714)

Neudecker, Reinhard, "Does God Visit the Iniquity of the Fathers upon their Children? Rabbinic Commentaries on Ex. 20,5b (Deut 5,9b)," *Gregorianum* 81(1) (2000): 5–24

Nicolas, Harris, *Treatise on the Law of Adulterine Bastardy* (London: W. Pickering, 1836)

Noonan, John T., Jr., *Contraception: A History of Its Treatment by Catholic Theologians and Canonists* (Cambridge, MA: Harvard University Press, 1986)

   "Marital Affection among the Canonists," *Studia Gratiana* 14 (1967): 489–99

   "Novel 22," in *The Bond of Marriage: An Ecumenical and Interdisciplinary Study*, ed. W. J. Bassett (Notre Dame/London: University of Notre Dame Press, 1968), 41–90

Novak, David, "Law and Religion in Judaism," in *Christianity and Law: An Introduction,* ed. John Witte, Jr. and Frank S. Alexander (Cambridge: Cambridge University Press, 2008), 33–52

Oberman, Heiko A., *The Roots of Antisemitism in the Age of Renaissance and Reformation* (Philadelphia: Fortress Press, 1984)

Ogden, Daniel, *Greek Bastardy in the Classical and Hellenistic Periods* (Oxford: Oxford University Press, 1996)

Orme, Nicholas, *Medieval Children* (New Haven, CT: Yale University Press, 2002)

Pagan, John Ruston, *Anne Orthwood's Bastard: Sex and Law in Early Virginia* (Oxford: Oxford University Press, 2003)

Paleotti, Gabriele, *De notis spuriisque* (Frankfurt am Main: Nicolai Bassaei, 1574), in *Tractatus universi juris,* vol. VIII/2: 45b–74b

Papiensis, Bernardus, *Summa Decretalium*, repr. edn., ed. Theodore Laspeyres (Graz: Akademische Druck und Verlagsanstalt, 1956)

Parkes, James W., *The Jew in the Medieval Community: A Study of His Political and Economic Situation*, 2nd edn. (New York: Hermon Press, 1976)

Passameneck, Stephen M., *Some Medieval Problems in Mamzeruth* (Cincinnati: Hebrew Union College Annual, 1966)

Pataui, Mntua Bonauito, *Tractatus de legitima filiorum*, in *Tractatus universi iuris,* VIII/1, 440a–445b

Penrose, J., *The Rev. Mr. Penrose's Account of the Behavior, Confession, and Last Dying Words of* ... *J. Williams for the Murder of Her Bastard Child* (Bristol, 1741)

Peters, Edward N., ed. and trans., *The 1917 or Pio-Benedictine Code of Canon Law in English Translation* (San Francisco: Ignatius Press, 2001)

Pollock, Sir Frederick and F. W. Maitland, *The History of English Law before the Time of Edward I*, 2nd edn. by S.F.C. Milsom, 2 vols. (Cambridge: Cambridge University Press, 1968)

Popenoe, David and Barbara DaFoe Whitehead, *The State of Our Unions* (Rutgers, NJ: National Marriage Project, 1998–2000)

Post, Stephen G., *More Lasting Unions: Christianity, the Family, and Society* (Grand Rapids, MI: Wm. B. Eerdmans, 2000)

Poudret, Jean-François, *Coutumes et coutumiers: Histoire comparative des droits des pays romands du XIIIe à la fin du XVIe siècle*, 6 vols. (Berne: Staempfli, 1998)

Presser, Stephen B., "The Historical Background of the American Law of Adoption," *Journal of Family Law* 11 (1972): 443–516

"Law, Christianity, and Adoption," in *The Morality of Adoption: Social-Psychological, Theological, and Legal Perspectives*, ed. Timothy P. Jackson (Grand Rapids, MI: Wm. B. Eerdmans, 2005), 219–45

Pringsheim, Fritz, *Gesammelte Abhandlungen*, 2 vols. (Heidelberg: C. Winter, 1961)

Pullan, Brian S., *Rich and Poor in Renaissance Florence: The Social Institutions of a Catholic State to 1620* (Oxford: Oxford University Press, 1971)

"Support and Redeem: Charity and Poor Relief in Italian Cities from the Fourteenth to the Seventeenth Century," *Continuity and Change* 3 (1988): 177–88

Pustilnik, Amanda C., "Private Ordering, Legal Ordering, and the Getting of Children: A Counterhistory of Adoption Law," *Yale Law and Policy Review* 20 (2002): 263–96

Quaesten, Johannes *et al.*, eds., *Ancient Christian Writers: The Works of the Fathers in Translation* (New York: Newman Press, 1982)

Quigley, Aileen, *King Bastard: The Story of William the Conqueror* (London: Hale, 1973)

Rau, Gerhard, Hans-Richard Reuter, and Klaus Schlaich, eds., *Das Recht der Kirche*, 4 vols. (Gütersloh: Chr. Kaiser, 1994–7)

Rawson, Beryl, "*Spurii* and the Roman View of Illegitimacy," *Antichthon* 23 (1989): 10–41

Reay, Barry, "Sexuality in Nineteenth-Century England: The Social Context of Illegitimacy in Rural Kent," *Rural History* 1(2) (1990): 219–47

Reekie, Gail, *Measuring Immorality: Social Inquiry and the Problem of Illegitimacy* (Cambridge: Cambridge University Press, 1998)

Reese, James M., *The Book of Wisdom, Song of Songs* (Wilmington, DE: Michael Glazier, Inc., 1983)

Reeve, Tapping, *The Law of Baron and Femme,* 2nd edn. (New York: Banks, Gould and Company, 1845)

Reid, Charles J., Jr., *Power over the Body, Equality in the Family: Rights and Domestic Relations in Medieval Canon Law* (Grand Rapids, MI: Wm. B. Eerdmans, 2004)

Reynolds, Philip L., *Marriage in the Western Church: The Christianization of Marriage during the Patristic and Early Medieval Periods* (Leiden: E. J. Brill, 1994)

and John Witte, Jr., eds., *To Have and to Hold: Marrying and Its Documentation in Western Christendom, 400–1600* (Cambridge: Cambridge University Press, 2007)

Rodgers, William C., *A Treatise on the Law of Domestic Relations* (Chicago: T.H. Flood and Company, 1899)

Rogers, Nicholas, "Carnal Knowledge: Illegitimacy in Eighteenth-Century Westminster," *Journal of Social History* 23 (1989): 355–75

Rose, Lionel, *The Massacre of the Innocents: Infanticide in Britain 1800–1939* (London: Routledge and Kegan Paul, 1986)

Rosellis, Antonii de, *De legitimatione,* in *Tractatus universi iuris,* vol. VIII/ 2, 75a–90a

Rubin, E. R., *The Supreme Court and the American Family* (Westport, CT: Greenwood Press, 1986)

Rufinus, *Summa Decretorum,* ed. Henrich Singer, repr. edn. (Aalen: Scientia Verlag, 1963)

Salmon, Mary Lynn, *Women and the Law of Property in Early America* (Chapel Hill, NC: University of North Carolina Press, 1986)

Salzberg, Marc, "The *Marckx* Case: The Impact of European Jurisprudence of the European Court of Human Rights' 1979 *Marckx* Decision Declaring Belgian Illegitimacy Statutes Violative of the European Convention on Human Rights," *Denver Journal of International Law and Policy* 13 (1984): 283–99

Sardis, Ludovici a, *De naturalis liberis ac eorum successione,* in *Tractatus universi iuris,* vol. VIII/2, 29b–45b

Scafidi, Benjamin, *The Taxpayer Costs of Divorce and Unwed Childbearing: First-Ever Estimates for the Nation and All Fifty States* (New York: Institute for American Values, 2008)

Schaff, Philip, ed., *The Creeds of Christendom, with a History and Critical Notes,* reprint of 6th edn. by David S. Schaff, 3 vols. (Grand Rapids, MI: Baker Books, 2007)

Schellekens, Joan, "Courtship, the Clandestine Marriage Act, and Illegitimate Fertility in England," *Journal of Interdisciplinary History* 25 (1995): 433–44

Schillebeeckx, Edward, *Marriage* (New York: Sheed and Ward, 1965)

Schmugge, Ludwig, *Kirche, Kinder, Karrieren: Päpstliche Dispense von der unehelichen Geburt in Spätmittelalter* (Zurich: Artemis & Winkler, 1995)

ed., *Illegitimät in Spätmittelalter* (Munich: R. Oldenbourg, 1994)

The Schottenstein Edition Talmud: The Gemara (Brooklyn: Mesorah Publications, 1990–)

Schouler, James, *A Treatise on the Law of Domestic Relations* (Boston: Little, Brown, and Company, 1870)

Schrader, Katharina, Gerda Mayer, Helga Fredebold, and Irene Fründ, *Vorehelich, ausserehelichen, uneheliche – wegen der grossen Schande: Kindestötung im 17. und 18. Jahrhundert* (Hildesheim: Gerstenberg, 2006)

Schroeder, H. J., *Councils and Decrees of the Council of Trent* (St. Louis, MO: B. Herder Book Co., 1941)

Disciplinary Decrees of the General Councils: Text, Translation, and Commentary (London: Herder, 1937)

Scott, James M., *Adoption As Sons of God* (Tübingen: J.C.B. Mohr (Paul Siebeck), 1992)

Scott, John, *The Fatal Consequences of Licentiousness: A Sermon, Occasioned by the Trial of a Young Woman for the Alleged Murder of Her Illegitimate Child*, 6th edn. (London: L.B. Seeley & Sons, 1828)

Scott, S. P., *The Civil Law*, repr. edn., 17 vols. (New York: AMS Press, 1973)

Scott, Susan and C. J. Duncan, "Interacting Factors Affecting Illegitimacy in Preindustrial Northern England," *Journal of Biosociological Science* 29 (1997): 151–69

Segusio, Henrici de [Hostiensis], *Summa aurea*, repr. edn. (Aalen: Scientia Verlag, 1962)

Selden, John, *De iure naturali et gentium, juxta disciplinam Ebraeorum libri septem* (London, 1640)

De successionibus ad leges Ebraeorum in bona defunctorum, new edn. (Frankfurt an der Oder: 1673)

Opera Omnia tam edita quam inedita in tribus voluminibus, 3 vols. (London, Guil. Bowyer, 1726)

Sexton, George, *The Causes of Illegitimacy Particularly in Scotland* (Edinburgh: Edmonston and Douglas, 1860)

Shaberg, Jane, *The Illegitimacy of Jesus: A Feminist Theological Interpretation of the Infancy Narratives* (New York: Crossroad, 1990)

Shahar, Shulamith, *Childhood in the Middle Ages* (London/New York: Routledge, 1990)

Sheehan, Michael M., "Illegitimacy in Late Medieval England," in Ludwig Schmugge, ed., *Illegitimität im Spätmittelalter* (Munich: R. Oldenbourg Verlag, 1994), 115–22

Shorter, Edward, "Illegitimacy, Sexual Revolution, and Social Change in Modern Europe," *Journal of Interdisciplinary History* 2(2) (1971): 237–72

The Making of the Modern Family (New York: Basic Books, 1977)

The Shulchan Aruch, trans. and ed. Eliyahu Touger (Brooklyn: Kehot, 2002)

Smith, Daniel Blake, *Inside the Great House: Planter Family Life in Eighteenth-Century Chesapeake Society* (Ithaca, NY: Cornell University Press, 1980)

Smith, Daniel Scott, "The Long Cycle in American Illegitimacy and Premarital Pregnancy," in Laslett *et al.*, *Bastardy and Its Comparative History,* 362–78

Smith, Sydney, *Elementary Sketches of Moral Philosophy* (New York, Harper and Bros., 1856)

Soloveitchik, Joseph B., *Family Redeemed: Essays on Family Relationships,* ed. David Shatz and Joel Wolowelsky (New York: Meorot Harav Foundation, 2002)

Spierling, Karen E., *Infant Baptism in Reformation Geneva: The Shaping of a Community, 1536–1564* (Aldershot: Ashgate, 2005)

Spitz, Rabbi Elie Kaplan, "Mamzerut," *The Committee on Jewish Law and Standards of the Rabbincal Assembly* (March 8, 2000): 558–86

Stephen, Henry John, *New Commentaries on the Laws of England (Partly Founded on Blackstone),* 4 vols. (London: Henry Butterworth, 1842)

Stevenson-Moessner, Jean, *The Spirit of Adoption: At Home in God's Family* (Louisville, KY: Westminster John Knox Press, 2003)

Stone, Lawrence, *The Family, Sex, and Marriage in England, 1500–1800* (San Francisco: Harper & Row, 1979)

Strebi, W., "Die Rechtsstellung der unehelichen Kinder in Kanton Luzern" (Diss. Berne, 1928)

Swinburne, Henry, *A Briefe Treatise on Testaments and Last Willes* (London: John Windet, 1590)

Symposium, "What's Wrong with Rights for Children?" *Emory International Law Review* 20 (2006): 1–239

Tanner, Norman P., ed., *Decrees of the Ecumenical Councils* (Washington, DC: Georgetown University Press, 1990)

The Teaching of the Twelve Apostles, Didache, or The Oldest Church Manual, 3rd rev. edn., ed. and trans. Philip Schaff (New York: Funk & Wagnalls, 1889)

Teichmann, Jenny, *Illegitimacy: An Examination of Bastardy* (Ithaca, NY: Cornell University Press, 1982)

Tertullian, trans. and ed. Gerald H. Rendall (New York: G.P. Putnam's Sons, 1931)

Thomas, Mason P., "Child Abuse and Neglect. Part I: Historical Overview, Legal Matrix, and Social Perspectives," *North Carolina Law Review* 50 (1972): 293–349

Tierney, Brian, *Medieval Poor Law* (Berkeley: University of California Press, 1959)

Tiffany, Walter C., *Handbook on the Law of Persons and Domestic Relations* (St. Paul, MN: West Publishing, 1896)

Tipton, Steven M. and John Witte, Jr., eds., *Family Transformed: Religion, Values, and Society in American Life* (Washington, DC: Georgetown University Press, 2005)

Tractatus universi iuris, duce, & auspice Gregorio XIII, vol. VIII/1–VIII/2 (Venice, 1584)

Treggiari, Susan, *Roman Marriage: Iusti Coniuges from the Time of Cicero to Ulpian* (Oxford: Clarendon Press, 1991)

The Trial of Alice Clifton, for the Murder of Her Bastard-Child (Philadelphia, 1787)

The Trial of Mary Gibbs for the Murder of Her Female Bastard Child (London, 1814)

Trible, Phyllis, *Texts of Terror: Literary-Feminist Readings of Biblical Narratives* (London: SCM Press, 2002)

 and Letty M. Russell, eds., *Hagar, Sarah, and Their Children: Jewish, Christian, and Muslim Perspectives* (Louisville, KY: Westminster John Knox Press, 2006)

Trumper, Tim, "The Metaphorical Import of Adoption: A Plea for Realization," *Scottish Bulletin of Evangelical Theology* 14 (1996): 129–45

 "The Theological History of Adoption," *Scottish Bulletin of Evangelical Theology* 20 (2002): 4–28, 177–202

Twinam, Ann, *Public Lives, Private Secrets: Gender, Honor, Sexuality, and Illegitimacy in Colonial Spanish America* (Stanford: Stanford University Press, 1999)

Ubaldi, Angelo degli, *Consilia* (Frankfurt am Main, 1575)

Vawter, Bruce, *On Genesis: A New Reading* (Garden City, NY: Doubleday & Company, Inc., 1977)

Vernier, Chester G., *American Family Laws: A Comparative Study of the Family Law of the Forty-Eight American States . . . (to Jan. 1, 1935)*, 5 vols. (Stanford: Stanford University Press, 1936)

von Balthasar, Hans Urs, *The Glory of the Lord: A Theological Aesthetics, vol. VI, Theology: The Old Covenant* (San Francisco: Ignatius Press, 1991)

von Rad, Gerhard, *Deuteronomy* (Philadelphia: The Westminster Press, 1966)

 Genesis (Philadelphia: The Westminster Press, 1961)

 Old Testament Theology, 2 vols. (New York: Harper & Brothers Publishers, 1962)

Waite, Linda J. and Maggie Gallagher, *The Case for Marriage: Why Married People Are Happier, Healthier and Better Off Financially* (New York: Broadway Books, 2001)

Walker, Timothy, *Introduction to American Law; Designed As a First Book for Students* (Philadelphia: P.H. Nicklin and T. Johnson, 1837)

Watson, Alan, *The Evolution of Law* (Baltimore, MD: Johns Hopkins University Press, 1985)

    The Law of Persons in the Later Roman Republic (Oxford: Clarendon Press, 1967)

    Legal Transplants: An Approach to Comparative Law (Charlottesville, VA: University of Virgina Press, 1974)

    The Making of the Civil Law (Cambridge, MA: Harvard University Press, 1981)

    Sources of Law, Legal Change, and Ambiguity (Philadelphia: University of Pennslyvania Press, 1984)

Watt, Jeffrey R., "The Impact of the Reformation and Counter-Reformation," in *Family Life in Early Modern Times, 1500–1789*, ed. David I. Kertzer and Marzio Barbagli (New Haven, CT: Yale University Press, 2001), 125–54

    The Making of Modern Marriage: Matrimonial Control and the Rise of Sentiment in Neuchâtel, 1550–1800 (Ithaca, NY: Cornell University Press, 1992)

Weindling, Paul, *Health, Race and German Politics between National Unification and Nazism, 1870–1945* (Cambridge: Cambridge University Press, 1989)

Weitnauer, Albert, *Die Legitimation des ausserehelichen Kindes im römischen Recht und in den Germanenrechten des Mittelalters* (Basel: Helbing & Lichtenhahn, 1940)

Wells, Robert, "Illegitimacy and Bridal Pregnancy in Colonial America," in *Bastardy and Its Comparative History*, ed. Peter Laslett *et al.*, 349–61

Westermann, Claus, *Genesis 12–36: A Commentary* (Minneapolis: Augsburg Publishing House, 1985)

White, J.D., "Legitimation by Subsequent Marriage," *Law Quarterly Review* 36 (1920): 255–67

Wilkerson, Albert E., ed., *The Rights of Children: Emergent Concepts in Law and Society* (Philadelphia: Temple University Press, 1973)

Wilpert, Paul, ed., *Lex et Sacramentum im Mittelalter* (Berlin: Walter de Gruyter, 1969)

Winterer, Hermann, *Die rechtliche Stellung der Bastarden in Italien von 800 bis 1500* (Munich: Arbeo, 1978)

Witte, John, Jr., "Ishmael's Bane: The Sin and Crime of Illegitimacy Reconsidered," *Punishment and Society* 5 (2003): 327–45

    Law and Protestantism: The Legal Teachings of the Lutheran Reformation (Cambridge: Cambridge University Press, 2002)

    The Reformation of Rights: Law, Religion, and Human Rights in Early Modern Calvinism (Cambridge: Cambridge University Press, 2007)

Religion and the American Constitutional Experiment, 2nd edn. (Boulder, CO: Westview Press, 2005)

and Frank S. Alexander, eds., *Law and Christianity: An Introduction* (Cambridge: Cambridge University Press, 2008)

and Robert M. Kingdon, *Sex, Marriage and Family in John Calvin's Geneva*, 3 vols. (Grand Rapids, MI: Wm B. Eerdmans, 2005–)

and Richard C. Martin, eds., *Sharing the Book: Religious Perspectives on the Rights and Wrongs of Proselytism* (Maryknoll, NY: Orbis Books, 1999)

and Johan D. van der Vyver, eds., *Religious Human Rights in Global Perspective: Religious Perspectives* (The Hague: Martinus Nijhoff Publishers, 1996)

Wohlhaupter, Eugen, *Aequitas canonica. Eine Studie aus dem kanonischen Recht* (Paderborn: F. Schöning, 1931)

Wolff, Hans Julius, "The Background of the Post-Classical Legislation on Legitimation," *Seminar* 3 (1945): 21–45

Zainaldin, Jamil S., "The Emergence of an American Family Law: Child Custody, Adoption, and the Courts, 1796–1851," *Northwestern University Law Review* 73 (1979): 1038–89

Zingo, Martin T. and Kevin E. Early, *Nameless Persons: Legal Discrimination against Non-Marital Children in the United States* (Westport, CT: Praeger, 1994)

Zunshine, Lisa, *Bastards and Foundlings: Illegitimacy in Eighteenth-Century England* (Columbus, OH: Ohio State University Press, 2005)

Index to biblical sources

Subject index